The Romanoffs
100 Years Later

Daniel A. Willis

Bygone Era Books

Published by:
Bygone Era Books, LLC
7665 E. Eastman Ave. #B101
Denver, CO 80231

ISBN 978-1-941072-43-1

Printed in the United States of America

TABLE OF CONTENTS

Introduction 1

Chapter 1: How Did We Get Here? 5

Chapter 2: Post-Revolution Romanoffs 39

Chapter 3: Declared Heads of the Imperial House 51

Chapter 4: Great-Nieces and Great-Nephews of Nicholas II 67

Chapter 5: Romanoff in All but Name 83

Genealogy of The Descendants of Nicholas I 95

INTRODUCTION

No historical royal family has captured the imagination or inspired dreams dripping in diamonds like the Imperial House of Russia, the Romanoffs. For most, their story ended in that damp and musty cellar in Ekaterinburg in July 1918. But that was only the end of one chapter.

Although the Bolsheviks did their level best to rid the world of the Romanoff name, they failed. There were survivors, and those survivors continued the family. Now, a century after the murders, it is an appropriate time to reflect on how the family has survived and what is their current situation. This book is written to introduce the current Romanoffs to the public.

There are a few technical notes. The most pressing is the spelling of names. When even writing is translated between two languages which use different alphabets, such as Russian and English, there are bound to be awkward spelling issues. This book does not attempt to give an exact transliteration of Russian names. The explanation of the large family connections is confusing enough without bogging the reader down with such barriers as language. Therefore, all Russian names have been anglicized, for example, instead of the Russian names Piotr, Mikhail, and Nikolai, I use their English counterparts Peter, Michael, and Nicholas.

The same is true for surnames. Nearly all members of the family living today use the spelling Romanoff, whereas previous generations used Romanov. In the text of the book I use the double f consistently for all names ending with that sound: Romanoff, Cheremeteff, Orloff, etc. However, in the genealogy I try to follow the spelling used by the individual.

For events that happened in Russia prior to the Revolution, I use the dates of the western calendar. This is because it is more familiar to the reader than the Orthodox calendar, which had between 10 and 13 days difference, depending on the century we are talking about. In the genealogy, I give both dates for such events.

In the biographical text, I tried very hard to not overwhelm the reader with genealogical minutia. There is a detailed genealogy at the end of the book for those whose seek that information. Therefore, I only use the Russian patronymics such as Alexandrovich or Nikolaevna only when it is necessary to clarify to whom I am referring. However, be warned: Nicholas is a very common name in the Romanoff family, and there often cases of three or four generations in a row using it. I have done my best to be as clear as I can be about the person to whom I am referring.

I hope I have made this book as easy to read, as I have tried to make it enjoyable.

Daniel A. Willis
February, 2018

Chapter 1
How did we get here?

Pre-Romanoff Russia

Before we can discuss the Romanoff family in the present day, we need to understand how we got to this point. So, here is a very brief history of the country of Russia and of the family that ruled it for three centuries.

Russia, as we know it today, covers one-eighth of the inhabitable land mass of the planet. At over 6.5 million square miles (17 m km^2), it is by far the largest single country, and home to 145 million people. It stretches from central Europe, across Asia, to the Pacific Ocean and from the Black Sea to the Artic. This vast empire had its beginnings in what amounted to not much more than city-states sprinkled around the northern region of the Black Sea. Yet, at its largest, in the mid-twentieth century, the Asian portion of the Russian Empire extended down to the borders of modern day Iran and Afghanistan.

Due to its size, Russia is a polyglot country with a large number of ethnicities, religions and cultures. It has been that way almost since its inception, and only added to this patchwork quilt as it grew.

The first tribes to enter the area of what we now call Russia are believed to have come up from the southern regions even before the rise of the Babylonian and Persian empires. They were nomadic people and did not establish permanent settlements, but roamed through the region between the Black and Caspian Seas, known as the Russian Steppes.

The first tribes to enter the area of what we now call Russia are believed to have come up from the southern regions even before the rise of the Babylonian and Persian empires. They were nomadic and did not establish permanent settlements but roamed through the region between the Black and Caspian Seas, known as the famous Russian Steppes.

The earliest permanent settlements were built by Greek merchants who established trading ports on the coast of the Black Sea and her northern connected neighbor, the Sea of Azov. This region, then called Bospora, was formed into a kingdom, which was later incorporated into the Roman Empire. During this time, their nomadic neighbors to the east were overrun by a Turkic people called the Khazars who established their own empire east of the Black Sea, from where they dominated the region until the eighth century.

When Rome fell as the center of the Empire in the early fifth century, and the Empire moved to

Constantinople, these Kazan regions gained significance in world affairs, especially in trade between the emerging powers of western Europe and the Islamic kingdoms of the near east. The rise of the Eastern Empire, or Byzantium, also pulled many of the Slavic tribes of central and eastern Europe even further east. These Slavic migrations culminated in the founding of Kiev, just north of the Black Sea, and Novgorod, at the eastern tip of the Baltic Sea.

Reaching the Baltic brought the Slavs into regular contact with the Scandinavian Vikings, called Varangians in the east. One such Varangian, Rurik, rose to prominence and was elected as the first Prince (*knyaz*) of Novgorod in about 860. All of the subsequent royal rulers of Russia and its predecessor states can claim descent from Rurik. Many of the Soviet-era rulers also claimed such descent, though with much less documented evidence.

Rurik and his many sons extended their rule southward until all of the Slavic tribes blended to form the first Slavic state, Kievan Rus. The sons founded their own princely houses and soon Kievan Rus was a confederation of small principalities bound together by their common goals of promoting trade up and down the river system between the Baltic and Black Seas.

Under Prince Vladimir I, Kievan Rus adopted Christianity in 988. A Slavic variant of Eastern Orthodoxy had been growing in the region for several years, and was one of the reasons the Russian language was not heavily influenced by Greek or Latin as the Slavs used their own language in the liturgy. The rest of Europe fell into the camps of using Latin or Greek, causing those languages to be the basis of most modern European languages. From the onset, the princes kept the church dependent upon them, thus cementing the relationship between Church and State until to the fall of the Empire in the twentieth century.

Over the next five hundred years, various western and central Asiatic kingdoms came and went, each being either trade partners or enemies-at-war with the early Russian state, depending which way the wind was blowing. The most serious, and longest, invasion and occupation came from the Mongols, called Tartars in Russia, who crossed over the Ural Mountains from Asia and passed through the Steppes, in the mid-1200s. They brought with them a new, merciless form of fighting, which the Russians were unable to repel. Whereas the Russians used European-style marching and lines of infantryman armed with straight swords, the Tartars rode on horseback, in no particular pattern, slicing their enemies at high speed with very sharp, curved blades.

In time, the Mongols were incorporated into Russian society. After a couple of generations, they were genetically well mixed with the Slavic peoples they had conquered. The Mongol Horde, or Golden Horde as they are often called, did not have an organized sense of government or culture, outside of military command. Therefore, the Russian traditions survived, and the descendants of Rurik continued to be vassal rulers, who exercised most of the political authority, but only as long as they paid tribute to the Khans of the Horde. This balancing act continued until 1380 when the Tartar Khans were finally defeated and expelled.

Tartar control had been waning during the previous century and, at the same time, Russia found itself under attack from its northwestern neighbors, whose power was consolidated in Sweden. Prince Alexander Nevsky, later made an Orthodox saint, led the forces that held the Swedes and Poles at bay. Meanwhile, his son, Danilo, moved further inland, into the wilds east of Kiev. There he founded the city of Moscow, often called Muscovy in the west. Danilo worked in close cooperation with the Tartar overlords and as a result was made Grand Prince of Moscow.

A quick note about the title Grand Prince. The Russian language did not have a separate word for Duke, therefore they used the title Grand Prince (*Velikii Knyaz)* to designate the rulers of each of the Russian territories, Moscow, Novgorod, and Kiev. It was not until French became the official court language, under Catherine the Great in the 1700s, that the title Grand Duke began to be used on a regular basis. Many English and French texts started using the term Grand Duke; first for the pre-Tsar rulers, and then for members of the imperial family.

One of the unsung heroes of Russian history is Ivan III, Grand Prince of Moscow. It was he who consolidated all of the Rus lands under one ruler by the 1480s. In theory, this would have made him the first Tsar, but that title was not adopted until after his death. The term Tsar is a Russianized version of Caesar, linking the Russian Empire back to Byzantium, and the classical Roman Empire before them. Although Ivan was the first ruler to be called "the Great," in hindsight he is largely overlooked in favor of his more famous grandson and namesake, Ivan the Terrible.

Ivan the Great did receive the title Grand Prince of all Russia after he annexed the lands of all the other Rurik princes, either by inheritance or by force. He forced the Kazan empire (in the Steppes) into becoming a puppet state with their Khan subservient to the Grand Prince. Towards the end of his reign, Lithuania invaded Novgorod. After eighteen months of war, Lithuania was defeated and forced to cede even more territory to Ivan. By the time of his death, in 1505, he had expanded his territory from the border with Poland to the Ural Mountains, which are the tradition dividing line between Europe and Asia.

Ivan's son, Vasili III, served mostly as a place holder. He annexed the last few remaining Russian provinces and kept potential foreign invaders at bay. However, most of his reign is considered a footnote to history, sandwiched as he was between the two powerful Ivans.

Ivan IV, called the Terrible by history, came to the throne in 1547. His nickname is something of a misnomer. The English use of the world terrible had different connotations at the time and was considered an appropriate translation for the Russian *Ivan Grozny*. In modern terms, a better translation would be Ivan the Formidable. Modern culture tends to focus on the outbursts of rage and mental instability that plagued Ivan, especially in his later years. During one such event, he accidently killed his eldest son and heir. However, he also accomplished many good things for Russia.

Most notably he expanded his territory well into Siberia. Ivan was a notable diplomat and patron of the arts and of trade. He was also the first leader to take the title of Tsar.

The first half of Ivan's life overlapped the last half of that of England's Henry VIII. One thing they had in common was their numerous wives. Ivan outdid Henry by marrying seven times. Another area where he outperformed his English contemporary was in producing heirs. He had three surviving sons, two of whom would become Tsar in due course. Despite this, Ivan's death in 1584 started the slide into Russia's famous "Time of Troubles."

It began during the reign of Ivan's son, Feodor I. He had little interest in, nor mental capacity for, statesmanship and left the running of the country to his wife's brother, Boris Godunoff. After the childless Feodor died, Boris claimed the throne and was elected Feodor's successor by the *Zemsky Sobor*, a national assembly of nobles and church leaders from around the country. His seven-year reign was plagued by unusually cold summers, which caused massive crop failures, resulting in a third of the population's starving to death.

Then came the appearance of three men who each claimed, successively, to be Dmitry, the youngest son of Ivan IV who was stabbed, in 1591, under circumstances that have never been fully explained. The official story was that he died from the stabbing, most likely murdered at the order of Godunoff, who was already planning to take the throne. However, it was also rumored at the time that the person in his grave was not Dmitry, but someone the superstitious assassins had killed instead of Dmitry, being afraid to spill royal blood.

Russia in circa 1500 at the end of the reign of Ivan IV
© Lena Dvorkina

The Russian Empire at its height ca.1913
©Lena Dvorkina

This led to a series of almost farcically short reigns of various princes of Rurikid descent, one of whom was the first man claiming to be the dead Dmitry. With the Russian government in complete disarray, Poland, which at the time also included Lithuania, took the opportunity to invade. Prince Waldyslaw, son of the Polish King Sigismund, took the Russian throne for himself and began to convert the vast nation to Roman Catholicism. During 1611 and 1612, tens of thousands died in uprisings against the Polish regime or on the battlefield.

The Russians finally abandoned their internal fighting and banded together to slowly and definitively push the Poles out and to restore the Orthodox Church. The Church responded by quickly putting forth a new candidate for the vacant throne, one who had no allegiance to any of the warring factions, yet still had Rurikid blood through his mother. Furthermore, he was the great-nephew of Tsaritsa Anastasia, the first wife of Ivan IV and mother of most of his children. His name was Michael Romanoff.

Russia under the Romanoffs

Michael, now Tsar Michael I, was only sixteen when he was elected. The nobility saw this as both a point for concern and an opportunity to try to influence the young Tsar. However, Michael retained his father, Feodor, as his primary advisor. Feodor was closely connected to the

Tsar Michael in his coronation robes

Church, so most of Michaels' guidance came from there. His reign was devoted to rebuilding his war-torn kingdom and making peace with Sweden and Poland.

Whereas Michael fathered several healthy daughters, he only had one son who lived to adulthood, his successor, Tsar Alexei I. Like his father, Alexei came to the throne at the age of sixteen. However, he fell into the trap of letting one of the several factions in the nobility have ascendency over the others. This led to many divisions in his government and even the Church. His two marriages created the biggest divide of all. He fathered several children, by his first wife, Maria Miloslavskya, but only three had a significant role in history: his successor, Feodor III; a half-witted son, Ivan; and a very capable daughter, Sofia. In his second marriage, to Natalia Naryshkina, he became father to most famous figure of Russian history, Peter the Great.

Feodor III was tsar for six years, and died at the age of twenty. His only child died in infancy, leading to a major uprising in Moscow over a divided succession. The two sides of the revolt were centered around the families of the two wives of Alexei I, the Miloslavskys and the Naryshkins. The former supported putting Ivan on the throne despite his mental incapacity. The latter supported Peter.

Peter was declared Tsar at the age of ten. However, the Miloslavskys spread the rumor that the Naryshkins had murdered the true heir, Ivan. Peter's mother produced Ivan to an angry mob to prove he was alive. It also proved he was not mentally fit to be Tsar. This did not prevent his supporters from storming the Kremlin

Peter the Great by Paul Delaroche

and slaughtering several of Natalia's relatives, right in front of young Peter's eyes. A truce was made by naming Ivan and Peter as co-Tsars with Ivan's sister Sofia as regent over both. As it turned out, this was ploy by Sofia and her co-conspirator, and perhaps lover, Prince Vasili Galitzine, to position themselves to claim the crown for Sofia. Vasili served as the head of government during the regency.

Peter's formative years were spent in semi-exile while Galitzine and Sofia ruled in his name. At the age of seventeen, he returned home to wrest his country back from his half-sister. He was successful in exiling Sofia to a nunnery, and Galitzine to frozen northern Siberia.

Peter's early reign was largely a transitional period. During the first five years, his mother wielded most of the control over the government. Meanwhile, Peter traveled to western Europe and learned about ship-building and diplomacy. He met with the constitutional monarchs of the west, as well as the remaining autocrats in Germany.

Peter brought what he learned in his travels back to Russia and began the painful task of pulling his kingdom into the eighteenth century, kicking and screaming the whole way. He instituted many reforms designed to westernize the nation. He also built a new capital, St. Petersburg, on the marshes of northern Russia, importing workers from all over Europe. In the last years of his nearly 40-year reign, Peter took a new, more western title, Emperor of All the Russians. This title would continue until the Revolution of 1917.

One thing that Peter failed to do was leave a clear succession. He practiced the ancient rule of designating his successor rather than establishing a set of rules to guide the process. His initial heir had been his son, Alexei, but he was tortured to death for supposedly conspiring with a foreign power to overthrow Peter. Evidence suggests that Alexei was only attempting to escape Peter's brutality, and that he had even offered to renounce the succession if only his father would leave him alone.

Most looked to Alexei's infant son, another Peter, as the true heir, however he was only nine when his grandfather died. The palace guard, who would often prove to be the final arbitrators in succession disputes, sided with Peter's second wife, Catherine. Her origins have never been fully documented, but she was known to have been a mere housemaid before she became Peter's mistress, and later, his wife. She was duly crowned Empress Catherine I which began a series a short reigns. She died in 1727 after only two years on the throne, she was followed by: Peter II (1727-30), the young son of Tsarevich Alexei; Empress Anna (1730-1740) the elder surviving daughter of Ivan V (Peter the Great's half-brother); and Ivan VI (1740-1741), the infant great-nephew of Empress Anna.

When an infant was placed on the throne, the place guard had had enough. Grand Duchess Elizabeth, the daughter of Peter the Great, had long been a favorite of the Russian Court. The Guard rallied behind Elizabeth and silently launched a coup d'état deposing the infant Tsar Ivan and his mother, the Regent Anna (named for her aunt the Empress). Elizabeth was kinder than most to her predecessors. Anna was merely exiled to northern Russia, where she died in childbirth five years later. Ivan was locked away in the Oreshek fortress just outside of St. Petersburg. He was stripped of his name and was known only as "Unnamed Prisoner #1," his true identity not even known by the commandant of the fortress.

Because of his tender age, he was not killed, but strict orders were given to the guards that if anyone should try to break him out, he was to be killed rather than allowed to leave. He remained in the prison, with minimal human contact until the day there was an effort to free him in 1762, when the guards carried out their orders. Ivan had lived through the reigns of Elizabeth and her successor, Peter III, before being murdered at the age of twnty-three, during the reign of Catherine the Great.

Elizabeth reigned for twenty years, putting most of her efforts into continuing the domestic policies of her father. She had not been trained for this role, but showed an uncanny knack for diplomacy. While many believed her to be lazy, allowing bills to lie about for months without her signature, this was often her way of allowing events to unfold a bit more to give her more guidance on which way to proceed on a given matter.

Once again, succession became an issue. Elizabeth had never married so had no children to whom to pass her throne. Her only real option was her nephew, Peter of Holstein-Gottorp, son of her elder sister, yet another Anna. As Peter grew into his teens, his maturity level did not. He retained the mentality of a prepubescent boy, who wanted to do nothing but play with his toy soldiers. When the time came to find him a wife, Elizabeth carefully sought out just the right girl. She needed someone from a foreign reigning house, but not one of the major powers which would then tie Russia to them. She wanted someone strong enough to guide Peter, but still allow him to be “the man” in charge. Elizabeth thought she found the perfect person in Princess Sophie of Anhalt-Zerbst.

As it turned out, Peter was more hopeless than even Elizabeth was willing to believe. When she died in 1762, Russia was on the brink of completely crushing Prussia under the rule of Frederick the Great in the Seven Years War. However, her nephew, now Peter III, who idolized the military discipline of the Prussians, and Frederick in particular, ordered a general retreat and offered very generous peace terms to Frederick. Needless to say, the Russian military, and especially the Palace Guard were not happy with their new Emperor. The final insult came when Peter ordered the guard to abandon their traditional green and beige uniforms in favor of blue and white ones patterned their Prussian counterparts.

Peter III had been Emperor only six months when the Palace Guard arrested him and forced him to sign an abdication order in favor of his wife. Princess Sophie had taken the Russian name Catherine upon her conversion to Orthodoxy, and was now declared Catherine II, Empress of Russia. She would go on to reign over the greatest expansion of Russia, not only geographically, but also in terms of becoming a world power.

Catherine modelled her court after Versailles, and introduced French as the court language. By this point, it had long been the official language of international diplomacy. Her reign was one of the longer ones at thirty-four years. During her reign, she expanded the empire to it largest size. Not only did she colonize

Siberia all the way to the Pacific, but she also crossed the Bering Strait and established the Alaskan colony in North America. She was the first to establish Russian trade with Japan.

One area she always considered a failure on her part was closing the divide between the wealthy and the poor. There was no middle class to speak of Russia. Although the large cities of Moscow and St. Petersburg had a merchant/tradesman class, the vast majority of Russian territory did not see this. There were the wealthy, aristocratic land owners, and the extremely poor serfs who were essentially slaves to them. When war arose, it was always these serf who were conscripted into service first to be mostly cannon fodder.

This led to the occasional peasant uprising, which were quickly suppressed by the military. However, one in particular broke out during Russia's war with the Ottoman Empire in the 1770s. A deserter named Pugachev riled up the Cossacks in the frontier lands east of the Volga, claiming to be Peter III, having escaped Catherine's prison. His revolt grew to tens of thousands, but came to an end when he attempted to take the eastern city of Kazan. He was ultimately executed, but the event was an early example of tensions boiling over in a slave-like populous, whom the elite few treated as sub-human, and often with barbaric cruelty.

Meanwhile, back in St. Petersburg, Catherine's love life was always a hot topic at court. She had a string of lovers, and when their relationship would end they would part as friends, with the Empress often giving them generous pensions of land and serfs. Her progressive attitude toward sexual behavior sparked a

Catherine the Great later in life

lot of rumors about her tastes, most of which were likely not true. The revolving door on her bedroom had begun even before she overthrew her husband.

Early in her marriage she discovered her husband suffered from a physical affliction that made sexual intercourse unbearable for him. Hence, there was no possibility of an heir being born, causing Catherine to fail in her primary duty as wife of the heir to the throne. The Empress Elizabeth suggested she would turn a blind eye if Catherine found another means of becoming pregnant. It did not take her long to find a willing partner in one Sergei Saltykoff. Meanwhile, the court physician was enlisted to find a cure for Peter's problem. It turned out to be a simple matter that could have been corrected if Peter were circumcised. His foreskin was too tight, preventing him achieving a full erection. However, Peter was deathly afraid of having a doctor cut him in any way and would not agree to the procedure to correct the problem.

There are several stories about how they got Peter to finally have it done. My favorite is that the doctor paid the ever reliable Palace Guard to get Peter drunk to the point of passing out and performed the simple procedure on the unconscious Tsarevich. When he asked, the next day, what had happened, the guards told him he had challenged them to a penis-measuring contest and had accidentally cut himself on a broken vodka bottle. The guards wisely informed Peter that he had won the contest.

Peter began making love to his wife, but Catherine continued her relationship with Saltykoff, as well. Since her relations with Peter were few in number, it is generally believed that Saltykoff was actually the father of Catherine's elder son, Paul, who would later become Emperor. The affair with Saltykoff ended and Catherine fell in love with Grigory Orloff, a member of the Palace Guard which was commanded by his brother, Alexei. Grigory, Alexei and their other brothers were instrumental in placing Catherine on the throne.

Not long after coming to the throne, Catherine had a second son, this one unquestionably from Orloff. He was named after his uncle Alexei and eventually given the title Count Bobrinskoy. Alexei would marry and have descendants, many of whom are living in the present day. The senior male line lives primary in France, with a junior line based in Chicago.

When Catherine died in 1796, she left a much stronger Russia than she had inherited. But she also left it in the hands of an emotionally unstable man in her son, Paul. Emperor Paul had grown to despise his mother and devised the Fundamental Laws of the Imperial Family, which will be examined in more detail in a later chapter. Basically, these were rules about whom a member of the imperial family could marry, and most importantly they established a set of rules for the succession. Notably, Paul selected a semi-Salic succession plan which prevented women from coming to the throne unless every male of the family was dead. At the time he passed these laws he had three sons, two of whom were married, but no grandchildren yet. As it turned out, neither of those two would have sons.

Despite his mental instability, Paul did institute some reform policies to offer limited rights to the serfdom of his vast empire. While this made him popular with the masses, it was not so with the nobility. He also alienated the military by reneging on treaties his mother had signed with several surrounding kingdoms, most notably Persia and Georgia, the latter being incorporated into the Russian Empire.

A conspiracy grew, which included members of both the military and the nobility, to rid the empire of Paul in favor of his eldest son, Alexander. In March 1801, the conspirators charged into Paul's bedroom and tried to force him to sign an abdication. He refused and was strangled to death. Though Tsarevich Alexander had no role in the plotting of the crime, he is believed to have known that the event was brewing. Whatever the case, he did not punish the conspirators and took the throne as Alexander I.

Alexander was a well-liked Emperor, a successful warrior, and as he got older, a very religious man. He was Emperor during the Napoleonic Wars of the early 1800s. At first Russia entered into an alliance with Napoleon's France, but after it became clear that Bonaparte intended to control all of Europe, there was a break between the two empires. This led to Napoleon's disastrous attempt to invade Russia. It was not so much the Russian army that stopped Napoleon as it was the Russian winter. After Napoleon was defeated at Waterloo, Alexander entered Paris as a liberator and was greatly admired by the French.

As Alexander aged, he became more withdrawn, and more religious. He began studying mysticism, and started showing signs of paranoia. His wife, Princess Luise of Baden, rechristened Elizabeth after her marriage, became ill in 1825, and the couple went to the southern parts of the Empire for its better climate. While there, the Emperor developed typhoid and died that November; Elizabeth following him a few months later.

For several years, a persistent rumor continued that Alexander had not died, but that he had disappeared, by his own free will, to live out a life of religious devotion and mysticism. A monk by the name of Feodor Kuzmich, who lived in the Siberian town of Tomsk, has been named as likely to have been the self-exiled Emperor. Alexander's tomb has supposedly been opened four times since his death, the most recent in 1921, and was always reported to be empty.

Whether he died in 1825 or not, he left no surviving children. Both of his daughters died in infancy. In the few days immediately following the announcement that the Emperor had died, there was some confusion between his heirs. The next-younger brother, Constantine, who was also childless, was the heir in accordance with the succession law. However, he had renounced his rights several years previously, an act that Alexander had chosen to keep secret. Therefore, the throne actually passed to the third son, Nicholas, only he did not know it.

As was the practice when a new Emperor came to the throne, members of the family would go to pledge their allegiance to him. Nicholas dutifully went to Constantine, only to find his brother pledging allegiance to him instead. They quickly sorted it out and Nicholas took the throne as Nicholas I.

By 1825, the imperial family was as large as it had ever been, Emperor Paul had fathered nine children, including four sons. His five daughters had all married into European royal houses and were the first generation of Romanoffs to begin alliances of blood throughout the continent. Royal families that descended from these marriages include those of Saxe-Weimar, Oldenburg, Württemberg, and the Netherlands.

In addition, Nicholas was already a father of a son and three daughters when he came to the throne, and would go on to three more sons after he ascended. The genealogy at the end of this book traces the many descendants of Nicholas I and his wife, the former Princess Luise of Prussia, rechristened Alexandra when she entered the Orthodoxy.

Nicholas, being a third son, was not meant to be Emperor and was not trained in the area of diplomacy. He was a military man through and through and ran his government, and his family in strict military fashion. During his thirty years in charge, he saw the beginning of industrialization in the major cities, and the implementation of several reforms for the vast farmlands. However, he also pursued a policy of "Russification" of the disparate peoples within his empire.

While his treatment of the large Jewish population, then numbering over two million people, was nowhere near the cruelty they would see in the twentieth century under the Soviets and the Nazis, they were still treated as the bottom rung of the ladder. Jewish men were conscripted into lengthy stints of military service. One way to escape this was to migrate to Ukraine and farm the land there, however, they had to pay for this and, thus, were rarely able to take care of their families. With each "reform" Nicholas passed concerning the Jews, there was always the option of converting to Orthodoxy and gaining more options.

Emperor Nicholas I is the common ancestor of all of the present-day Romanoffs. They are divided into four groups, each descended from one of Nicholas' sons: Alexander, Constantine, Nicholas, and Michael. A fifth group of descendants were also considered members of the imperial family and that was the Dukes of Leuchtenberg, descended from Nicholas' daughter, Maria. The Leuchtenbergs are all but extinct now, the last males being a middle-aged bachelor and his elderly father.

Also extinct in the male lines are the descendants of Nicholas I's sons, Constantine and Nicholas. The last Romanoff from the Constantine branch was Princess Catherine, the Grand Duke's great-great-granddaughter who died in 2007. Among her family members is her grandson, the American Broadway and television actor Sebastian Arcelus.

The last male Romanoff descended from the third son and namesake, Grand Duke Nicholas, was his great-great-grandson, Dmitry Romanoff, who was the Chairman of the Romanoff Family Association at the time of his death at the end of 2016. This line does still have a few Romanoff princesses left, the three daughters of Dmitry's elder brother, yet another Nicholas. This line produced another television actress, this one in Italy, through a line of female descent: Nicoletta Consolo, who has adopted the screenname of Nicoletta Romanoff.

When Emperor Nicholas I died in 1855, he was succeeded by his eldest son as Alexander II. Alexander was a different sort of emperor. His views were far more liberal than any of his predecessors, or his successors for that matter. His most famous decree was the emancipation of the serfs in 1861. While this freed the overwhelming majority of the population of the empire, in reality it moved them up from being slaves to be being share-croppers, much like the similar emancipation of the slaves did in the United States.

One major problem Alexander inherited from his father was the Crimean War. The war was nominally started over the question of religious freedom in the Holy Land, which was under the control of the Islamic Turks of the Ottoman Empire. However, the real issue at hand was that the Ottomans were declining in their power and Russia was poised to take advantage of the situation and claim more territory in Crimea. England and France vowed to prevent this in the name of keeping a balance of power in the region.

Most of Europe sided with England, France and their unlikely alliance with the Ottomans. The combined might of so many countries was simply too much for the Russians to oercome and they lost the war. While it was Nicholas I who started this war, it was his son who had to mop up afterwards. For Russia, the war was not only costly in human lives but also money. Alexander inherited a nearly bankrupt treasury.

In addition to many spending cuts, Alexander also established a system of more local control with limited local taxation, authorized to ease the financial burden from the national coffers. His single largest one-item effort to pay off the war debts was the sale of the Alaskan territory to the United States in 1867. This vast colony of only 700 Russian settlers had become a financial burden for Russia to maintain, and even the US Secretary of State who instigated the deal, William Seward, was considered a laughing stock for making the purchase. However, he got the last laugh from his grave, when vast quantities of oil were discovered under the surface. One can only imagine the even higher tensions that would have existed during the Cold War, if Soviet Russia had had such a large portion of North America under its control. The small island of Cuba caused the United States enough headaches by itself.

Alexander II's family life was as different as was his governmental style. He had been duly married to a Princess in accordance with the Fundamental Laws. It was a successful union in that they had eight children, all but two were boys. However, like most of the men of his family, Alexander had a mistress. In a move reminiscent of Peter the Great, he married the mistress after his wife died. This was upsetting enough to his children, but he had the poor taste to do it less than a month after the Empress' death.

The second wife was from one of the old Rurik families, and as such, not considered equal under the Fundamental Laws. Therefore, their marriage was considered morganatic and she was given the title Princess Yourievsky, which she shared with their children who were all born prior to their marriage. After the assassination, Alexander III arranged for the Princess to have a generous pension under the condition she did not claim the right to live in any of the imperial palaces. She established new homes in Paris and on the French Riviera. Though popular in French society, she was always viewed by the Romanoffs with disdain. But, living on to 1922, she survived, where many of them did not.

In what must be one of the greatest ironies of history, Alexander was often the subject of assassination attempts by those who sought to bring about a social revolution against the autocracy of imperial Russia. That Alexander II, who was the most liberal of all the Tsars or Emperors, and who granted greater freedoms to his own people, should be such a target is a great testament to the Russian masses' lack of education. Only the upper classes could read or write, so the vast majority could not even read a newspaper, nor understand that this Emperor was actually working for their betterment.

One such attack on the Emperor left him unscarred, but had far-ranging effects on his family. In December 1879, the imperial family was returning to St. Petersburg from a vacation in Livadia, Crimea. A group calling themselves the People's Will (*Narodnaya Volya*) set off a bomb along the train tracks as the imperial train passed. The car carrying the Emperor and his wife was undamaged. But the car carrying his son, Tsarevich Alexander and his family, was blown completely off the tracks and crushed. The Tsarevich, later Alexander III, was a very large man with a broad back and shoulders. He used his size to hold up the collapsing railway car ceiling long enough for his wife and young children to escape. While he survived the incident, the younger Alexander was never quite fit again. His premature death is attributed to this attempt, which elevated an unprepared Nicholas II to the throne.

Alexander II, The Liberator of the Serfs

Fifteen months later, the assassins would finally take their prize. In March 1881, Alexander II was travelling by coach through the streets of St. Petersburg, where three members of the People's Will were standing along the route. The first two each threw their bombs, the second mortally wounding the Emperor. He died a couple of hours later in the same study where he had signed both the Emancipation of the Serfs twenty years earlier, and just that same day, a limited constitution which would have created a parliamentary system, — and thus, a constitutional monarchy. The following morning the new emperor, Alexander III, found the constitution on his father's desk and threw it in the trash.

Alexander III was an emperor in the mold of his grandfather, Nicholas I. He sought to limit many of the liberal reforms of his father, implementing the practice of Russification again. He decreed Russian would be taught to everyone in the empire, even though it now stretched into German, Polish, and several Asian language speaking lands.

In foreign affairs, he was a man of peace. No major conflicts arose during his reign, but then his reign was mercifully short. Even in marriage he picked a bride from a neutral country, Denmark. Like all other Romanoff wives before her, Princess Dagmar took a new name upon joining the Orthodoxy. She is known to history as Empress Maria, however her diminutive size, a stark contrast to her massive husband, earned her the name Minna among her family.

Alexander and Minna had five surviving children, three boys and two girls. However, the middle son,

George, died at the age of twenty-eight from tuberculosis. It would be the four remaining siblings that would bear the brunt of the horrors to come. Alexander, weakened in the 1879 attempt on his father's life, died in late 1894, leaving his throne to a woefully unprepared Nicholas II.

Over the past century, no effort has been made to spare the amount of ink that has been used to describe the last Emperor of Russia, Nicholas II. Since the point of this book is to focus on the living, we will limit this to a brief few paragraphs, which I acknowledge, will not do the topic justice.

Neither Alexander II nor the III saw the need to include Nicholas in discussions of state. During the grandfather's time, he was too young, and his father was too busy pursuing immortality by refusing to die, a pursuit he failed at miserably. One of the first things Nicholas said upon his father's death was, "But I don't know how to rule." The best that could be said about the situation, was that the man knew his shortcomings.

Nicholas inherited his father's ministers, who expected him to be as tough as his father. His own personality and temperament were not compatible with that form of government, but he did not have the ability to assert himself enough to avoid it. It did not help that he was surrounded by women with stronger wills than his own. In many ways, his mother and wife, both from more liberal countries than Russia, were even more autocratic than the new emperor.

Nearly everything Nicholas did as Emperor either made matters worse for the Russian people or simply failed. Whether it was his complete lack of domestic

Nicholas and Alexandra surround by their children:
(Clockwise from the bottom) Alexei, Anastasia, Tatiana, Olga, Maria

policy or the defeats the Russians were suffering militarily, first in the war with Japan, and then the First World War, the mood for social change was stoked to a fevered pitch.

In March 1917, the long simmering pot of dissatisfaction with imperial rule boiled over. Riots broke out in St. Petersburg, Prompted by the mounting hardships of war, overpopulation, and under production of food. All rule of law completely collapsed. Members of the Duma, Russia's quasi-parliament, joined with socialists to form a provisional government, one that did not include a Tsar.

Nicholas, who was at the war front, still got the message loud and clear. He abdicated, not only for himself, but also for his 13-year-old son, Alexei. The boy suffered from hemophilia and was in no condition to take the throne. Thus, the crown technically passed to Nicholas's brother, Michael, who had the good sense to refuse it.

Nicholas returned to St. Petersburg to be with his family. They were under house arrest in one the palaces until the following August. The Provisional Government sent them to Tobolsk in the Urals for their own protection as revolutionary tensions were rising again in the capital.

That October, the Bolsheviks seized control of the government, placing Vladimir Lenin as the chief executive. In April, after the harshness of the Siberian winter had passed, the family, were transferred to Ekaterinburg, deep within southern Siberia, along with four remaining attendants. It was here that the whole group of them: the Emperor, the Empress, their five children, their doctor, their cook, the Empress' maid, the Emperor's valet, and the Tsarevich's dog would all be murdered in the early hours of 17 July 1918.

Lenin did his best to completely rid the world of the Romanoff family. Nicholas's brother, Michael, had been murdered near Perm a month earlier. The night after the murder of the Emperor and his family, the Empress' sister, Grand Duchess Elizabeth who was herself the widow of a Romanoff, and five Romanoff cousins were thrown into a mining pit outside of Alapaevsk, some 80 miles (128 km) northeast of Ekaterinburg. Hand grenades were thrown in after them, and then kindling which was set afire.

The following January, four more grand dukes who had been arrested during the Bolshevik Revolution, were executed in the Fortress of St. Peter and St. Paul. This brought the number of Romanoffs dead at Bolshevik hands to nineteen. There were other cousins who met their ends during the same time period, but as casualties of war. And one grand duke died in Tashkent, in present-day Uzbekistan, from the flu during the 1918-19 pandemic.

Yet, there were survivors.

CHAPTER 2

POST-REVOLUTION ROMANOFFS

As noted before, the male-line Romanoffs fall into four lines of descent, each from one of the sons of Nicholas I: Emperor Alexander II and the Grand Dukes Constantine, Nicholas, and Michael. Before discussing the various Romanoff cousins, we first need to have a look at the titles of the imperial family.

Before Nicholas I came to the throne, there were never very many members of the imperial family living at one time. This changed with his healthy bloodlines. The number of Grand Dukes and Grand Duchesses, along with the financial allowances each got, soon threatened to bankrupt the Empire. So in 1886, Alexander III issued a decree that would regulate the imperial titles.

The title Grand Duke or Grand Duchess would be limited to the children of the Emperor and the children of the sons of the Emperor. Any further generations would be titled Prince or Princess of Russia. If a Prince married unequally, the marriage would be considered morganatic. The wife and any children of their marriage would be given separate titles, which would be considered inferior to the titles of the full members of the imperial house. This brings us back to the survivors who were a mixture of Grand Dukes and Princes.

From the senior-most line, that of Alexander II, we already know that Nicholas II, his children, and his brother were murdered. However, both of his sisters, Olga and Xenia managed to get out alive. Xenia, and her mother the Dowager Empress, the widow of Alexander III, were rescued from Crimea by the British battleship *HMS Marlborough*. King George V sent the ship at the insistence of his mother, Queen Alexandra, who was the Dowager Empress' sister.

Xenia had married Grand Duke Alexander, a second cousin from the youngest branch of the family. He, their seven children and two grandchildren born thus far, were all carried to safety along with his wife and mother-in-law. Alexander and Xenia separated shortly after this, with Alexander settling in Paris, and Xenia, going to England with the children.

The other sister, Olga, and her husband, Col. Nicholas Kulikovsky, remained behind in an effort to assist the so-called White Army, which rose up in opposition to the Bolsheviks. Many in the White Army were not necessarily monarchists, so the coalition they formed was more of a case of "the enemy of my enemy is my friend." As the White movement failed, she was forced to flee further and further from the heartland of Russia until she was evacuated by the Allies to Serbia.

From there she joined her mother in the latter's native Denmark. By this time Olga and Nicholas had two small sons in tow, Tikhon and Guri.

Their brother, Grand Duke Michael, had married unequally and had a son who was titled Count George Brassoff, who was still a child under ten during the Revolution. Not realizing that Countess Brassoff and her young son were the family of the would-be Emperor, a lower level Soviet official gave them an exit visit to visit relatives in Sweden. Needless to say, they never returned. Sadly, George was killed in a car crash in France at the age of twenty-one.

Nicholas II's only uncle still living at the time of Revolution was his father's youngest brother, Paul. Paul would be one of the Grand Dukes executed in the Fortress of Saint Peter and Saint Paul in January 1919. Paul had five children. The younger three were from his second, morganatic marriage and carried the titles Prince and Princess Paley. The young Prince Paley was one of the victims to be thrown in the mine shaft with Grand Duchess Elizabeth. His mother and sisters were permitted to leave Russia and went to France.

Paul's two children by his first, royal wife were also spared. The daughter Maria, already a divorced mother, married a soldier named Poutiatin and was able to leave under her married name, as the Soviets did not realize her imperial identity. Her brother, Grand Duke Dmitry, was one of the conspirators who plotted and carried out the assassination of the monk Rasputin, a mystic who had developed a very powerful hold on the Emperor and Empress prior to his death. Because of his actions, he was exiled to the southern border with Persia. From there it was easy to make his way to Paris after the Empire crumbled.

The eldest uncle of Nicholas II was Grand Duke Vladimir, who died in 1909. He left three sons, Cyril, Boris and Andrei. All three got out of Russia during the Revolution. Cyril took the controversial route of befriending the local Red leaders in St. Petersburg and essentially schmoozed himself and his family into Finland, which then declared its independence from Russia a short time after. They would later join his mother and brothers in southern France. In 1924, after it was clear Nicholas and Michael were both dead, Cyril, the next male in the line of succession, declared himself Emperor-in-Exile, something for which the Dowager Empress never forgave him. She went to her grave holding out hope at least one the family she left in Russia would come out alive.

Boris and Andrei's escape was much more adventurous. When the Bolsheviks took control, the brothers lived together in the imperial palace of Tsarskoie-Selo, along with their mistresses. All of them fled to the Caucasus where their mother had a villa in one of the spa towns. The Bolsheviks caught up with them eventually, arrested them and sentenced them to death. By the wildest stroke of luck, the executioner had once been a starving artist in Paris, whom Boris had helped out by buying some of his artwork. The executioner remembered his early patron and set both of the brothers free. After quite a few hardships, they made their way to the Black Sea where they were able to escape by boat.

L-R Grand Dukes Andrew, Cyril, and Boris

The second branch of the family, those descended from Grand Duke Constantine, were hit almost as hard by the Bolsheviks as the elder branch had been, except they did not have as many survivors.

Constantine's eldest son, another Nicholas, had been a problem child most of his youth. He finally got into so much trouble that Alexander III exiled him to Tashkent in present-day Uzbekistan. There he married a local girl and had two sons who were given the title Prince Iskander. The elder son was killed in the Civil War fighting for the Whites; the younger managed to get out and settle in France with his second wife. The first wife, and their two children remained in the Soviet Union. Both of the children lived into the 1990s, and the daughter was even able to attend the burial ceremony for the Emperor's family in 1998, almost exactly a year before her death. Neither sibling had children.

Constantine's second son and namesake did not live to see the Revolution which claimed the lives of three of his children. The eldest son, Ioann, had two small children, who were not even of school age, when he was thrown into that mineshaft outside of Alapaevsk. His daughter, Catherine, who was born in 1915, would be the last Romanoff born in Russia before the Revolution. She would also be the last living pre-Revolutionary Romanoff, not dying until 2007. Her brother, Vsevelod, although married three times, died in 1973 with no children. Ioann had two brothers and three sisters whon got out alive. Only two of them married, and while one sister had two children, she had no grandchildren.

The third son of Emperor Nicholas I was his namesake, Grand Duke Nicholas . His family was very compact, a wife and two sons. A notorious womanizer, it was once said of Nicholas that he loved all women, except his wife, whom he referred to as "government-issued." Their marriage was effectively over within five years, but she never granted him the divorce he would have liked. Eventually, he lived openly with his long-time mistress, the ballerina Catherina Chislova, who gave him five more children.

The two legitimate sons, Nicholas Jr. and Peter, both survived the Revolution by staying just ahead of the advancing Bolsheviks in Crimea. Ultimately, they were evacuated along with the Dowager Empress and her party, who were their next-door neighbors. Nicholas Jr., called Nikolasha within the family, and Peter married a set of sisters, daughters of the King of Montenegro. The elder brother died childless, and the younger left three children, two daughters, and a son, Roman.

Prince Roman married a Russian Countess and took a different attitude towards the Fundamental laws than his cousins. He took the position that the Empire had ended, and there was no Emperor. Therefore, he did not require permission to marry or pass on his titles. This attitude was shared by his two sons, Nicolas and Dmitry. As such, he did not request, nor did he receive a title for his wife. By his reckoning, she was Her Highness Princess Prascovia of Russia. The heads of the Imperial House viewed her as simply Mrs. Roman Romanoff.

Roman and several of his cousins, who were also first generation Princes of Russia laid the groundwork for the formation of the Romanoff Family Association,

Grand Duke Peter with son Prince Roman and grandson Prince Nicolas
©RoyalRussia

although he did not live to see the plan fulfilled. The RFA, which is still active today, has long maintained that it is up to the Russian people to determine if they wish to restore the monarchy, and to choose who that monarch should be. To this end, they do not recognize anyone as the Head of the Imperial House.

Both of Roman's sons served as presidents of the RFA. Nicolas died in 2014, followed two years later by Dmitry. Nicolas left three daughters by his Italian wife. Dmitry, though married twice, never fathered any children.

The junior most branch of the Romanoff family, the descendants of Nicholas I's youngest son, Michael, are now also the senior most in terms of relationship to the last Emperor.

The youngest of Michael's six sons died of natural causes at age nineteen, and only two of the remaining five survived the Bolsheviks. Sergei perished in the Alapaevsk mine shaft in the summer of 1918, and Nicholas and George were two of the four Grand Dukes shot in the Fortress of Saint Peter and Saint Paul in 1919.

Michael's younger surviving son Alexander married Nicholas II's sister, Xenia, therefore his descendants are the great-grand nephews and nieces of the Tsar.

The other survivor was also a Michael, Grand Duke Michael Jr. He defied the Emperor and married Countess Sophie of Merenberg, herself a morganatic daughter of Prince Nikolaus of Nassau. Michael argued that their marriage fit the Fundamental Laws since Sophie was from a reigning foreign house. Alexander III disagreed. In his mind, her morganatic status removed her from the definition of "from a reigning house." His

Grand Duke Michael and his children

defiance in marrying her anyway earned Michael exile from Russia, an act which spared his life as he was living in England at the time of the Revolution.

Michael's only son died unmarried in 1959, but Michael has numerous descendants via his two daughters. Many of them are now in the British nobility, such as the Duke of Westminster and the Marquess of Milford Haven.

Grand Duke Alexander and his wife, Grand Duchess Xenia were the parents of a daughter, Irina, followed by six sons: Andrei, Feodor, Nikita, Dmitri, Rostislav, and Vasili. Irina was married to the famous, or infamous depending on your point of view, Prince Felix Yousoupoff. Felix was the principle organizer of the successful plot to kill Rasputin. Though initially exiled for the murder, Felix and Irina did return just prior to the Revolution and were able to leave with most of the Yousoupoff family jewels and two paintings by Rembrandt, the sale of which helped maintain the family in exile. Alexander and all of his children were among those evacuated by the British on *HMS Marlborough*. A detailed account of their time hiding in Crimea, and evacuation, is detailed in Alexander's two-part autobiography, *Once a Grand Duke* and *Always a Grand Duke*.

The six sons of Alexander and Irina will be discussed in a later chapter. It is their descendants who make up the majority the current living Romanoffs.

Alexander's only sister, Anastasia, married the Grand Duke of Mecklenburg-Schwerin. She leaves many descendants living today, including the royal families of Denmark and Prussia via her two daughters

Alexandrine, wife of King Christian X of the former, and Cecilie, wife of Crown Prince Wilhelm of the latter.

The remainder of this book will look more closely at the living descendants of these survivors.

CHAPTER 3

THE DECLARED HEIRS OF THE EMPIRE

Before meeting the current claimants to the throne, we need to have a discussion about the Fundamental Laws of the Russian as they apply to the succession. Below is the language of these laws which are found in Chapter Two of the Fundamental Laws[1]:

25. The Imperial Throne of all the Russias is hereditary within the Imperial House presently reigning.
26. Inseparable from the Imperial Throne of All the Russias are the Thrones of the Kingdom of Poland and the Grand Duchy of Finland.

---

[1] Copied from www.russianlegitimist.org/the-fundamental-laws on 21 Jan 2018.

27. Both sexes have the right of succession to the Throne, but this right belongs by preference to the male sex according to the principle of primogeniture. With the extinction of last male issue, succession to the Throne passes to the female by right of substitution.
28. Accordingly, succession to the Throne belongs in the first place to the eldest son of the reigning Emperor, and after him to all his male issue.
29. With the extinction of this male issue, succession passes to the branch of the second son of the Emperor and his male issue, with the extinction of the second male issue, succession passes to the branch of the third son, and so forth.
30. When the last male issue of the Emperor's sons is extinct, succession remains in the same branch, but in the female issue of the last reigning Emperor, as being being nearest to the Throne, and therein it follows the same order, with preference to a male over the female person, but the female person from whom this right directly proceeds never loses this right.
31. With the extinction of this branch the succession passes to the female issue of the branch of the eldest son of the Emperor-Progenitor, wherein the nearest relative of the last reigning Emperor in the branch of his son succeeds, the eldest in this descending line, or if unavailable, in a collateral line, and if this relative is lacking, then the male or female person who takes her place by substitution with preference, as above, for a male over a female person.

32. When these branches too are extinct, succession passes to the female issue of the sons of the Emperor-Progenitor, following the same order, and after that to the male issue of the eldest daughter of the Emperor-Progenitor, and when that too is extinct, to her female issue, following the order established for the female issue of the Emperor's sons.
33. With the extinction of the male and female issue of the eldest daughter of the Emperor-Progenitor, succession passes first to the male and then to the female issue of the second daughter of the Emperor-Progenitor and so forth
34. A younger sister, even if she has sons, does not deprive her elder sister of her right, even if the latter is unmarried, but a younger brother succeeds before her his elder sisters.
35. When the succession reaches a female branch which is already reigning on another throne, it is left to the person who succeeds to make a choice of faith and throne and, together with that person's heir, to renounce the other faith and throne, if such a throne is tied by Law with a religious denomination. If there is no renunciation of faith, the succession passes to the person next in order.
36. Children born of a marriage between a person of the Imperial Family and a person not of corresponding dignity, that is not belonging to any royal or sovereign house, have no right of succession to the Throne.

Paraphrasing this all in a nutshell, males come first. When all male lines become extinct, then the throne goes to the female relative closest to the Emperor, and follows the same rules within her descendants before passing on to the next female. The issue of equal marriage is addressed only in paragraph 36. What is not addressed is what happens if a person of female descent who is not born into the imperial house marries beneath their rank. For example, if the claim to the throne were to pass to the nearest relatives of the current claimants, Grand Duchess Maria and her son, that would be the Leiningen family and their internal marriage rules are much more lax than that of the Romanoffs. The answer to that question may not be that far off, as we shall see shortly.

How this all applied in practice to the family of Nicholas II, was that when he abdicated for himself and his only son Alexei, next in line was his brother, Michael. Michael did not marry a person of equal dignity, or rank. His wife was born merely a Miss Cheremetevskya. Therefore, his son had no succession rights.

Here is where the semi-Salic nature of the law kicks in. Rather than going to one of Nicholas II's sisters, the throne passed to the next male in line. This would be the line of Alexander III's next younger brother, Vladimir, who was already dead, but he left three surviving sons. The eldest of these sons was Cyril, who declared himself Emperor-in-Exile after being assured by the Soviet government that Nicholas, Alexei, and Michael were all dead.

Before we move on from Cyril, there is a little discussion about his marriage. All marriages of members of the imperial family required the approval of the

Emperor. Cyril picked badly when he chose to marry Princess Victoria of Great Britain, a granddaughter of both Queen Victoria and of Emperor Alexander II. To begin with she was his first cousin, a closeness of relationship forbidden by the Russian Orthodox Church. Secondly, she was divorced. While this alone was not enough to disqualify her as an imperial bride, the fact that she was divorced from the Empress' brother made her, at best, unwelcome. With these three strikes against her, Nicholas refused permission for the couple to marry.

Cyril and Victoria eloped and got married anyway in Bavaria. They were duly banished for defying the Emperor, and the marriage was not recognized as valid in Russia. Cyril and Victoria lived first near her mother in Coburg, and then on the French Riviera. Along the way, they had two daughters who were considered illegitimate by the Russian Court.

In time, the Emperor's anger cooled, and as the winds of war were approaching hurricane strength, he invited Cyril and his family to return to Russia in the name of circling the wagons for war. He gave his approval for the marriage, but only after Cyril got dispensation from the Church, and the Emperor raised the two daughters to their regular rank as Princesses of Russia. This placed Cyril back in the succession, along with his children.

After the Revolution, Victoria gave birth to a son, Wladimir, who succeeded his father as Head of the Imperial House in 1938. Like his father, Wladimir's marriage also requires some discussion. He chose

Princess Leonida Bagration as his bride. Her family had once ruled the Kingdom of Georgia.

Since the passage of the Pauline Laws, now called the Fundamental Laws, marriage to Russian nationals was considered forbidden as they were not from royal or sovereign houses. There is some room for argument here that the old Rurik princely houses were former reigning houses before the consolidation of Russia under Ivan III. But the attitude within the Empire was generally against this. It was believed that Emperor Paul intended to specifically exclude these families as potential imperial mates, in order to prevent any the relatives of his mother's lovers from entering the imperial family.

So, if it follows that the Rurik families were not eligible, it would also follow that other Russian princely families would also not be eligible and that would include the Bagrations. The hair that was split there, however, is that Georgia was not annexed into Russia until after the passage of the Pauline Laws, and therefore it was a foreign royal house at that time. The issue first arose in 1911, when Princess Tatiana, of the Constantine branch of the Romanoffs, became engaged to Leonida's cousin, Prince Constantine Bagration. Then, the decision was made that the marriage was not considered equal, and that Tatiana had to renounce her extremely remote succession rights in order to marry a Bagration.

When Wladimir wanted to marry someone from the same house in 1948, his cousins cried foul. By this time, many of them had also married unequally, and some even to Rurik princesses. However, Vladimir had one advantage. He was now head of the House himself and was the final arbitrator of what constituted an equal marriage. So it essentially came down to the old saying, "It's good to be King." Wladimir died in 1992, followed by his wife eighteen years later. They left an only child, a daughter, Maria.

Grand Duchess Maria Wladimirovna

Born in 1953, Maria succeeded her father, Waldimir, as Head of the Imperial House in 1992. However, this move was not without controversy. Most of the question surrounds the equality of her parents' marriage. Her father added fuel to the fire by announcing she would be his heir while there were still other male dynasts living. In the end, Wladimir outlived them all, rendering that point of contention moot.

But the marriage issue remains. Maria's claim to Headship of the House is recognized by nearly everyone, except all other members of the Romanoff family. She does represent the imperial family at foreign royal events such as weddings and funerals. Most recently, she attended the 2017 funeral of King Michael of Romania.

The finances of this branch of the Romanoff family were always on shaky grounds. Wladimir's grandmother, Grand Duchess Maria Pavlovna, managed to smuggle some of her jewels out of Russia and their sale supported the family for a time. Many of these jewels were purchased by Queen Mary of Great Britain, an avid collector, and are now in the possession of the present Queen.

Grand Duchess Maria Wladimirovna

When Wladimir married Leonida, he was marrying a divorced woman with a 13-year-old daughter, Helen. Leonida's first husband was Sumner Moore Kirby, from a wealthy family in Pennsylvania, who were business partners with F.W. Woolworth. Kirby and Leonida lived in Paris, but were divorced in 1937. Afterwards, he ran afoul of the Nazi occupiers and was sent to Buchenwald by the Vichy regime. He did not survive. Half of his fortune was left to his daughter, Helen. Helen never married, and she provided significant support for her mother and her second family. With assistance from her half-sister, Maria was able to attend college in Madrid, Paris and Oxford, where she studied Russian history and literature.

In 1976, Maria married Prince Franz Wilhelm of Prussia, a descendant of the last German Kaiser via his youngest son. The marriage lasted ten years before ending in divorce, but did provide Maria with her much needed heir George. Prior to the marriage, Franz Wilhlem converted to Orthodoxy and took the name Michael Pavlovich. He was given the title Grand Duke of Russia by his father-in-law. After the divorce, he returned to Germany, and to his "maiden name."

Maria continues to live in Madrid, where she was raised, but visits Russia often. She carries out typical royal duties suhc as laying cornerstones, cutting ribbons, and helping with raising funds and awareness where it is needed for the people of Russia.

When the remains of Emperor Nicholas II and his family were discovered in 1991 a protracted effort began to confirm their authenticity. In the end, DNA testing against living matrilineal relatives of the imperial family as well as the servants who perished with them conclusively proved the remains were indeed those murdered in Ekaterinburg in 1918. Despite this, the Church took a position of skepticism, which was then adopted by Maria. In 1998, on the eightieth anniversary of the murders, the remains were reburied in the imperial crypt with great pomp. Nearly every Romanoff living attended. Notably missing were Maria and her son.

Grand Duke George Mikhailovich

Like the other members of his immediate family, Grand Duke George, heir-apparent to the headship of the imperial house, has lived his life in controversy. The difference is, little of it was of his own doing.

To begin with, when he was born in 1981, his grandfather immediately gave him the title Grand Duke of Russia, despite there still being other Romanoff dynasts living. One such dynast, Prince Vasili, nephew of Nicholas II, and then president of the Romanoff Family Association, promptly responded by issuing a statement, "That the Romanoff Family Association hereby declares that the joyful event in the Prussian Royal House does not concern the Romanoff Family Association since the newborn prince is not a member of either the Russian Imperial House or of the Romanoff family."

Haviong been raised mostly in France, a further complication came when the French authorities refused

Grand Duke George of Russia, Prince of Prussia

to issue the tyke a passport in the name Grand Duc Georges de Russie, instead of the legal name he inherited from his father, Georg Prinz von Preussen. His parents separated the next year, and his father declared his son to be a Prussian royal. "I always carry it [George's German passport] with me. It says he is Prince George of Prussia" (translated from the German). Once the family returned to Spain, George's name and title were more readily accepted.

Although entitled to both Grand Duke of Russia and Prince of Prussia, he only uses the latter. He is also now legally surnamed Romanoff rather than Hohenzollern like his father. George has little interaction with his father, but regularly accompanies his mother when his own business needs allow it. One charity that is near to his heart is the Imperial Foundation for Cancer Research, which raises funds to seek new treatments, and hopefully one day, cures for various types of cancer. The foundation is based in St. Petersburg.

Like his mother, George attended Oxford. After this he worked at the European Parliament as an assistant to the Commissioner for Transport and Energy. He later worked at the European Commission's Directorate-General for Atomic Energy and Security, and then a nickel-mining company. In 2014, he started his company, Romanoff & Partners, based in Brussels which promotes Russian businesses in the rest of Europe.

Since his family had maintained a strict adherence to the Fundamental Laws as they pertain to equal marriages, the pressure will be on George to find a princess to marry. In a few years he will be fifty. The longer he waits to marry to stronger that pressure will be.

If he does not marry, or if he marries unequally, the Headship of the house will leave the Romanoff family. In accordance with the Fundamental Laws, the next heir is the grandson of Wladimir's elder sister, the Princess of Leiningen.

Prince Karl Emich of Leiningen (aka Emperor Nicholas III)

Although the Leiningen family has not been a reigning princely family since the collapse of the Holy Roman Empire in 1806, they were among the families to retain their sovereign status, thus making them equal in birth to the reigning houses, including the Romanoffs. The senior male of this family is Prince Karl Emich (b.1952).

However, he is not the head of the Leiningen family. His second marriage was not in accordance with the house laws, so he was disinherited by his father and the headship of the house passed to his younger brother Andreas. There is room here to argue that he would also be banned from the Russian succession for the same reason. If that is the case, then Andreas would be next. His marriage to Princess Alexandra of Hanover is uqestionably equal, and their eldest son has recently married a Princess of Prussia.

In recent years, Prince Karl Emich has joined the choir singing the tune that Wladimir and Leonida's marriage was not equal, and that he is the rightful Head

Prince Karl Emich zu Leiningen
(aka Emperor Nicholas III of Russia)

of the Imperial House. In 2013, he converted to Orthodoxy, taking the name Nicholas Kirillovich, and with the support of the Monarchist Party of Russia, he has agreed to assume the title Emperor Nicholas III.

The Monarchist Party has spent the last few years attempting to purchase land outside of Russia to declare a sovereign state as the "Romanov Empire." In December 2017, the Chairman of the party, Anton Bakoff, announced such a purchase has been made of some islands belonging to the African nation of Gambia.

While most monarchists outside of this political party take the pretensions of Karl Emich/Nicholas III with a grain of salt, the fact does remain that until Grand Duke George marries equally and produces heirs, the Russian Imperial House is careening for an uncertain succession.

CHAPTER 4

Nicholas II's Great-Nieces and Great-Nephews

Nicholas II was one of the five children of Alexander III to survive childhood. However, the only ones to survive the Revolution were his two sisters Xenia and Olga. As mentioned previously, the older, Xenia, married her second cousin, Grand Duke Alexander, and Olga married a military man, Col. Nicholas Kulikovsky.

Olga and Col. Kulikovsky, as I refer to him to avoid mixing him up with his brother-in-law, the more famous Nicholas, had two sons, Tikhon and Guri, both of whom are now deceased. Since Col. Kulikovsky was a commoner, neither her nor his children received any titles. The elder son, Tikhon married three times, but left an only daughter, Olga, when he died in 1993. Olga is now Mrs. Joe Cordeiro and the mother of four sons, all in their late teens and early twenties. Olga is a motivational speaker and empowerment coach.

Guri, on the other hand, fathered three children, all by the first of his two wives. While all three have remained out of the spotlight, Guri's grandson, Paul Kulikovsky, warrants some recognition.

Paul Kulikovsky
Great-Grandson of Grand Duchess Olga Alexandrovna

Paul was raised in Denmark where his grandfather, Guri, returned after initially emigrating to Canada with his parents. He was the son Guri's only daughter, Ksenia (sometimes spelled Xenia) and Ralph Jones. Paul's education and early career were in the fields of business and management. A fluent Russian speaker, Paul has since moved to Moscow permanently.

Although, technically, he is not a Romanoff, being descended through a female line, as a close relation to the last Tsar, he is often interviewed about his ancestors' heritage and their place in history. Living in Russia also makes him more easily accessible to the Russian media than his far-flung Romanoff cousins around the world.

Paul's two daughters remain in Denmark, near their mother, Paul's first wife. His second wife, Ludmilla, is a Russian national.

Paul Kulikovsky

Descendants of Grand Duchess Xenia Alexandrovna

Grand Duchess Xenia, the elder of Nicholas II's sisters, lived out her life after the Revolution in England, at Frogmore Cottage, a "grace and favor" residence in the grounds of Windsor Castle, that was granted to her by her first cousin, King George V. In the 1930s this was changed for Wilderness House in the grounds of Hampton Court Palace, where she died in 1960.

She and Grand Duke Alexander had seven children, a daughter followed by six sons, the last of whom died in 1989. Their daughter, Irina, was married to Prince Felix Yousoupoff, the principle conspirator in the murder of Rasputin. She had an only daughter, who was the mother and grandmother of only daughters as well. Princess Irina's great-granddaughter finally broke the chain by having two children, both of whom are, of course, daughters, now in their teens.

Grand Duchess Xenia's eldest son, Prince Andrei, married twice. He had three children with his first wife. Donna Elisabetta Sasso-Ruffo, a daughter an then two sons. With his second wife Nadine McDougall, he had a fiurth child, a daughter. Both the elder daughter, Xenia, and elder son, Michael, lived into their eighties but left no children. The younger son, Andrew, is the head of this branch of the family.

Prince Andrew Andreievich Romanoff

Andrew Romanoff, as a U.S. citizen, technically does not carry a title. However, he is entitled to be called Prince Romanovsky, in accordance with the title given his mother, Donna Elisabetta Sasso-Ruffo. Although she was from an old Italian noble family, was not from a sovereign house and therefore her marriage to Prince Andrei was not considered equal. As none of Grand Duchess Xenia's sons married equally, the title Princess Romanovsky became the standard handed out by Grand Duke Cyril, and later his son, Wladimir. However, none of the children of these marriages ever used these titles preferring to be known as Prince or Princess Romanoff instead, and legally use the surname Romanoff, somewhat to the chagrin of Grand Duke Cyril and his descendants.

Andrew was born in London and was raised in his grandmother's grace and favor residences. His father, in his role as the eldest son, remained with the Grand Duchess and was her primary caregiver. While his parents sought to raise him as a sensible person, living in their reduced circumstances, they also taught him all the mannerisms and protocol of royalty. He was raised speaking both Russian and English fluently.

Their quiet family life was interrupted by World War II. His mother, who was already suffering from the advanced stages of cancer, died during a bombing raid. Her death certificate lists her cause of death as cancer,

L-R: Peter, Andrew Jr, Andrew Sr., Alex

but Andrew always maintains that it was the Nazi bombing that killed her, after part of their ceiling collapsed. In 1942, Andrew joined the Royal Navy. While it was standard practice for royalty to be granted an officer's commission, he chose to go in as an enlisted man and perform all of the duties of a regular sailor.

He emigrated to America after the war, at the invitation of his uncle, Prince Vasili, and settled the San Francisco Bay region. His career path was one of much variety. Over time, he worked in grocery stores, hydroponic farms, a shipping brokerage, car inpentry, and as a jeweler.

Like his father, he showed early signs of artistic ability. Having no formal education in art, Andrew used a variety of mediums as his way to relax. After retiring from the day-to-day types of jobs that had maintained him, he devoted his life to his art. His designs, mostly framed works which combine drawings and shrunken plastic landscapes, have won critical acclaim, and draw heavily on American folk art. His art has been exhibited worldwide.

Andrew has been married three times. His first marriage to Helen Dourneva ended after eight years and produced one son Alexis, generally known as Alex. He owns his own accounting firm and is married, but has no children. By his second marriage to Kathleen Norris, who was a granddaughter of noted American authors Kathleen and Charles Gilman Norris, Andrew fathered two more sons, Peter and Andrew. Peter's love is cars, and his positions have always been in connection with them, whether as a mechanic, or a salesman. Like his older brother, he too is married but has no children. The younger Andrew works in the business management field. He and his wife, Elizabeth Flores, are the parents of a daughter, Natasha, a recent college graduate with a degree in Psychology.

After the death of Kathleen in 1967, Andrew remained single for many years before finding a kindred artistic spirit in Inez Storer, a successful painter who mixes magical realism with faux-Native American motifs. The two have been married since 1987. Like many of the Romanoffs, since the end of the empire, Andrew Romanoff has published a memoir, *The Boy Who Would Be Tsar*, which is heavily illustrated with his own artwork.

Princess Olga Andreievna Romanoff

Andrei's second wife, Nadine McDougall, brought Provender House, in Kent, to the marraige. The origins of the house date back to the fourteenth century. Since 1912, the house has been passed from mother to daughter, and is now owned by Andrei and Nadine's daughter, Olga.

When Andrei married the second time, he moved out of his mother's residence and into Provender House. This is where Olga was raised. After she inherited the property herself, Olga used the sale of what was left of the Romanoff heirlooms to refurbish the ancient house and open it to the public as a museum and a wedding and event facility.

Princess Olga Romanoff
©John Paul Brooke/ScopeFeatures.com

Through spending time with her imperial grandmother, Olga had befriended a young Prince Charles, Prince of Wales. Her name was often mentioned in a popular press pastime of the late 60s and early 70s, that of guessing whom Prince Charles would marry. The pre-teen Lady Diana Spencer wasn't on anyone's radar back then.

Ultimately, in 1975, Olga married a man a little lower on the table of precedence, Thomas Mathew, a member of the Irish Gentry. His father, Francis, had once been the managing editor of *The Times*. The couple had four children, but sadly the youngest died aged only seventeen months. Of the three surviving children only the eldest, Nicholas, is married. He is the father of three children.

Both Olga and her second son, Francis, have appeared on reality television. Olga was a consultant who gave advice to contestants on *Australian Princesses*, inspired by the marriage of fellow Aussie Mary Donaldson to Crown Prince Fredrik of Denmark. Francis, meanwhile, actually competed as a contestant on the Ukraine version of *The Bachelor*. Since he is still not married we can only assume he did not win. Luckily, he has a successful career as a freelance photograp[her to fall back on.

Late in 2017, a year after the death of Prince Dmitry Romanovich, Olga was elected as President of the Romanoff Family Association. She is the fifth person to hold the position and the first female.

The descendants of Grand Duchess Xenia's next three sons are now all extinct in the male line. Prince Feodor lived out his life in France and had an only son,

Michel (1923–2008), who also had an only son Michel (1959–2001). The younger Michel had a daughter, Tatiana, but never married her mother. The mother, Mercedes Ustrell, later married the elder Michel, who legally adopted his granddaughter.

Prince Nikita had two sons, Nikita (1923–2007) and Alexander (1929–2002), who both married, but only Nikita had offspring, an only son, Feodor, known to his friends as Theo. Sadly, in 2007, Theo died, shortly after his father, as a young unmarried man, without children. The only survivor from this family is the widow of Alexander, Maria, who was born Donna Maria Valguarnere, of the noble family of the Princes di Nescemi in Italy.

Prince Dmitry's only child was a daughter, Nadejda (1933–2002). She married twice, the first time to Brian Allen, by whom she had three children, Penny, Marina and Alex. Penny married back into the Russian nobility when she married Prince Emmanuel Galitzine. She is now a mother of two and a grandmother of one. Marina is also a grandmother, via her only son. Alex remains unmarried.

This brings us to Grand Duchess Xenia's fifth son, Rostislav. He was married three times. His first wife was Princess Alexandra Galitzine. This is one of the marriages that is used as a comparison to that of Grand Duke Wladimir with Princess Leonida Bagration. Alexandra was from a junior branch of the family that once ruled Lithuania as Grand Dukes, the same way Leonida was from a junior branch of the family that once ruled the Kingdom of Georgia. Rostislav's younger brother, Vasili married a princess from a different line of the same family. By this reckoning, the descendants of Rostislav's first marriage should have succeeded as Head of the Imperial House ahead of Wladimir's daughter, Maria. The wrinkle in this plan is that his only son by the Galitzine marriage, Rostislav Jr, died before Wladimir, and *his* marriage disqualified him and his children under the Fundamental Laws.

Rostislav's later marriages were unquestionably unequal. The second, to American Alice Eilken, was the love affair that ended the his first marriage, and the third was to a minor Austrian noble, Hedwig von Chappuis. When he died in 1978, Rostislav left two children, Rostislav Jr. by his first wife, and Nicholas by his second.

The elder son, known as Rosti, was raised in Illinois by his mother and step-father, meat-packing tycoon Lester Amour. He later made his hopme in England from the 1990s. Rosti married two ladies from Chicago's upper society, Stephena Cook in 1960, and Christia Ipsen twenty years later. Stephena was a descendant of Congressman Daniel Cook (1794–1827) for whom the county that contains central Chicago was named.

Christia Ipsen was previously married to John Odell and brought a son, Erik, with her to her marriage with Rosti. Rosti adopted Erik, who is now known as Erik Odell-Romanoff. After Rosti's death, Christia remarried, to the Honourable David Russell, now the 5th Baron Ampthill.

By his first marriage, Rosti fathered a daughter, named Stephena for her mother. The younger Stephena has been married to Chicago businessman William Boggess III since 1988, but they have no children. By his second marriage, Rosti had three more children,

Rostislav III, Nikita, and Alexandra. Rosti contracted a rare illness, while attending the reburial of the Emperor and his family in 1998, and fell into a coma upon his return to England. He died six months later. Through his mother, Rosti had inherited a sizable fortune. He added to this in his career as a banker which is what took him to London to live. Upon his death, his widow and children were all well provided for.

Prince Rostislav Rostislavovich of Russia

Rosti's elder son, also named Rostislav, was known within his family as Mouse, most likely due to his very slender frame. Considering that the senior male-lines have either become extinct, or seem to be destined to, young Prince Rostislav will likely one day be the senior male representative of the Romanoff Family. In acknowledgment of this genealogical fact, he has recently been elected Vice-President of the Romanoff Family Association.

He is also the only male member of the family to return permanently to Russia. After being born in America and raised in England, he moved to Moscow in 2009. A budding watercolorist, he is best known for his watches designs. In 2010, he was appointed director of Petrodvorets Watch Factory, maker of the prestigious Raketa watches. Petrodvorets is Russia's oldest existing factory, and was founded by Rostislav's ancestor, Peter the Great.

Prince Rostislav Romanoff

In more recent years, with his improving Russian, he has been featured in several documentaries about his famous ancestors, and shares duties with Paul Kulikovsky, representing the family at historical and cultural events.

Though not married, he has fathered a son with Foteini Georganta, a Greek-born playwright who is based in London. They have named him Michael, and call him Misha, a common nickname that is also the Russian word for mouse.

The rest of Rostislav's immediate family remain out of the limelight. His younger siblings attended the reburial of the Emperors family with their parents in 1998, but for the most part they live their own lives, with Nikita now in New York and Alexandra in England.

Prince Rostislav Alexandrovich's second son, Nicholas, had a very different life. He was raised by his mother, Alice Eilken, in the Chicago area and had almost no contact with his royal father who had returned to England. Nicholas grew up in what would be considered the lower middle-class by American standards. He was married twice, and after a varied career of working for others started up a mail order business.

Prince Rostislav never sought permission for his second marriage, nor did Alice or her children receive any title from Grand Duke Wladimir, who was then Head of the Imperial House. Perhaps the feeling was that since they were being raised as Americans, they could not carry titles anyway. Whatever the case, Nicholas lived and died as plain Mr. Nick Romanoff. In 2000, he was killed in a car crash in Las Vegas, where he had made his home.

Nick left behind three grown children by his first marriage, Nick Jr., Dan, and Heather. Each of them have two children of their own. Nick Jr. also had a firstborn son, Cory, but the youngster met a tragic end at the hands of his mother's boyfriend, after she and Nick had divorced. The boyfriend was rightfully convicted of child abuse resulting in death and sentenced to a lengthy prison term.

In order to begin anew, Nick moved to California and found a new love. They now have two beautiful teenaged daughters, who were born in San Diego. His brother Dan is married to Korean emigre Soo Kim, and their pre-teen children, a daughter and a son, were born in Chicago. The baby sister, Heather, a school teacher, is married to Joey Munao, and also has a son and a daughter of similar ages to their cousins from Uncle Dan. So, the future of the male-line of the Romanoffs falls to these four grandsons of Prince Rostislav Alexandrovich: Rostislav, Nikita, Nick, and Dan. So far, there is only legitimate son among them, Dan's son, Jackson.

The youngest son of Grand Duchess Xenia was Prince Vasili (1907–1989). As mentioned previously, he married a Galitzine princess, who should be considered of equal rank if the Bagrations are. However, since his only child was a daughter, and he was outlived by Grand Duke Wladimir, the opportunity to claim to the throne never passed to this line.

His daughter, Marina, married in 1967 to William Beadleston, a fine art dealer based in New York. They have four children, three daughters and a son. The daughters are now married with their own families, nut the son, Nicholas, has remained single. After her divorce from Beadleston, Marina moved to Aspen, Colorado with her children. Most of them still live in western Colorado. Marina has recently remarried, to Dr. Daniel Stanberry, a chiropractor.

CHAPTER 5

Romanoff in all but name.

There are two remaining branches of the Romanoff family but they do not carry the Romanoff name. These are the Princes Ilyinsky and Princes Yourievsky, both the products of an unequal alliance by a tsar or grand duke. As we have seen, the descendants of Princes of Russia who married unequally were given the title Prince Romanovsky, which they generally shortened to Romanoff. However, when the groom in such a match was of grand ducal level, or even an Emperor, a new title was created altogether.

Such was the case when Alexander II married Catharina Dolgurka, his mistress and the mother of his three youngest children. Although she already carried the title princess, being a member of one of the old Rurik families, Alexander elevated her to a new title, Princess Yourievskya, to use as a married name. This title passed to three surviving children.

The elder of the two daughters, Olga married a man who was the product of another morganatic marriage, Count Georg on Merenberg, son of Prince Nikolaus of Prince Nikolaus of Nassau and Natalia Puskin, daughter of the famous poet and playwright. Georg's sister, Sophie, married Grand Duke Michael Mikhailovich, and was granted the title Countess de Torby. Olga does still have living descendants in the female line, who married into the noble families of von Rinteln and the Counts Loris-Melikoff.

The younger daughter, Katerina, married Prince Alexander Bariatinsky, and had two sons. However, this line has been extinct since 1992.

The only survivng son, Prince George Yourievsky (1872–1913) also married a fellow morganaut, Countess Alexandra Zarnekau, whose father was a Duke of Oldenburg. George and Alexandra had an only son, Prince Alexander (1901–1988), who in turn left an only son, Prince Hans-Georg.

Prince Hans-Georg Yourievsky

Hans-Georg, is one of the last two great-grandchildren of Emperor Alexander II. We shall meet the other one shortly. His parents made Switzerland their home in the 1950s and this is where Hans-Georg was raised, speaking both German and English. He has since learned some Russian but does not consider himself fluent in it.

He attended college and studied business administration which he turned into a successful career in the field of computer technology. An avid sportsman, some of his technology has been developed to assist with training and measuring the success of world-class athletes.

Since the fall of the Soviet Union, he has spent considerable energy reconnecting with the land of his ancestors. For example, he now sits on the Board of the European University at St. Petersburg. He also travels often to Russia to participate in events commemorating his ancestors.

When the first Princess Yourievsky was essentially sent into exile, after the assassination of Alexander II, she was given a considerable allowance from the imperial treasury. With wise investments, the family has maintained a respectable fortune, some of which Hans-Georg uses today for philanthropic goals aimed at helping the poorest who were left behind, when Russia became a capitalist country in the 1990s.

Prince Hans George Yourievsky

Our next descendant to discuss was born a Romanoff, but it turned out she wasn't. But first a little background. Grand Duke Paul, the youngest son of Alexander II by his first wife, pulled a stunt similar to his father. His royal wife had in childbirth with their second child, Dmitry. Although, he began his affair with Olga Karnovich Pistohlkors after his wife's death, if was she who still had a husband. She eventually gained a divorce and, despite overwhelming opposition from his family, the two were married in 1903, by which time they already had one son and Olga was pregnant with their second child.

This led to exile for Paul, so he established a home in Paris where he and Olga lived quite happily with their children. In time, Paul was forgiven and welcomed back to Russia just three months before World War I started. The following year, the Emperor granted Olga the title Princess Paley, which was extended to her children by Grand Duke Paul. Their only son, Vladimir, was among those killed in the mineshaft in Alapaevsk with Grand Duchess Elizabeth. He was only twenty-one at the time. Paul himself fell to the Bolsheviks the following January, being one of the four grand dukes executed in the Fortress of Saint Peter and Saint Paul.

Princess Paley was permitted to leave Russia with her daughters after her husband and son were murdered. She lived on to 1929, and died in Paris. The younger daughter, Natalia became a model and actress in the early days of French cinema. She married twice but, since both of her husbands were gay, it is not surprising that she did not have any children.

The elder daughter, Irina, also married twice. Her first husband was Prince Feodor, one of the six sons of Grand Duchess Xenia, Nicholas II's sister. We have already discussed their son, Prince Michel. She had another child, Princess Helene, however, it was revealed that Helene was not Feodor's daughter, but that of Irina's lover, Count Hubert de Monbrison. Feodor soon divorced Irina, but she did not marry Helene's father until 1950, when their daughter was nearly sixteen years old. So, although Helene was named Romanoff, she was only a Romanoff descendant via her mother. She is also the second living great-grandchild of Alexander II, again through her mother.

Now in her eighties, Helene still lives in France, having outlived both of her own husbands. She also had children by each one, but did not follow her mother's tricky path. She had her children while actually married to their fathers. As the eldest of the grandchildren are in their thirties, it is possible she will live to see her great-grandchildren. Of course, this family lives outside of the public eye, so it is quite possible those great-grandchildren already exist and we have just not heard about it yet.

Before Grand Duke Paul ran off with Princess Paley, he had been married to Princess Alexandra of Greece, and had two imperial children as well, Grand Duchess Maria and Grand Duke Dmitry. Maria lived a quixotic life, well described in her two-part autobiography, *The Education of a Princess* (1930) and *A Princess in Exile* (1932).

Grand Duke Dmitry also gained fame, but for all the wrong reasons. First, he was one of the co-conspirators with Prince Felix Yousoupoff in the murder of Rasputin. His exile for this act saved him from the Bolsheviks. Although he likely never reciprocated the feelings, he could thank his survival to being the object of a crush Felix had developed on the very handsome young prince. In his own memoirs, Felix admitted this was the reason he recruited Dmitry to assist with the murder.

Later, after the Revolution, Dmitry's model-like good looks landed him in an affair with Coco Chanel. An amateur chemist, he is credited with concocting the formula for her signature perfume, Chanel No. 5. Dmitry was famous for bouncing from the beds of one wealthy lady to another. One of them actually managed to get him to alter. She was Audrey Emery, heiress of a real-estate fortune based in Cincinnati, Ohio.

Not being from a royal family, the marriage was morganatic, and Grand Duke Cyril granted her the title Princess Romanovsky-Ilyinsky, the second part a reference to Dmitry's estate of Ilyinskoie in Russia, of course, lost to the Communists. As a matter of practicality, she simply called herself Princess Ilyinsky. When their only child was born, he was given the name Prince Paul Ilyinsky. Technically, he lost the title when he asserted his US citizenship, after initially living in France. However, his children continue to use the title socially to the present day. Dmitry and Audrey did not remain married long. Afterwards, she married another prince, this one from Georgia, but that marriage failed too. After that she chose to be called Mrs. Audrey Emery.

Dmitry's son, Paul Ilyinsky (1928–2004), inherited his mother's wealth. He returned with her to the United States as a child, later joining the US Marine Corps. He served as a war photographer during the Korean War and afterwards retired a lieutenant colonel. He lived in Cincinnati, serving on the board of Emery Industries, the company founded by his mother's family. He married and had four children. Later in life, he and his wife retired to Florida, where Paul was elected to be mayor of Palm Beach three times, after serving ten years as a city councilman.

Princes Dmitry and Michael Ilyinsky

The children of Prince Paul Ilyinsky were legally surnamed Romanoff-Ilyinsky, but were generally just called Ilyinsky. As anyone who grew up during the 50s and 60s might guess, having a Russian last name during the height of the Cold War was a difficult thing to live with. For the elder son, it was doubly hard, having been given a patently Russian first name, Dmitry, as well. To ease the way, he anglicized it to Tim.

Michael, a common name in English as well as Russian, had an easier time of it. The boys grew up in one of the swankier neighbors of Cincinnati, bookending their two sisters, Paula and Anne in age. While Michael is now on his third marriage, Tim got it right the first time and is still married to his college sweetheart, the former Martha McDowell. Tim and Martha now live in Connecticut with their three daughters nearby. The elder daughters are married and are starting families of their own.

Princes Dmitry (Tim) & Michael Ilyinsky with their wives.

Michael, an unofficial historian of the Romanoff family learned to embrace his Russian heritage after his first trip to the country in the late 1980s. He has since been back many times, and is a leading figure among matters pertaining to the extended Romanoff clan. He has also served in various positions within the Romanoff Family Association, which takes the position that all Romanoffs born after the Revolution are equal, even if their name is Ilyinsky.

By his first marriage, Michael fathered his only child, now a young lady in her twenties. Since he and his elder brother only have daughters, and Prince Hans-Georg Yourievsky has no children at all, the three of them are the last of the male-line descendants of Emperor Alexander II.

So yes, there are still Romanoffs remaining one hundred years after the brutal murders of the Tsar and much of his family. However, their numbers are dwindling fast, and it is looking as if only one branch will potentially carry on the name in the male line. The youngest of that line is a completely untitled half-American, half-Korean little boy named Jackson Romanoff.

God Save the Tsar!

Most of the surviving Romanoffs in 1998 in St. Petersburg
when they gathered for the reburial of the last Emperor and his family

THE DESCENDANTS OF NICHOLAS I

Nicholas I Pavlovich, **Emperor of All the Russians** (14/25 Jun 1796 Gatchina – 6/18 Feb1855 St. Petersburg) son of Paul, Emperor of All the Russians & Duchess Sophie (Maria Feodorovna) of Württemberg; suc. brother, Alexander I, 19 Nov 1825

= 19 Jun/1 Jul 1817 St.Petersburg; **Princess** Friederike Luise **Charlotte** Wilhelmine **of Prussia** (renamed **Alexandra** Feodorovna) (13 Jul 1798 Charlottenburg – 20 Oct/1 Nov 1860 Tsarskoie-Selo, near St. Petersburg) daughter of Friedrich Wilhelm III, King of Prussia & Duchess Luise of Mecklenburg

I. **Alexander II** Nikolaievich, **Emperor of All the Russians** (17/29 Apr 1818 Moscow – 1/13 Mar 1881 St. Petersburg) assassinated; suc. father 1855

=1 16/28 Apr 1841 St. Petersburg; **Princess** Maximiliane Wilhelmine Auguste Sophie **Marie of Hesse and By Rhine** (renamed **Maria** Alexandrovna) (8 Aug 1824 Darmstadt – 28 May/9 Jun 1880 St. Petersburg) daughter of Ludwig II, Grand Duke of Hesse and By Rhine & Princess Wilhelmine of Baden

=2 (morg.) 6/18 Jul 1880 St. Petersburg; **Princess Catherine** Mikhailovna **Dolgoruka**, cr. **Princess Yourievskya** (22 Oct/3 Nov 1847 Moscow– 15 Feb 1922 Nice) daughter of Prince Michael Dolgoruky & Vera Vichnecskya; cr. Princess Yourievskya 5/17 Feb 1880

issue of 1st:

A. **Grand Duchess Alexandra** Alexandrovna **of Russia** (18/30 Aug 1842 St. Petersburg – 16/28 Jun 1849 St. Petersburg)

B. **Grand Duke Nicholas** Alexandrovich, **Tsarevich of Russia** (8/20 Sep 1843 Peterhof – 24 Apr 1863 Nice) Tsarevich from 1855

C. **Alexander III** Alexandrovich, **Emperor of All the Russia** (26 Feb/10 Mar 1845 Peterhof – 21 Oct/2 Nov 1894 Livadia) suc. father 1881
= 28 Oct/9 Nov 1866 St. Petersburg; **Princess** Marie Sophie Friederike **Dagmar of Denmark** (renamed **Maria** Feodorovna) (26 Nov 1847 Copenhagen – 13 Oct 1928 Villa Hvidore, near Copenhagen) daughter of Christian IX, King of Denmark & Princess Luise of Hesse-Cassel

1. **Nicholas II** Alexandrovich, **Emperor of All the Russians** (24 Apr/6 May1868 Peterhof – 18 Jul 1918 Yekaterinburg) murdered with his wife and all of his children; suc. father 1894; abdicated for himself and his son 4/17 Mar 1917
= 14/26 Nov 1894 St. Petersburg; **Princess** Victoria **Alix** Helene Beatrice **of Hesse and By Rhine** (renamed **Alexandra** Feodorovna) (9 Jun 1872 Darmstadt – 18 Jul 1918 Yekaterinburg) daughter of Ludwig IV, Grand Duke of Hesse and By Rhine & Princess Alice of Great Britain

a. **Grand Duchess Olga** Nikolaievna **of Russia** (3/15 Nov 1895 St. Petersburg – 18 Jul 1918 Yekaterinburg)

b. **Grand Duchess Tatiana** Nikolaievna **of Russia** (30 May/11 Jun 1897 Peterhof – 18 Jul 1918 Yekaterinburg)

c. **Grand Duchess Maria** Nikolaievna **of Russia** (14/26 Jun 1899 Peterhof – 18 Jul 1918 Yekaterinburg)

d. **Grand Duchess Anastasia** Nikolaievna **of Russia** (5/18 Jun 1901 Peterhof – 18 Jul 1918 Yekaterinburg)

e. **Grand Duke Alexei** Nikolaievich, **Tsarevich of Russia** (30 Jul/21 Aug 1904 Peterhof – 18 Jul 1918 Yekaterinburg)

2. **Grand Duke Alexander** Alexandrovich **of Russia** (26 May/7 Jun 1869 St. Petersburg – 20 Apr/2 May 1870 St. Petersburg)

3. **Grand Duke George** Alexandrovich **of Russia** (27 Apr/9 May 1871 Tsarskoie-Selo – 9 Aug 1899 Abbas Tournon, Caucasus) Heir-Presumptive to Imperial Throne from 1894

4. **Grand Duchess Xenia** Alexandrovna **of Russia** (25 Mar/6 Apr

1875 St.Petersburg – 20 Apr 1960 Middlesex, England)
= 1894; ♦**Grand Duke Alexander of Russia** (1866 – 1933)
see: page

5. **Grand Duke Michael** Alexandrovich **of Russia** (de jure **Emperor Michael II**) (22 Nov/4 Dec 1878 St.Petersburg – Jul 1918 near Perm) murdered; technically suc. brother 1917 but never accepted Crown
   = (morg.) 15 Oct 1911 Vienna; **Natalia** Sergeievna **Cheremetevskya**, cr. **Countess Brasova** (27 Jun/9 Jul 1880 Moscow – 26 Jan 1952 Paris) daughter of Serge Cheremetevsky & Julia Sventitskya; =1st Vladimir Walffert; cr. Countess 1911
   a. **Count George** Mikhailovich **Brasov** (14 Jul/6 Aug 1910 Moscow – 2 Jul 1931 Auxerre)
6. **Grand Duchess Olga** Alexandrovna **of Russia** (1/13 Jun 1882 Peterhof – 24 Nov 1960 Toronto, Ontario)
   =1 28 Jul/9 Aug 1901 Gatchina (dv.1916); ♦**Duke Peter** Friedrich Georg **of Oldenburg** (9/21 Nov 1868 St. Petersburg – 11 Mar 1924 Biarritz) son of Duke Alexander of Oldenburg & Princess Eugenia Romanovskya, Duchess of Leuchtenberg
   =2 1/14 Nov 1916 Kiev; **Nicholas** Alexandrovich **Kulikovsky** (5/17 Nov 1881 Evsyratoska – 11 Aug 1958 Cooksville, Ontario, Canada) son of Alexander Kulikovsky & Evdokia Harin
   issue of 2nd (none by 1st):
   a. **Tikhon** Nikolaievich **Kulikovsky** (4/17 Aug 1917 Villa Ai-Todor, Crimea – 8 Apr 1993 Toronto, Ontario)
      =1 19 Apr 1942 Copenhagen (dv.1956); **Agnete** Carla **Petersen** (17 May 1920 Ballerup, Denmark – 2 Aug 2006 St. Jacobs, Ontario) daughter of Carl Petersen & Helga Nielsen; she =2nd Egon Petersen[2]
      =2 29 Sep 1959 Toronto; **Livia Sebesteyn** (17 Dec 1925 Budapest – 17 Jul 1982 Mississauga, Ontario) daughter of Aladár Sebesteyn & Helene Adler
      =3 8 Jun 1986 Toronto; **Olga** Nikolaievna **Pupynina** (*20 Sep 1926 Valjevo, Serbia) daughter of Nicholas Pupynin & Nina Kopernicka;

---

[2] They do not appear to have been related.

she =1st … Burton
issue of 2nd (none by others):
I) **Olga** Tikhonovna **Kulikovsky** (*9 Jul 1964 Toronto)
= 2 Jun 1994 Hamilton, Ontario; **Jose Cordeiro** (…)
A) **Peter** James **Cordeiro** (*Dec 1994)
B) **John** Alexander **Cordeiro** (*1996)
C) **Michael** Andrew **Cordeiro** (*1999)
D) **Victor Cordeiro** (*2001)

b. **Guri** Nikolaievich **Kulikovsky** (23 Apr 1919 Novo-Minskya, Caucasus - 11 Sep 1984 Brockville, Ontario)
=1 10 May 1940 Copenhagen (dv.1956); **Ruth Schwartz** (6 Feb 1921 – 22 Jul 2015 Copenhagen)
=2 …; Tamara Azanta (**Aza**) **Gagarina** (1 Aug 1927[3] – 5 Aug 2012 Ontario, Canada) =1st ... Lefebvre
issue of 1st (none by 2nd):
I) **Ksenia** Gurievna **Kulikovsky** (*19 Jun 1941 Ballerup)
=1 6 Nov 1961 Toronto (dv.1967); **Ralph Jones** (*28 Dec 1939)
=2 7 Jul 1967 Copenhagen (dv.1973); **Finn Larsen** (*14 Aug 1940 Copenhagen) son of Paul Larsen & Ella …
=3 26 Jun 1981 Greve, Denmark; **Aage Nielsen** (*2 May 1948 Nyköping) son of Carl Nielsen & Dagny …
issue of 1st:
A) **Paul** Edward **Kulikovsky** (*17 Dec 1960 Ottawa, Canada)
=1 2 Dec 1989 Copenhagen (dv.); **Kirsten Hansen** (*24 Mar 1959 Koege) daughter of Paul Hansen & Ruth …
=2 16 Jan 2004 London, England; **Ludmilla** Anatolievna **Antonova** (…) daughter of Anatoli Antonov & Olga ...
issue of 1st:
1) **Maiken Kulikovsky-Hansen** (*17 Mar 1990 Copenhagen)
2) **Zandra Kulikovsky-Hansen** (*16 Nov 1991 Copenhagen)

---

[3] Most sources give 1924 as her year of birth, but it is listed as 1927 on her gravestone.

issue of 2nd:

B) **Vivian Larsen** (*29 Dec 1962 Copenhagen)
= 21 Aug 1993 Ryslinge; **Bjarne Andersen** (20 Sep 1959 Kotagiri, India – 17 Sep 2014 Odense) son of Jos Andersen & Inger Rosenlund

1) **Anja** Rosenlund **Andersen** (*18 Jul 1988 Copenhagen) (twin)
= 15 Jul 2017 Vejle, Denmark; **Flemming Bjørnskov Pedersen** (...) son of Holger Bjørnskov Pedersen & Bodil ...

a) **Alfred Bjørnskov Pedersen** (*2016)

2) **Mathias Andersen** (*18 Jul 1988 Copenhagen) (twin)

3) **Philip Anderson** (*18 Jun 1997 Copenhagen)

C) **Peter Larsen** (*18 Dec 1966 Copenhagen)
has issue by **Anita** Luna **Hougaard** (*9 Jun 1965 Copenhagen) daughter of Fleming Christenen & Else ...; she = Jan Thomsen

1) **Ditte** Kulikovsky **Hougaard** (*2 Jan 1992 Glostrup)

2) **Theis** Steen **Hougaard Thomsen** (...)
has issue with **Jeanette ...** (...):

a) **Sally ...** (*2016)

issue of 3rd:

D) **Vibeke Nielsen** (*26 Nov 1981 Roskilde)
has issue by **Allan Vestergaard** (…):

1) **Cecilie Vestergaard Nielsen** (*31 Mar 2006 Roskilde)

II) **Leonid** Gurievich **Kulikovsky** (2 May 1943 Ballerup – 27 Sep 2015 Katherine, Northern Territory, Australia)

III) **Alexander** Gurievich **Kulikovsky** (*29 Nov 1948 Toronto)

D. **Grand Duke Vladimir** Alexandrovich **of Russia** (10/22 Apr 1847 St. Petersburg – 4/17 Feb 1900 St. Petersburg)
= 16/28 Aug 1874 St. Petersburg; **Duchess Marie** Alexandrine Elisabeth Eleonore **of Mecklenburg** (renamed **Maria** Pavlovna) (14 Nov 1854 Ludwigslust – 6 Sep 1920 Contrexéville, France) daughter of Friedrich Franz II, Grand Duke of Mecklenburg-Schwerin & Princess Auguste Reuss

1. **Grand Duke Alexander** Vladimirovich **of Russia** (1/13 Jul 1875

Tsarskoie-Selo – 4/16 Mar 1877 St. Petersburg)

2. **Grand Duke Cyril** Vladimirovich, **Head of the Imperial House of Russia** (30 Sep/12 Oct 1876 Tsarskoie-Selo – 13 Oct 1938 Neuilly) suc. cousin, Grand Duke Michael (Michael II), as Head of House 1918
= 8 Oct 1905 Tegernsee; (his first cousin) ♦**Princess Victoria Melita of Edinburgh, Princess of Saxe-Coburg and Gotha** Duchess of Saxony, Princess of Great Britain and Ireland (25 Nov 1876 Malta – 2 Mar 1936 Amorbach) daughter of Prince Alfred, Duke of Edinburgh, Duke of Saxe-Coburg and Gotha & Grand Duchess Maria of Russia

a. **Grand Duchess Maria** Kirillovna **of Russia** (2 Feb 1907 Coburg – 27 Oct 1951 Madrid)
= 25 Nov 1925 Coburg; Friedrich **Karl** Eduard Erwein, **Prince of Leiningen** (13 Feb 1898 Strassbourg – 2 Aug 1946 Saransk, Russia) died in Prisoner of War camp; son of Emich, Prince of Leiningen & Princess Feodora of Hohenlohe-Langenburg; suc. father 18 Jul 1939

I) **Emich** Kyrill Ferdinand Hermann, **Prince of Leiningen** (18 Oct 1926 Coburg – 30 Oct 1991 Amorbach) suc. father 1951
= 10 Aug 1950 Rastede; **Duchess Eilika** Stephanie Elisabeth Thekla Juliana **of Oldenburg** (2 Feb 1928 Lensahn – 26 Jan 2016) daughter of Hereditary Grand Duke Nikolaus of Oldenburg & Princess Helene of Waldeck and Pyrmont

A) **Princess Melita** Elisabeth Bathildis Helene Margarita **of Leiningen** (*10 Jun 1951 Amorbach)
= 14 Apr 1978 Karlsruhe; **Horst Legrum** (20 Jun 1929 Karlsruhe – 19 Sep 1994 Karlsruhe)
no issue

B) **Prince Karl-Emich** Nikolaus Friedrich Hermann **of Leiningen** (*12 Jun 1952 Amorbach) deprived of succession rights by father
=1 8 Jun 1984 Amorbach (civil) & 16 Jun 1984 Neuenstein (rel); **Princess Margarita** Katharina Elisabeth **of Hohenlohe-Oehringen** (28 Apr 1960 Munich – 27 Feb 1989 near Allershausen) daughter of

Kraft, Prince of Hohenlohe-Oehringen & Katharina von Siemens
=2 (morg.) 24 May 1991 Munich (civil) & 15 Jun 1991 Venice (rel) (dv.1998); **Gabriele** Renate **Thyssen** (*1 Apr 1963 Frankfurt) daughter of Helmut-Friedhelm Horney & Renate Kerkhoff; adopted by step-father Bodo Thyssen; =2nd Karim IV, Aga Khan changing her name to Inaara Begum Aga Khan
=3 8 Sep 2007 Amorbach (civil) & 7 Jun 2008 Pappenheim (rel); **Countess Isabel von und zu Egloffstein** (*12 Mar 1975 Bamberg) daughter of Count Albrecht von und zu Egloffstein & Countess Inge von der Recke von Volmerstein
issue of 1st:
1) **Princess Cäcilie** Maria Stephanie **of Leiningen** (*10 Jun 1988 Frankfurt)
issue of 2nd:
2) **Theresa** Anna Elisabeth **Prinzessin zu Leiningen** (*26 Apr 1992 Frankfurt)
issue of 3rd:
3) **Prince Emich** Albrecht Karl **of Leiningen** (*12 Apr 2010)

C) **Andreas, Prince of Leiningen** (*27 Nov 1955 Frankfurt) suc. father 1991
= 5 Oct 1981 Amorbach (civil) & 11 Oct 1981 Gmunden (rel); **Princess Alexandra** Irene Margaretha Elisabeth Bathildis **of Hanover** Duchess of Brunswick-Lüneburg, Princess of Great Britain and Ireland (*18 Feb 1959 Hanover) daughter of Ernst August, Prince of Hanover & Princess Ortrud of Schleswig-Holstein-Sonderburg-Glücksburg
1) **Hereditary Prince Ferdinand** Heinrich Emich Christian Karl **of Leiningen** (*12 Aug 1982 Frankfurt)
= 16 Sep (civil) & 5 Oct (rel) 2017 Amorbach; ♦**Viktoria Luise** Kira Ehrengard **Prinzessin von Preussen** (*2 May 1982 Berlin) daughter of Prince Friedrich Wilhelm of Prussia & Ehrengard von Reden

no issue

2) **Princess Olga** Margarita Valerie Elisabeth Stephanie Alexandra **of Leiningen** (*23 Oct 1984 Frankfurt)

3) **Prince Hermann** Ernst Johann Albrecht Paul **of Leiningen** (*13 Sep 1987 Frankfurt)
= 25 Mar (civil) & 1 Jul (rel) 2017 Amorbach; **Isabelle** Franziska Sophie **Heubach** (*1988) daughter of Hans Heubach & Gabriele ...
no issue

D) **Princess Stephanie** Margarita **of Leiningen** (*1 Oct 1958 Frankfurt)

II) **Prince Karl** Wladimir Ernst Heinrich **of Leiningen** (2 Jan 1928 Coburg – 28 Sep 1990 Jerusalem)
= 14 Feb 1957 Amorbach (civil) & 20 Feb 1957 Cannes (rel) (dv.1968); **Princess Maria Louisa of Bulgaria** Princess of Saxe-Coburg and Gotha, Duchess of Saxony (*31 Jan 1933 Sofia) daughter of Boris III, King of the Bulgarians & Princess Giovanna of Savoy; =2nd Bronislaw Chrobok

A) **Prince** Karl **Boris** Frank Martwart **of Leiningen** (*17 Apr 1960 Toronto)
=1 14 Feb 1987 Westfield, New Jersey (dv.1996); **Millena Manova** (22 Aug 1962 Sofia – 20 Nov 2015 Greenwich, Connecticut) daughter of Waldimir Manov & Elly Nedeva
=2 11 Sep 1998 Neptune, New Jersey; **Cheryl** Anne **Riegler** (*9 Aug 1962 Jersey City) daughter of Henry Riegler & Janice Rankin
issue of 1st:

1) **Prince Nicholas** Alexander Karel Friedrich **of Leiningen** (*25 Oct 1991 Philadelphia)

issue of 2nd:

2) **Prince Karl Heinrich of Leiningen** (*17 Feb 2001 Long Branch, New Jersey)

3) **Princess Juliana** Elisabeth Maria **of Leiningen** (*19 Sep 2003 Long Branch)

B) **Prince Hermann** Friedrich Roland Fernando **of Leiningen** (*16 Apr 1963 Toronto)

= 11 Mar (civil) & 16 May (rel.) 1987 Oakville; **Deborah Cully** (*2 Feb 1961 Belfast, Northern Ireland)

1) **Princess Tatiana** Victoria Maureen **of Leiningen** (*27 Aug 1989 Toronto)
= 17 Jun 2017 Ancaster, Ontario; **Clayton Reynolds** (*28 Feb 1990)
no issue

2) **Princess Nadia** Christine Ruth **of Leiningen** (*16 Dec 1991 Toronto)

3) **Princess Alexandra** Sophia Marie **of Leiningen** (*18 Dec 1997 Toronto)

III) **Princess Kira** Melita Feodora Marie Viktoria Alexandra **of Leiningen** (18 Jul 1930 Coburg – 24 Sep 2005 London)
= 1963; ♦**Prince Andrej of Yugoslavia** (1929 – 1991)
see: page

IV) **Princess Margarita** Ileana Viktoria **of Leiningen** (9 May 1932 Coburg – 16 Jun 1996 Überlingen)
= 5 Jan 1951 Sigmaringen (civil) & 3 Feb 1951 Amorbach (rel); **Friedrich Wilhelm** Ferdinand Josef Maria Manuel Georg Meinrad Fidelis Benedikt Michael Hubert, **Prince of Hohenzollern** (3 Feb 1924 Umkirch – 16 Sep 2010 Umkirch) son of Friedrich, Prince of Hohenzollern & Princess Margarete of Saxony; suc. father 6 Feb 1965

A) **Karl Friedrich** Emich Meinrad Benedikt Fidelis Maria Michael Gerold, **Prince of Hohenzollern** (*20 Apr 1952 Sigmaringen) suc. father 2010
=1 17 May 1985 Sigmaringen (civil) & 15 Jun 1985 Beuron (rel) (dv.2010); **Countess Alexandra** Petra Sofie **Schenk von Stauffenburg** (*25 May 1960 Detmold) daughter of Count Clemens Schenk von Stauffenburg & Countess Clementine von Wolff Metternich zur Gracht
=2 17 Jul 2010 Schloss Umkirch; **Katharina de Zomer** (*16 Jul 1959 Hamburg)
issue of 1st (none by 2nd):

1) **Hereditary Prince Alexander** Friedrich Antonius Johannes **of Hohenzollern** (*16 Mar 1987 New York)

2) **Princess Philippa** Marie Carolina Isabelle **of Hohenzollern** (*2 Nov 1988 New York)

3) **Princess Flaminia** Pia Eilika Stephanie **of Hohenzollern** (*9 Jan 1992 Munich)
4) **Princess Antonia** Elisabeth Georgina Tatiana **of Hohenzollern** (*22 Jan 1995 Munich)
B) **Prince Albrecht** Johannes Hermann Meinrad Stephan **of Hohenzollern** (*3 Aug 1954 Umkirch)
= 8 Sep 2001 Rome; **Nathalie Rocobado de Viets** (*10 Nov 1970 Hamburg) daughter of Claus Viets & Hortensia Rocabado
1) **Princess Josephine** Marie Isabelle Sophia Margarete **of Hohenzollern** (*31 Oct 2002 Munich)
2) **Princess Eugenia** Bernadette Maria Theresa Esperanza **of Hohenzollern** (*8 Jun 2005 Munich)
C) **Prince Ferdinand** Maria Fidelis Leopold Meinrad Valentin **of Hohenzollern** (*14 Feb 1960 Sigmaringen)
= 10 May 1996 Sigmaringen (civil) & 3 Aug 1966 Csicsó, Slovakia (rel); **Countess Ilona** Marie-Therese Renee Franziska **Kalnoky de Köröspatak** (*9 Mar 1968 Bruck) daughter of Count Aljós Kalnoky de Köröspatak & Baroness Sieglinde von Oer
1) **Prince Aloys** Maria Friedrich Karl **of Hohenzollern** (*6 Apr 1999 Berlin)
2) **Prince Fidelis** Maria Anton Alexis Hans **of Hohenzollern** (*25 Apr 2001 Berlin)
3) **Princess Victoria** Margarita Sieglinde Johanna Isabella Maria **of Hohenzollern** (*28 Jan 2004 Berlin)
V) **Princess Mechtilde** Alexandra **of Leiningen** (*2 Jan 1936 Würzburg)
= 24 (civil) & 25 (rel) Nov 1961 Amorbach; **Karl Anton Bauscher** (*26 Aug 1931 Grafenwöhr) son of Rudolf Scholl & Hedwig Ficher
A) **Ulf** Stephan Karl Heinz **Bauscher** (*20 Feb 1963 Frankfurt)
B) **Berthold** Alexander Erik **Bauscher** (*31 Oct 1965 Bamberg)
= 29 Mar 1991 Überlingen (civil) & 30 Mar 1996 Meersburg (rel); **Anett** Christin **Kuhfuss** (*8 Jun 1966 Ludwigsburg) daughter of Erik Kuhfuss & Christin

Richter
1) **Franka** Silke Stephanie **Bauscher** (*12 Sep 1996 Frankfurt
2) **Erik** Johann Berthold **Bauscher** (*13 Aug 1998 Ludwigsburg)
3) **Lorenz** Martin Julius **Bauscher** (*20 Apr 2002 Tamm)
C) **Johann** Karl Joachim Fritz Markwart **Bauscher** (*2 Feb 1968 Bamberg)
= ...; **Katja Jäger** (...)
no issue
VI) **Prince Friedrich Wilhelm** Berthold **of Leiningen** (18 Jun 1938 Würzburg – 31 Aug 1998 Miesbach)
=1 9 Jul 1960 Würzburg (dv.1962); **Karin** Evelyn **Goss** (*27 May 1942 Nuremberg – 28 Jul 2016)
=2 23 Aug 1971 Gmunden; **Helga Eschenbacher** (5 Jan 1940 Gmunden – 29 Mar 1999 Buchen) daughter of Hans Eschenbacher & Sofie Theobald
no issue
VII) **Prince Peter Viktor of Leiningen** (23 Dec 1942 Würzburg – 12 Jan 1943 Würzburg)
b. **Grand Duchess Kira** Kirillovna **of Russia** (9 May 1909 Paris – 8 Sep 1967 St.Briac)
= 1938; **♦Louis Ferdinand, Prince of Prussia** (1907 – 1994)
see: page
c. **Grand Duke Wladimir** Kirillovich, **Head of the Imperial House of Russia** (13 Aug 1917 Borga, Finland – 21 Apr 1992 Miami, Florida) suc. father 1938
= 13 Aug 1948 Lausanne; **Princess Leonida** Georgeievna **Bagration-Moukhranskya** (23 Sep 1914 Tiblisi – 23 May 2010 Madrid) daughter of Prince George Bagration-Moukhransky & Elena Zlotkova; =1st Sumner Kirby
I) **Grand Duchess Maria** Vladimirovna, **Head of the Imperial House of Russia** (*23 Dec 1953 Madrid) suc. father 1992
= 4 Sep 1976 Dinard (civil) & 22 Sep 1976 Madrid (rel) (dv.1985); **Prince Franz Wilhelm** Viktor Christoph Stephan **of Prussia** (*3 Sep 1943 Grünberg) son of Prince

Karl Franz Joseph of Prussia & Princess Henriette of Schoenaich-Carolath; was baptised into the orthodox religion as **Michael** Pavlovich and granted title **Grand Duke of Russia** by father-in-law, but no longer uses either name or title

A) **Grand Duke George** Mikhailovich **of Russia**, Prince of Prussia (*13 Mar 1981 Madrid)

3. **Grand Duke Boris** Vladimirovich **of Russia** (12/24 Nov 1877 St. Petersburg – 9 Nov 1943 Paris)
= (morg.) 12 Jul 1919 Genoa; **Zenaida** Sergeievna **Rachevskya** (22 Oct/3 Nov 1898 Dvinsky – 30 Jan 1963 Paris) daughter of Serge Rachevsky & Polyxena Bartholomai; =1st … Elisseev and =3rd Constantin Djanumov
no issue

4. **Grand Duke Andrew** Vladimirovich **of Russia** (2/14 May 1879 Tsarskoie-Selo – 30 Oct 1956 Paris)
= (morg.) 30 Jan 1921 Cannes; **Mathilda Krzesinska** (renamed **Maria** Feodorovna and cr. **Princess Krassinskya** 1921 (20 Aug/1 Sep 1872 Ligovo – 7 Dec 1971 Paris) daughter of Felix Krzesinski & Julia Demininska
a. **Prince Vladimir** Andreievich **Krassinsky** (30 Jun/13 Jul 1902 Strelona – 23 Apr 1974 Paris)

5. **Grand Duchess Elena** Vladimirovna **of Russia** (17/29 Jan 1882 Tsarskoie-Selo – 13 May 1957 Athens)
= 1902; ♦**Prince Nicholas of Greece** (1872 – 1938)
see: page

E. **Grand Duke Alexei** Alexandrovich **of Russia** (2/14 Jan 1850 St. Petersburg – 27 Nov 1908 Paris)
has issue by **Alexandra** Vassilievna **Zhukovskya** (12 Nov 1842 Düsseldorf – 26 Aug 1899 Baden-Baden) daughter of Vassili Zhukovsky & Elisabeth von Beutern; she is rumored to have married Grand Duke Alexei in 1870 in Italy, but no evidence has surfaced supporting such a marriage; she later married Christian von Wohrmann:

1. **Count Alexei** Alexeievich **Belevsky-Zhukovsky** (14 Nov 1871 Salzburg – 1932 Tiblisi) murdered by the Communists; cr. Count 9/21 Mar 1884
=1 3/15 Aug 1884 Ilynskoie (dv.); **Princess Maria** Petrovna

Troubetzkoya (24 May/5 Jun 1872 Tsarskoie-Selo – 20 Mar 1954 Neuilly) daughter of Prince Peter Troubetzkoy & Princess Elizabeth Beloskya-Belozerskya
=2 …; **Baroness Natalia** Vladimirovna **Schoeppingk** (…) daughter of Baron Vladimir Schoeppingk & Sofia Ermolovna
issue of 1st (none by 2nd):
a. **Countess Elizabeth** Alexaeivena **Belevskya** (25 Jun/7 Jul 1896 Moscow – 30 Jul 1975 Princeton, New Jersey)
=1 Jan 1917 Moscow; **Peter** Dmitrievich **Ghika-Perevoschikov** (24 Feb/8 Mar 1872 Moscow – 28 Jun 1937 Florence) son of Peter Ghika-Perovschikov & Katharina Moscina
=2 Jul 1939; **Arthur** Vincent **Lourie** (2/14 May 1892 St. Petersburg – 13 Oct 1966 Princeton)
issue of 1st (none by 2nd):
I) **Maria** Petrovna **Ghika-Perovschikova** (14/27 Oct 1917 Odessa – 1 Aug 1990 Grasse)
= 13 Oct 1943 Paris (dv.1960); **Lucien Teissier** (22 Aug 1908 Marseilles – Feb 2006 Toulouse) son of Louis Teissier & Louise Ségond
A) **Alexis Teissier** (*27 Aug 1946 Neuilly)
= 1972 (dv.1980); **Allana Chesebro** (…)
no issue
B) **Marie Beatrice** Svetlana **Teissier** (*19 Mar 1951 Neuilly)
II) **Dmitri** Petrovich **Ghika-Perevoschikov** (25 Jan 1920 Rapollo – 23 Aug 1960 Neuilly)
= May 1944 (dv.1947); **Marina** Nikolaievna **Ouroussova** (…) daughter of Nicholas Ouroussov
no issue
b. **Countess Alexandra** Alexeievna **Belevskya** (19 Feb/2 Mar 1899 Moscow – 12 Oct 1994 New York) her name at time of death was Alexandra Fells. It is unclear if she shortened Flevitzky to Fells or if she remarried
=1 9 Sep 1925 Berlin (dv.1950); **Henry de Lepp** (29 Jan/10 Feb 1897 – 25 May 1956 Annesse) son of Peter-Abraham de Lepp & Eva Willems
=2 20 Nov 1965 New York; **George Flevitzky** (1904 St.

Petersburg – 11 May 1960 St. Petersburg) son of Ivan Flevitzky & Vera Domanevskya
no issue

c. **Countess Maria** Alexeivna **Belevskya** (13/26 Oct 1901 Moscow – 19 Aug 1996 Cormeilles)
=1 17 Sep 1922 Berlin; **Vladimir** Sergeievich **Sverbeev** (24 Oct/5 Nov 1892 Yalta – 3 Jan 1951 Neuilly) son of Serge Sverbeev & Anna Brezobrazova
=2 28 Oct 1959 New York; **Vladimir** Alexandrovich **Yanuchevsky** (28 May/9 Jun 1887 St. Petersburg – 13 Feb 1970 Paris) son of Alexander Yanuchevsky & Lydia Tchernya
issue of 1st (none by 2nd):
I) **Elizabeth** Sergeievna **Sverbeeva** (*28 Aug 1923 Berlin)
=1 9 Nov 1947 New York (dv.1951); **Alexander** Georgeievich **Tarsadze** (9/22 Jan 1901 Tiblisi – 18 Mar 1978 New York) son of George Tarsadze & Princess Elizabeth Eristova
=2 9 May 1965 New York; **Charles Byron-Patrikiades** (15 Dec 1918 Istanbul – 28 Nov 2013 New York City) son of Antoine Patrikiades & Sophia Byron
no issue

d. **Count Serge** Alexeievich **Belevsky-Zhukovsky** (5/18 Feb 1904 Moscow – 27 Nov 1953 Los Angeles)
= 26 Jan 1925 Paris; **Nina** Sergeievna **Botkina** (6 May 1901 Bern, Switzerland – 16 Oct 1966 Vevey) daughter of Serge Botkin & Nina von Butzow
I) **Countess Hélène** Sergeievna **Belevskya** (*31 Aug 1920 Paris)
=1 17 Nov 1949 (dv.1956); **Nicholas** Alexeievich **Mojaisky** (*17 Aug 1928 Paris) son of Alexei Mojaisky & Olga Weriguina
=2 9 Jul 1956 Paris; **Count Cyril** Mikhailovich **Nieroth** (14 Apr 1930 Boulogne – 28 Jun 2005 Paris) son of Count Michael Nieroth & Countess Katharina Kleinmichel
issue of 1st:
A) **Alexis** Nikolaievich **Nieroth** (*20 Dec 1951 Boulogne) adopted by step-father 1975
= 31 May 1975 Sea Cliff, New York; **Pamela**

Waldbauer (*17 Mar 1953) daughter of Robert Waldbauer & Mary Hammel

1) **Katherine** Alexeievna **Nieroth** (*27 Feb 1983 in Connecticut)

= 11 Jun 2011 Siascnet, Mass.; **John Ghirardelli** (...)

a) **Emma Ghirardelli** (*2015)

2) **Christopher** Alexeievich **Nieroth** (*23 Aug 1989 in Connecticut)

issue of 2nd:

B) **Count Peter** Kirillovich **Nieroth** (12 Jun 1957 Neuilly – 26 May 2002 Paris)

C) **Countess Elizabeth** Kirillovna **Nieroth** (*2 Feb 1966 Houston, Texas)

F. **Grand Duchess Maria** Alexandrovna **of Russia** (5/17 Oct 1853 Tsarskoie-Selo – 24 Oct 1920 Zurich)

= 10/23 Jan 1874 St. Petersburg; **Prince Alfred** Ernest Albert **of Great Britain** and Ireland, **Duke of Edinburgh and Strathearn** Earl of Ulster and Kent, **Duke of Saxe-Coburg and Gotha** Duke of Saxony (6 Aug 1844 Windsor – 30 Jul 1900 near Coburg) son of Prince Albert of Saxe-Coburg and Gotha & Victoria, Queen of the United Kingdom; cr. Duke of Edinburgh etc. 24 May 1866; suc. uncle, Ernst II, as Duke of Saxe-Coburg and Gotha 22 Aug 1893

Until 1917 issue was additionally titled Prince/ss of Saxe-Coburg and Gotha, Duke/Duchess of Saxony:

1. **Prince Alfred** Alexander William Ernest Albert **of Edinburgh, Hereditary Prince of Saxe-Coburg and Gotha** (15 Oct 1874 London – 6 Feb 1899 Merano)

2. **Princess Marie** Alexandra Victoria **of Edinburgh** etc. (29 Oct 1875 Kent – 10 Jul 1938 Sinaia, Romania)

= 10 Jan 1893 Sigmaringen; **Ferdinand** Viktor Albert Meinrad, **King of Romania** Prince of Hohenzollern (25 Aug 1865 Sigmaringen – 20 Jul 1927 Sinaia) son of Leopold, Prince of Hohenzollern & Infanta Antonia of Portugal; suc. uncle, Carol I, 10 Oct 1914

Children were additionally titled Prince/ss of Hohenzollern:

a. **Carol II, King of Romania** (15 Oct 1893 Sinaia – 4 Apr 1953 Estoril, Portugal) renounced succession rights 25 Dec 1925 but claimed the Throne 6 Jun 1930; abdicated 6 Sep 1940

=1 (morg) 31 Aug 1918 Odessa (ann.1919); Joana Marie Valentia (**Zizi**) **Lambrino** (3 Oct 1898 Roman, Romania – 11 Mar 1953 Paris) daughter of Constantin Lambrino & Euphrosine Alcaz; marriage was considered illegal under Romanian law
=2 10 Mar 1921 Athens (dv.1928); ♦**Princess Helen of Greece** (3 May 1896 Athens – 28 Nov 1982 Lausanne) daughter of Constantine I, King of the Hellenes & Princess Sophie of Prussia; granted style of Queen Mother of Romania 1940
=3morg 3 Jun 1947 Rio de Janeiro (civil) & 19 Aug 1949 Lisbon (rel); **Elena Lupesu** (cr. **Princess of Hohenzollern**) (15 Sep 1895 Hertza – 29 Jun 1977 Estoril) daughter of Nicholas Wolf & Elisabeth Falk; cr. Princess 1949 by the Prince of Hohenzollern
issue of 1st:
I) Mircea Gregor **Carol von Hohenzollern** (8 Jan 1920 Budapest – 27 Jan 2006 London)
=1 22 Mar 1944 Paris (dv.1960); **Hélène** Henriette **Nagavitzine** (*26 May 1925 Paris) daughter of Paul Nagavitzine & Marguerite Brissot; =2nd Michael Raina
=2 20 Dec 1960 Paris (dv.1977); **Thelma** Jeanne **Williams** (15 Nov 1930 Nashville, Tennessee – 5 Jun 1988 Rutland, Vermont) daughter of Richard Williams & Josephine Owens
=3 27 Jun 1984 London; **Antonia Colville** (29 May 1939 Bracken, England – 13 Jun 2007) daughter of Edward Colville & Barbara Denney; =1st Gary Ropner
issue of 1st:
A) **Paul** Philippe **von Hohenzollern** (*3 Aug 1948 Paris) calls himself Prince Paul of Romania, but was not recognized as such by King Michael
= 15 Sep 1996 Bucharest; **Lia Triff** (*23 Feb 1949 Great Lakes, Illinois) daughter of Thomas Triff & Elizabeth Andrea; =1st Melvin Belli
1) **Carol** Ferdinand **von Hohenzollern** (*11 Jan 2010 Bucharest)
issue of 2nd:

B) Ion Georg Nicolas **Alexander von Hohenzollern** (*1 Sep 1961 Poole, Dorset)

issue of 2nd:

II) **Michael, King of Romania** (25 Oct 1921 Sinaia – 5 Dec 2017 Lausanne) suc. grandfather 1927; lost Throne to father 1930; suc. father 1940; deposed 30 Dec 1947
= 10 Jun 1948 Athens; **Princess Anne** Antoniette Françoise Charlotte **of Bourbon-Parma** (18 Sep 1923 Paris – 1 Aug 2016 Morges, Swirzerland) daughter of Prince René of Bourbon-Parma & Princess Margarethe of Denmark

A) **Crown Princess Margarita of Romania** (*26 Mar 1949 Lausanne) suc. father as Head of the Royal House 2017
= 21 Sep 1996 Lausanne; **Radu Duda** (cr. **Prince of Romania**) (*6 Jul 1960 Iasi, Romania) son of Rene Radu & Gabriela Constadade; cr. Prince Jan 2008 by father-in-law
no issue

B) **Princess Helen of Romania** (*15 Nov 1950 Lausanne)
=1 20 Jul 1983 Durham (civil) & 24 Sep 1983 Lausanne (rel) (dv.1991); Leslie **Robin Medforth-Mills** (8 Dec 1942 Sproatley, York – 2 Feb 2002 Geneva) son of Cyril Mills & Nora Medforth
=2 18 Aug 1998 Peterlee; **Alexander** Philip Nixon **McAteer** (*22 Oct 1964 Easington)
issue of 1st (none by 2nd):

1) **Nicholas** Michael **de Roumanie-Medforth-Mills** (*1 Apr 1985 Geneva) cr. Prince by grandfather 1 Apr 2010 but deprived of title and succession Jul 2015
= Dec 2017 London; **Alina** Maria **Binder** (*26 Jan 1988 Constanta, Romania) daughter of Heiz Binder & Rodica Iancu
no issue[4]

[4] Nicholas is currently involved in a dispute with Nicoleta Cirjan over the paternity of her daughter, Iris Jean Cirjan (*9 Feb 2016 Bucharest). She claims Nicholas is the father, but she has yet to agree to a paternity test.

2) **Elisabeta-Karina de Roumanie-Medforth-Mills** (*4 Jan 1989 Newcastle-upon-Tyne)

C) **Princess Irina of Romania** (*28 Feb 1953 Lausanne)
=1 10 Feb 1983 Lausanne (civil) & 11 Feb 1984 Phoenix, Arizona (rel); **John Kreuger** (*3 Aug 1945 Solna, Sweden) son of Torsten Kreuger & Diana Gedberg
=2 2 Nov 2007 Reno, Nevada; **John** Wesley **Walker** (*30 Dec 1945 Douglas, Missouri) son of John Walker & Lucy Hall
issue of 1st (none by 2nd):

1) **Michael** Torstan de Roumanie **Kreuger** (*25 Feb 1985 Coos Bay, Oregon)
= 26 Feb 2011 Sisters, Oregon; **Tara** Marie **Littlefield** (*1981) daughter of James Littlefield & Cynthia ...; =1st Wyatt Cleaver

a) **Kohen Kreuger** (*28 Mar 2012)

2) **Angelika** Margarita Bianca **Kreuger** (*29 Dec 1986 Coos Bay)
= 25 Oct 2009 Myrtle Point, Oregon; **Richard Knight** (*31 Oct 1984 Coos Bay) son of Randy Akins & Suzanne Knight

a) **Courtney Knight** (*31 May 2007 Coos Bay)
b) **Diana Knight** (*2 May 2011)

D) **Princess Sophie of Romania** (*29 Oct 1957 Tatoi, Greece)
= 29 Aug 1998 Neuilly (dv.); **Alain-Michel** Léonce **Biarneix** (also called **Alain-Michel de Laufenborg**) (*10 Jul 1957
Nancy) son of Robert Biarneix & Nadine Besillon

1) **Elisabeta-Maria** Bianca Elena **Biarneix** (*15 Aug 1999 Paris)

E) **Princess Maria of Romania** (*13 Jul 1964 Hellerup)
= 16 Sep 1995 New York (dv.2000); **Kazimierz Mystkowski** (*13 Sep 1958 Las-Toczyowo, Poland) son of Eugeniusz Mystkowski & Janina Wadelowska
no issue

b. **Princess Elisabeth** Charlotte Josephine Alexandra Victoria **of Romania** etc. (12 Oct 1894 Sinaia – 15 Nov 1956 Cannes)

= 2 Feb 1921 Bucharest (dv.1935); ♦**George II, King of the Hellenes** (19 Jul 1890 Tatoi – 1 Apr 1947 Athens) son of Constantine I, King of the Hellenes & Princess Sophie of Prussia
no issue

c. **Princess Marie of Romania** etc. (4 Jun 1900 Gotha – 22 Jun 1921 London)
= 8 Jun 1922 Belgrade; **Aleksandar I, King of Yugoslavia** (16 Dec 1888 Centinje, Montenegro – 9 Oct 1934 Marseilles) assassinated; son of Petar I, King of Serbia, Croatia, and Slovenia & Princess Zorka of Montenegro; suc. father 16 Aug 1921; declared King of Yugoslavia 3 Oct 1929

I) **Peter II, King of Yugoslavia** (6 Sep 1923 Belgrade – 3 Nov 1970 Denver, Colorado) suc. father 1934 (under regency of cousin, Prince Paul, until 2 Mar 1941); monarchy was abolished 29 Nov 1945
= 20 Mar 1944 London; **Princess Alexandra of Greece** (25 Mar 1921 Athens – 30 Jan 1993 Burges Hill, England) daughter of Alexander, King of the Hellenes & Aspasia Manos (see below)

A) **Crown Prince Alexander of Yugoslavia** (*17 Jul 1945 London) suc. father as Head of the Royal House 3 Nov 1970
=1 1 Jul 1972 Seville (dv.1985); **Princess Maria da Gloria** Henriqueta Dolores Lucia Micaela Rafaela Gabriela Gonzaga **of Orleans and Bragança** (*13 Dec 1946 Petrópolis, Brazil) daughter of Prince Pedro of Orleans and Bragança & Princess Maria de la Esperanza of the Two Sicilies; =2nd Ignacio de Mendia, Duke of Segorbe
=2 20 (civil) & 21 (rel) Sep 1985 London; **Katherine** Clairy **Bates** (*13 Nov 1943 Athens) daughter of Robert Bates & Anna Dosti; =1st Jack Andrews
issue of 1st (none by 2nd):

1) **Prince Peter of Yugoslavia** (*5 Feb 1980 Chicago)

2) **Prince Philip of Yugoslavia** (*15 Jan 1982 Falls Church, Virginia) (twin)
= 7 Oct 2017 Belgrade, Serbia; **Danica Marinkovic**

(*17 Aug 1986 Belgrade) daughter of Milan Marinmkovic-Cile & Beba ...

a) due 2018

3) **Prince Alexander of Yugoslavia** (*15 Jan 1982 Falls Church) (twin)

II) **Prince Tomislav of Yugoslavia** (9 Jan 1928 Belgrade – 12 Jul 2000 Oplenac, Serbia)

=1 5 (civil) & 6 (rel) Jun 1957 Salem, Germany (dv.1981); ♦**Princess Margarita** Alice Thyra Viktoria Marie Louise Scholastica **of Baden** (14 Jul 1932 Schloss Salem – 15 Jan 2013 London) daughter of Berthold, Margrave of Baden & Princess Theodora of Greece

=2 16 Oct 1982 Bourneville, England; **Linda** Mary **Bonney** (*22 Jun 1949 London) daughter of Holbrook Bonney & Joan Evans

issue of 1st:

A) **Prince Nikolas of Yugoslavia** (*15 Mar 1958 London)

= 30 Aug 1992 Faaborg (civil) & 22 Nov 1992 Düsseldorf (rel) (dv.); **Ljilana Licanin** (*27 Dec 1959 Zemun) daughter of Lazar Licanin & Marija Sowie

1) **Princess Marija of Yugoslavia** (*4 Aug 1993 London)

has issue by **Enzo ...**:

a) **Enzo ...** (*2012)

b) a daughter (*2013)

B) **Princess Katarina of Yugoslavia** (*28 Nov 1959 London)

= 5 Dec 1987 London (dv.2011); George **Desmond** Lorenz **de Silva** (*13 Dec 1939 Ceylon, Sri Lanka) son of Edmund de Silva & Esmé Nathanialsz

1) **Victoria** Marie Esmé Margarita **de Silva** (*16 Sep 1991 London)

issue of 2nd:

C) **Prince George of Yugoslavia** (*25 May 1984 London)

= 15 Jul 2017 Oplenac, Serbia; **Fallon** Misti Kristin Elizabeth **Rayman** (...) daughter of ... Rayman & Elizabeth ...

no issue

D) **Prince Michael of Yugoslavia** (*15 Dec 1985 London)
= 23 Oct 2016 Oplenac; **Ljubica Ljubislavljevic** (*21 Sep 1989 Belgrade) daughter of Milorad Ljubislavljevic & Vera Sokolovic
no issue

III) **Prince Andrej of Yugoslavia** (28 Jun 1929 Bled – 7 May 1990 Irvine, California)
=1 1 (civil) & 2 (rel) Aug 1956 Kronberg (dv.1962); ♦**Princess Christina** Margarethe **of Hesse** (10 Jan 1933 Kronberg – 21 Nov 2011 Gersau) daughter of Prince Christoph of Hesse and Princess Sophie of Greece; =2nd Robert van Eyck
=2 18 Sep 1863 Kent (civil) & 21 Oct 1963 Amorbach (rel) (dv.1972); ♦**Princess Kira** Melita Feodora Marie Viktoria Alexandra **of Leiningen** (18 Jul 1930 Coburg – 24 Sep 2005 London) daughter of Karl, Prince of Leiningen and Grand Duchess Maria of Russia
=3 30 Mar 1974 Palm Springs, California; **Eva Marie Anjelkovich** (*26 Aug 1926 Varnjacka-Banja, Serbia) daughter of Milan Anjelkovich & Ena Jovanovich; =1st Frank Lowe
issue of 1st:

A) **Princess Maria Tatiana of Yugoslavia** (*18 Jul 1957 London)
= 30 Jun 1990 St.Paul de Vence; **Gregory** Per Edward Anthony Michael **Thune-Larson** (*11 Aug 1953 London) son of Knut Thune-Larson & Solveig Tandberg
1) **Sonja** Tatiana **Thune-Larson** (*29 Oct 1992 Cagnes-sur-Mer)
2) **Olga** Kristin **Thune-Larson** (*26 Oct 1995 Cagnes-sur-Mer)

B) **Prince Christopher of Yugoslavia** (4 Feb 1960 London – 14 May 1993 Glengedale) killed when struck by a car while riding a bicycle

issue of 2nd (none by 3rd):

C) **Princess Lavinia** Marie **of Yugoslavia** (*18 Oct 1961 London)
=1 20 May 1989 London (dv.1993); **Erastos** Dimitrious

Sidiropolous (*31 Mar 1942 Alexandria, Egypt) son of Aristotle Sidiropolous & Evniki Klonos
=2 4 Oct 1998 London; **Austin Prichard-Levy** (20 Jan 1953 Roma, Australia – 5 Jan 2017 London) son of Hermann Levy & Brenda Prichard
issue of 1st:
1) **Andrej** Aristotle **Sidiropolous** (*22 Feb 1990 London)
issue of 2nd:
2) **Luca** Orlando Christopher **Prichard-Levy** (*14 Feb 2000 London)
Princess Lavinia also has issue by **Roy** Rexford **Finnimore** (…):
3) **Nadya-Marie Sidiropolous** (*11 Dec 1987 London) adopted by step-father 1990

D) **Prince Karl Wladimir** Kirill Andrej **of Yugoslavia** (*11 Mar 1964 London)
= 18 Apr 2000 London; **Birgitte Müller** (*7 Jul 1960 Bad Salzuflen) daughter of Helmut Müller & Gerda Martha; =1st Wolfgang Staudte
no issue

E) **Prince Dmitrij** Ivan Mihailo **of Yugoslavia** (*21 Apr 1965 London)

d. **Prince Nicolas of Hohenzollern** (formerly **Prince of Romania**) (18 Aug 1903 Sinaia – 9 Jul 1978 Madrid) deprived of royal rank 9 Apr 1937; cr. Prince of Hohenzollern 15 Jan 1947
=1 24 Oct 1931 Bucharest; **Joana** Lucia **Dumitrescu-Doletti** (24 Sep 1907 Bucharest – 19 Feb 1963 Lausanne) daughter of Ion Dumitrescu & Nella Theodoru; =1st Radu Savianu
=2 13 Jul 1967 Lausanne; **Thereza Lisboa Figueira de Melo** (10 Jun 1913 Rome – 30 Mar 1997 Madrid) daughter of Jeronymio Figueiro de Melo & Candida Lisboa; =1st Andres Piorti Boulton
no issue

e. **Mother Alexandra** (formerly **Princess Ileana of Romania**) (5 Jan 1909 Bucharest – 21 Jan 1991 Youngstown, Ohio)
=1 26 Jul 1931 Sinaia (dv.1954); **Archduke Anton** Maria

Franz Leopold Blanka Karl Joseph Ignaz Raphael Michael Margarita Nicetas **of Austria** Prince of Hungary and Bohemia, Prince of Tuscany (20 Mar 1901 Vienna – 22 Oct 1987 Mondsee) son of Archduke Leopold Salvator of Austria & Princess Blanca of Bourbon
=2 19 Jun 1954 Newton, Massachusetts (dv.1965); **Stefan** Virgil **Issarescu** (5 Oct 1906 Turnu-Severin, Romania – 21 Dec 2002 Providence, Rhode Island) son of Ionn Issarescu & Virginia Popescu
issue of 1st (none by 2nd):

I) **Archduke Stefan of Austria** etc. (15 Aug 1932 Mödling – 12 Nov 1998 Farmingham, Michigan)
= 28 Aug 1954 Milton, Massachusetts; Mary **Jerrine Soper** (19 Jun 1931 Boston – 14 Jul 2015 Commerce, Michigan) daughter of Charles Soper & Agnes McNeil
Issue is entitled to Archduke of Austria, etc. but use Habsburg-Lothringen as a surname as U.S. citizens.

A) **Archduke Christopher of Austria**, etc. (*26 Jan 1957 Boston)
=1 1 May 1987 Mt.Tamapais, California (dv.1994); **Elizabeth** Ann **Blanchette** (*22 Jan 1967 Peoria, Illinois) daughter of Larry Popejoy & Regina Keller
=2 15 Oct 1994 Clarkston, Michigan (dv.2001); **Catherine Ripley** (*5 Sep 1958 Pontiac, Michigan) daughter of Anthony Ripley & Anna Brunner
issue of 1st:

1) **Archduchess Saygan** Genevieve **of Austria**, etc. (*31 Oct 1987 Marin City, California)
has issue by **Leigh** Thomas **Schultes** (...):

a) **Wulfric** Aurelius **Habsburg-Schultes** (*10 Dec 2011 Novi, Michigan)

2) **Archduke Stefan** Christopher **of Austria**, etc. (*19 Jan 1990 Southfield, Michigan)
= 18 Oct 2014 Illinois; **Natalie Corder** (...)
no issue

issue of 2nd:

3) **Archduchess Maria Antonia of Austria**, etc. (*1 Oct 1997 Commerce, Michigan)

B) **Archduchess Ileana von Habsburg** (*4 Jan 1958 Detroit)
= 26 Jun 1979 Farmington Hills; **David Snyder** (*18 Nov 1956 Pontiac) son of Loyce Snyder & Laura Hutton
1) **Alexandra** Marie **Snyder** (*18 Aug 1984 Southfield)
= 25 Jun 2006; **Matthew Tillard** (...)
a) **Aaron** Nicholas **Tillard** (*5 Apr 2011 Holland, Michigan)
b) **Oliver** Stefan **Tillard** (*21 Apr 2013)
2) **Nicholas** David **Snyder** (*27 Feb 1987 Southfield)
= 28 Jul 2012 Michigan; **Jacqueline Jones** (...)
a) **Theoden** Adama **Snyder** (*13 May 2014)
3) **Constanza** Ileana **Snyder** (*23 Jun 1994 Southfield)
= 13 Aug 2016 Cedar, Michigan; **Calvin** Edward **Kuyers** (*1992) son of Michael Kuyers & Roberta Boone
no issue
C) **Archduke Peter of Austria**, etc. (*19 Feb 1959 Detroit)
=1 27 Jun 1981 Farmington Hills (dv.1985); **Shari** Suzanne **Reid** (*11 Sep 1960 Highland Park, Michigan) daughter of William Reid & Barbara Miller
=2 17 Jun 1989 Union Lake, Michigan; **Lauren Klaus** (*9 May 1956 Detroit) daughter of Martin John Klaus & Vera Kruk
issue of 2nd (by adoption – none by 1st):
1) **Oksana** Nicole **Habsburg** (*8 May 1991 Saratov, Russia)
has issue by **Amir Cavill** (...)
a) **Arya Cavill** (*18 Sep 2014)
2) **Alexander** Stefan **Habsburg** (*30 Jan 1996 Vilsk, Russia)
3) **Tatiana** Julia **Habsburg** (*28 Feb 1997 Saratov)
D) **Archduchess Constantza of Austria**, etc. (*2 Oct 1960 Detroit)
=1 16 Jan 1987 Franklin, Michigan (dv.1995); **Mark** Lee **Matheson** (*15 Feb 1958 Grosse Pointe, Michigan) son of Robert Matheson & Lois Dove; =1st Debra Kalita
=2 8 Nov 1997 Marietta, Georgia; **Michael** Dale **Bain**

(*4 Jan 1962 Rockwood, Tennessee) son of Eugen Bain & Betta Long
no issue

E) **Archduke Anton of Austria**, etc. (*7 Nov 1964 Detroit)
= 5 Nov 1991 Aurora, Ohio; **Ashley** Byrd **Carrell** (23 Aug 1966 Nashville – 24 Oct 2002 Geauga, Ohio) daughter of William Byrd & Paula Anderson
no issue

II) **Archduchess Maria Ileana of Austria** etc. (18 Dec 1933 Mödling – 11 Jan 1959 Rio de Janeiro) killed in a plane crash
= 6 (civil) & 7 (rel) Dec 1957 Vienna; **Count Jaroslav** Franz Josef Ignaz Maria **Kottulinsky,** Baron Kottulin, Krzizkowitz und Dobrenzenicz (3 Jan 1917 Graz – 11 Jan 1959 Rio de Janeiro) killed in plane crash; son of Count Karl Kunata Kottulinsky & Countess Maria Theresia von Meran

A) **Countess Maria Ileana Kottulinsky** etc. (25 Aug 1958 Klagenfurt – 13 Oct 2007 Brussels)
= 10 Oct 1997 Neudaughter; **Noel van Innis** (*15 Dec 1939 Tierlemont)
no issue

III) **Archduchess Alexandra of Austria** etc. (*21 May 1935 Sonneberg)
=1 31 Aug 1962 Mondsee (civil) & 3 Sep 1962 Salzburg (rel) (ann.1972, dv.1973); **Duke Eugen Eberhard** Albrecht Maria Joseph Ivan Rilsky Robert Ulrich Philipp Odo Carl Hubert **of Württemberg** (*2 Nov 1930 Karlsruhe) son of Duke Albrecht of Württemberg & Princess Nadejda of Bulgaria
=2 22 Aug 1973 Mondsee (civil) & 29 Dec 1973 Salzburg (rel); **Baron Viktor** Franz Clemens Otto Johann Hermann Julia Maria **von Baillou** (*27 Jun 1931 Vienna) son of Baron Clemens von Baillou & Magdalena Mirck
no issue

IV) **Archduke Dominic of Austria** etc. (*4 Jul 1937 Sonneberg)
=1 11 Jun 1960 Houston, Texas (dv.1999); Virginia **Engel**

von Voss (31 Mar 1937 Houston – 27 Sep 2010 Vienna) daughter of Friedrich von Voss & Mildred McKibben
=2 14 Aug 1999 North Salem, New York; Emmanuela (**Nella**) **Mlynarska** (*14 Jan 1948 Afula, Israel) daughter of Yadidia Mlynarski & Raissa Fogel
issue of 1st (none by 2nd):
A) **Archduke Sandor of Austria**, etc. (*13 Feb 1965 Vienna)
=1 15 May 2000 Berndorf (dv.2009); **Priska Vilcsek** (*18 Mar 1959 Hofheim) daughter of Herberth Vilcsek & Ela Haidhofer
=2 2010 (civil) & 19 Nov 2011 Vienna (rel.); **Herta** Margarete **Reyländer** (*19 Feb 1961)
issue of 1st (none by 2nd):
1) **Archduke Constantin of Austria**, etc. (*11 Jul 2000 Vienna)
B) **Archduke Gregor of Austria**, etc. (*20 Nov 1968 Vienna)
= 13 Aug 2011 Los Angeles; **Jacquelyn Frisco** (*17 Nov 1965 Los Angeles)
no issue
VI) **Archduchess Maria Magdalena of Austria** etc. (*2 Oct 1939 Sonneberg)
= 27 (civil) & 29 (rel) Aug 1959 Mondsee; **Baron Hans Ulrich von Holzhausen** (*1 Sep 1929 Windischgarten) son of Baron Kurt von Holzhausen & Mary Heipsler
A) **Baron Johann** Friedrich Anton **von Holzhausen** (*29 Jul 1960 Salzburg)
= 23 Sep 2001 Wartberg; **Brunilda Castejon-Schneider** (*14 Jul 1962 Madrid)
1) **Baron Laurenz von Holzhausen** (*21 Jun 2001 Vienna)
B) **Baron Georg** Ferdinand **von Holzhausen** (*16 Feb 1962 Salzburg)
= 30 Apr 1993 Vienna (civil) & 22 May 1993 Julich (rel); **Countess Elena** Maria Viktoria Ingeborg **von und zu Hohensbroech** (*1 May 1965 Kellenberg) daughter of Count Reinhart von und zu Hohensbroech &

Archduchess Immaculata of Austria
1) **Baron Alexander** Justinian Victor Christoph **von Holzhausen** (*28 Nov 1994 Vienna)
2) **Baron Tassilo** Johannes Christoph Donatus **von Holzhausen** (*4 May 1997 Vienna)
3) **Baron Clemens** Antonius Philipp Ferdinand **von Holzhausen** (*26 Apr 2003 Vienna)

C) **Baroness Alexandra** Maria **von Holzhausen** (*22 Jan 1963 Salzburg)
= 12 Jul 1985 Salzburg (civil) & 7 Jul 1985 Kirchberg (rel); **Christof** Alexander Rudolf Michael **Ferch** (*4 Aug 1959 Salzburg) son of Rudolf Ferch & Countess Elisabeth Coreth zu Coredo
1) **Ferdinand** Georg Botho **Ferch** (*17 Oct 1986 Salzburg)
2) **Leopold** Anton David **Ferch** (*18 Aug 1988 Wels)
3) **Benedikt** Peter Nikolaus **Ferch** (*2 Mar 1993 Munich)
4) **Elisabeth** Patricia Katherina **Ferch** (*22 Feb 1995 Munich)

IV) **Archduchess Elisabeth of Austria** etc. (*15 Jan 1942 Sonneberg)
= 3 Aug 1964 Mondsee; **Friedrich** Josef **Sandhofer** (*1 Aug 1934 Salzburg) son of Joseph Sandhofer & Emma Waldeck

A) **Anton** Dominic **Sandhofer** (*26 Oct 1966 Salzburg)
= 28 (civil) & 29 (rel) May 1993 Innsbruck; **Katarzyna** Marta **Wojkowska** (*23 Nov 1962 Warsaw) daughter of Wladzimierz Wojkowski & Maria Janina Redler
1) **Dominik** Alexander **Sandhofer** (*7 Jan 1994 Innsbruck)

B) **Margareta** Elisabeth **Sandhofer** (*10 Sep 1968 Salzburg)
= 20 Jun 1992 Salzburg; **Ernst** Helmut Klaus **Lux** (*13 Sep 1954 Graz) son of Ernst Lux & Wiefrede Theimer
1) **Mauritio** Maria Ernst **Lux** (*29 Apr 1999 Innsbruck)
2) **Dorian** Augustinus Maria **Lux** (*12 May 2001 Vienna)

C) **Andrea** Alexandra **Sandhofer** (*13 Dec 1969 Innsbruck)

= 30 Aug 1996 (civil) & 14 Jun 1997 (rel) Salzburg; **Jörg** Michael **Zarbl** (*25 Sep 1970 Wels) son of Horst Zarbl & Theresia Mauerbauer

1) **Ferdinand** Hans Friedrich Konstantin Maria **Zarbl** (*8 Dec 1996 Salzburg)

2) **Benedikt** Bonifatius Maria Manfred Rainer **Zarbl** (*19 Feb 1999 Salzburg)

D) **Elisabeth** Victoria Magdalena **Sandhofer** (*16 Nov 1971 Innsbruck)

f. **Prince Mircea of Romania** (3 Jan 1913 Bucharest – 2 Nov 1916 Buftea)

3. **Princess Victoria Melita of Edinburgh** etc. (renamed **Victoria** Feodorovna) (25 Nov 1876 Malta – 2 Mar 1936 Amorbach)
=1 19 Apr 1894 Coburg (dv.1901); **Ernst Ludwig** Albert Karl Wilhelm, **Grand Duke of Hesse and By Rhine** (25 Nov 1868 Darmstadt – 9 Oct 1937 Schloss Wolfsgarten) son of Ludwig IV, Grand Duke of Hesse and By Rhine & Princess Alice of Great Britain; suc. father 13 Mar 1892; a republic was declared 8 Nov 1918
=2 1905; ♦**Grand Duke Cyril of Russia** (1876 – 1938)
issue of 1st:

a. **Princess Elisabeth** Marie Alice Victoria **of Hesse and By Rhine** (11 Mar 1895 Darmstadt – 16 Nov 1903 Skierniewice)

issue of 2nd:
see: page

4. **Princess Alexandra of Edinburgh** etc. (1 Sep 1878 Coburg – 16 Apr 1942 Langenburg)
= 20 Apr 1896 Coburg; **Ernst** Wilhelm Friedrich Karl Maximilian, **Prince of Hohenlohe-Langenburg** (13 Sep 1863 Langenburg – 11 Dec 1950 Langenburg) son of Hermann, Prince of Hohenlohe-Langenburg & Princess Leopoldine of Baden; suc. father 9 Mar 1913

a. **Gottfried** Hermann Alfred Maximilian Viktor, **Prince of Hohenlohe-Langenburg** (4 Mar 1897 Langenburg – 11 Jun 1960 Langenburg) suc. father 1950
= 20 Apr 1931 Langenburg; ♦**Princess Margarita of Greece** (18 Mar 1905 Athens – 24 Apr 1981 Bad Wiesse) daughter of Prince Andrew of Greece & Princess Alice of Battenberg

I) **Kraft** Alexander Ernst Ludwig Georg Emich, **Prince of Hohenlohe-Langenburg** (25 Jun 1935 Schwabisch Hall – 16 Mar 2004 Schwabisch Hall) suc. father as Prince 11 Jun 1960
=1 5 Jun 1965 Langenburg (civil) & 16 Jul 1965 Zwingenburg (rel) (dv.1990); **Princess Charlotte** Alexandra Marie Clothilde **of Croy** (*31 Dec 1938 London) daughter of Prince Alexander of Croy & Anne Campbell; =2nd Baron Johann von Twickel
=2 22 May 1992 Graz; **Irma** Gisela Christine **Popesch** (*19 Jun 1946 Graz) daughter of Eugen Popesch & Gisela Spanring
issue of 1st (none by 2nd):
A) **Princess Cecilie** Margarita Dorothea **of Hohenlohe-Langenburg** (*16 Dec 1967 Crailsheim)
=1 6 Jun 1998 Cadouin (dv.2008); **Count Cyril** Amedeo **de Commarque** (*12 Aug 1970 Perigueux) son of Godefroy, Marquis de Commarque & Vera de Witt
=2 5 Aug 2015; **Ajoy Mani** (...)
no issue
B) **Philipp** Gottfried Alexander, **Prince of Hohenlohe-Langenburg** (*20 Jan 1969 Crailsheim) suc. father 2004
= 6 Sep 2003 Langenburg (civil) & 13 Sep 2003 Diessen (rel); **Saskia Binder** (*15 Jan 1973 Munich)
1) **Hereditary Prince Max** Leopold Ernst Kraft Peter **of Hohenlohe-Langenburg** (*22 Mar 2005 Munich)
2) **Prince Gustav** Philipp Friedrich Alexander **of Hohenlohe-Langenburg** (*28 Jan 2007 Bad Mergentheim)
3) **Princess Marita** Saskia Friedelind Charlotte Beatrix **of Hohenlohe-Langenburg** (*23 Nov 2010 Bad Mergentheim)
C) **Princess Xenia** Margareta Anne **of Hohenlohe-Langenburg** (*8 Jul 1972 Crailsheim)
= 13 Aug 2005 Obertaufkirchen (civil) & 26 Aug 2006 Langenburg (rel); **Maximilian** Gabriel **Soltmann** (*10 Dec 1973 Munich) son of Dieter Soltmann & Marie Kayser-Eichburg

1) **Ferdinand** Gabriel Kraft **Soltmann** (*5 Nov 2005 Bad Mergentheim)

2) **Louisa** Marei C harlotte **Soltmann** (*6 Apr 2008)

II) **Princess Beatrix** Alice Marie Melita Margarethe **of Hohenlohe-Langenburg** (10 Jul 1936 Schwabisch Hall – 15 Nov 1997 Langenburg)

III) **Prince** Georg **Andreas** Heinrich **of Hohenlohe-Langenburg** (*24 Nov 1938 Schwabisch Hall)
= 14 Aug 1969 Hirchburg-Aich (civil) & 9 Sep 1969 Burghausen (rel); **Princess Luise** Pauline Amélie Vibeke Emma **of Schönburg-Waldenburg** (*12 Oct 1943 Frankfurt) daughter of Prince Georg of Schönburg-Waldenburg & Countess Pauline zu Castell-Castell

A) **Princess Katharina** Clementine Beatrix **of Hohenlohe-Langenburg** (*21 Nov 1972 Munich)
= 28 Sep 2002 Munich; **Prince Nikolaus** Carl Ferdinand **of Waldeck and Pyrmont** (*2 Nov 1970 Limburg) son of Prince Volkwin of Waldeck and Pyrmont & Baroness Orlina von Gaublenz

1) **Princess Laetitia** Antoinette Julia Tatjana Felicitas **of Waldeck and Pyrmont** (*2 Dec 2003 Munich)

2) **Princess Alexia** Natalie Luise Tatjana Maresa **of Waldeck and Pyrmont** (*20 Jun 2006 Munich)

B) **Princess Tatiana** Louise **of Hohenlohe-Langenburg** (*10 Feb 1975 Munich)
= 30 Sep (civil) & 9 Oct (rel.) 2010 Munich; **Hubertus Stephan** (*21 Nov 1970 Gräfelfing)

1) **Carl Stephan** (*22 Jan 2012 Munich)

IV) **Prince Rupprecht** Sigismund Philipp Ernst **of Hohenlohe-Langenburg** (7 Apr 1944 Langenburg – 8 Apr 1978 Munich) (twin)

V) **Prince Albrecht** Wolfgang Christof **of Hohenlohe-Langenburg** (7 Apr 1944 Langenburg – 23 Apr 1992 Berlin) (twin)
= (morg.) 23 Jan 1976 Berlin; **Maria-Hildegard Fischer** (*30 Nov 1933 Freibourg) daughter of Max Fischer & Johanna Fredler

A) **Ludwig Prinz zu Hohenlohe-Langenburg** (*21 Apr

1976 Berlin)

b. **Princess Marie Melita** Leopoldine Viktoria Feodora Alexandra **of Hohenlohe-Langenburg** (18 Jan 1899 Langenburg – 8 Nov 1967 Munich)
= 15 Feb 1916 Coburg; Wilhelm **Friedrich** Christian Günther Albert Adolf Georg, **Duke of Schleswig-Holstein-Sonderburg-Glücksburg** (23 Aug 1891 Grunholz – 10 Feb 1965 Grunholz) son of Friedrich Ferdinand, Duke of Schleswig-Holstein-Sonderburg-Glücksburg & Princess Caroline Mathilde of Schleswig-Holstein-Sonderburg-Augustenburg; suc. father 29 Jan 1934

I) **Hereditary Prince Hans** Albert Viktor Alexander Friedrich Ernst Gottfried August Heinrich Waldemar **of Schleswig-Holstein-Sonderburg-Glücksburg** (12 May 1917 Schloss Louisenlund – 10 Aug 1944 Zedlinsk, Poland) killed in action

II) **Prince Wilhelm** Alfred Ferdinand **of Schleswig-Holstein-Sonderburg-Glücksburg** (24 Sep 1919 Schloss Louisenlund – 17 Jun 1926 Kiel)

III) Friedrich Ernst **Peter, Duke of Schleswig-Holstein-Sonderburg-Glücksburg** (30 Apr 1922 Schloss Louisenlund – 30 Sep 1980 Bienebeck) suc. father 1965
= 9 Oct 1947 Glücksburg; **Princess Marie-Alix of Schaumburg-Lippe** (*2 Apr 1923 Bückeburg) daughter of Prince Stephan of Schaumburg-Lippe & Duchess Ingeborg of Oldenburg

A) **Princess Marita of Schleswig-Holstein-Sonderburg-Glücksburg** (*5 Sep 1948 Schloss Louisenlund)
= 21 May 1975 Grunholz (civil) & 23 May 1975 Glücksburg
(rel); **Baron Wilfrid** Eberhard Manfred **von Plotho** (*10 Aug 1942 Bliesdorf) son of Baron Manfred von Plotho & Baroness Ingrid von Schroder

1) **Baron Christoph von Plotho** (*14 Mar 1976 Eckernförde)
= 10 Jul 2010; **Anahita Varzi** (...)

a) **Baron Antonius** Casimir Cyrus **von Plotho** (*2013)

2) **Baroness Irina von Plotho** (*28 Jan 1978 Eckernförde)
= 11 Jun 2016; **Julius** Ferdinand **von Bathmann-Hollweg** (*1977) son of Christoph von Bethmann-Hollweg & Baroness Sophie von Maltzan zu Wartrnberg und Penzlin
a) a son (*2017)

B) **Christoph, Prince of Schleswig-Holstein-Sonderburg-Glücksburg** (*22 Aug 1949 Schloss Louisenlund) suc. father but chooses not to use title Duke
= 23 Sep 1981 Damp (civil) & 3 Oct 1981 Glücksburg (rel); **Princess Elisabeth of Lippe-Weissenfeld** (*28 Jul 1957 Munich) daughter of Prince Alfred of Lippe-Weissenfeld & Baroness Irmgard von Wehrborn
1) **Princess Sophie of Schleswig-Holstein-Sonderburg-Glücksburg** (*9 Oct 1983 Eckernförde)
= ...; **Anders Wahlquist** (*1968)
2) **Hereditary Prince Friedrich-Ferdinand of Schleswig-Holstein-Sonderburg-Glücksburg** (*19 Jul 1985 Eckernförde)
= 2017; **Anjuta Buchholz** (...) daughter of Martin Buchholz & Gisela Winmkelmann
no issue
3) **Prince Constantin of Schleswig-Holstein-Sonderburg-Glücksburg** (*14 Jul 1986 Eckernförde)
4) **Prince Leopold of Schleswig-Holstein-Sonderburg-Glücksburg** (*5 Sep 1991 Eckernförde)

C) **Prince Alexander of Schleswig-Holstein-Sonderburg-Glücksburg** (*9 Jul 1953 Bienebek)
= 29 Aug 1994 Munich (civil) & 3 Sep 1994 Mallorca (rel); **Barbara Fertsch** (*27 Jul 1961 Friedberg) daughter of Fritz-Wilhelm Fertsch & Elke Gaidetzka
1) **Princess Helena of Schleswig-Holstein-Sonderburg-Glücksburg** (*25 Jan 1994 Hamburg)
2) **Prince Julian** Nicolaus **of Schleswig-Holstein-Sonderburg-Glücksburg** (*20 Oct 1997 Prague)

D) **Princess Ingeborg of Schleswig-Holstein-**

Sonderburg-Glücksburg (*9 Jul 1956 Bienebek)
= 31 May 1991 Hamburg (civil) & 1 Jun 1991 Schloss Glücksburg (rel); **Nikolaus** Albert **Broschek** (*30 May 1941 Munich) son of Curt Broschek & Ida Harms
1) **Alexis** Nikolaus Peter Johannes **Broschek** (*12 Dec 1995 Hamburg)

IV) **Princess Marie Alexandra** Caroline Mathilde Viktoria Irene **of Schleswig-Holstein-Sonderburg-Glücksburg** (9 Jul 1927 Schloss Louisenlund – 12 Dec 2000 Friedrichshafen)
= 22 Jul 1970 Grunholz (civil) & 25 Jul 1970 Louisenlund (rel); **Douglas Barton Miller** (*8 Dec 1929 San Francisco) son of Douglas Barton Miller & Marriet Deter
no issue

c. **Princess Alexandra** Beatrice Leopoldine **of Hohenlohe-Langenburg** (2 Apr 1901 Coburg – 26 Oct 1963 Langenburg)

d. **Princess Irma** Helene **of Hohenlohe-Langenburg** (4 Jul 1902 Langenburg – 8 Mar 1986 Heilbronn)

e. **Prince Alfred of Hohenlohe-Langenburg** (16 – 18 Apr 1911 Langenburg)

5. **Princess Beatrice** Leopoldine Victoria **of Edinburgh** etc. (20 Apr 1884 Kent – 13 Jul 1966 Sanlucar de Barrameda, Spain)
= 15 Jul 1919 Coburg; **Prince Alfonso** Maria Francisco Diego **of Orleans, Infante of Spain, Duke of Galliera** (12 Nov 1886 Madrid – 10 Aug 1975 Sanlucar de Barrameda) son of Prince Antoine of Orleans, Duke of Galliera & Infanta Eulalia of Spain; suc. father 24 Dec 1930, passed title to son 14 Jul 1937

a. **Prince Alvaro** Antonio Fernando Carlos Felipe **of Orleans, Duke of Galliera** (20 Apr 1910 Coburg – 22 Aug 1997 Monte Carlo) suc. father 1937
= 10 Jul 1937 Rome; **Carla Parodi-Delfino** (13 Dec 1909 Milan – 27 Jul 2000 Sanlucar de Barrameda) daughter of Leopoldo Parodi-Delgino & Lucia Henry

I) **Gerarda de Orleans-Borbón** (*25 Aug 1939 Rome)
=1 26 Jul 1963 New York City (dv.1977); **Harry** Freeman **Saint** (*13 Feb 1941 New York) son of Ellis Saint & Rachel Freeman
=2 17 Nov 1990 Monaco (dv.1998); **Ignacio** Enrique

Romero Solis, Marqués de Marchelina (*30 Oct 1937 Seville) son of Ignacio Romero Orborne, Marqués de Marchelina & Miguelina de Solis de la Vega; =1st Conseulo Fernandez de Cordoba Ybarra
issue of 1st (none by 2nd):
A) **Carla** de Orleans-Borbón **Saint** (*22 May 1967 New York)
=1 19 Sep 1992 Riverdale, New York (dv.2001); **John** Stephan **Lilly** (*20 Mar 1965 Chicago) son of Terence Lilly & Elizabeth Fischer
=2 23 Jun 2001; (her stepfather's stepson) **Nicolas de Haro y Fernández de Córdoba** (*13 Oct 1965 Seville) son of Joquin de Haro y Rodas & Consuelo Fernández de Córdoba y Ybarra
issue of 2nd (none by 1st):
1) **Nicolas de Haro y Saint** (*1 Jan 2001 Seville)
2) **Sofia de Haro y Saint** (*19 May 2004 Seville)
3) **Mateo de Haro y Saint** (*10 May 2007 Seville)
B) **Marc** de Orleans-Borbón **Saint** (*30 Mar 1969 New York)
=1 10 Dec 1990 New York (civil) & 6 Jul 1991 Murs (rel) (dv.1995); **Dorothée** Sophie **Horps** (*17 Feb 1968 Rennes) daughter of Michael Horps & Alix de Cherisey
=2 22 May 2009 Seville; **Amparo Barón y Fernández de Córdoba** (*4 Dec 1968 Seville) daughter of Ignacio Barón y Rojas-Marcos & Amparo Fernández de Córdoba y Ybarra (cousin to Nicolas de Haro y Fernández de Córdoba, above)
no issue
II) **Alfonso de Orleans-Borbón** (23 Aug 1941 Rome – 7 Sep 1975 Houston, Texas)
= 12 Jan 1996 Naples; **Donna Emilia Ferrera-Pignatelli** dei principi di Strongoli (6 Apr 1940 Naples – 22 Dec 1999 Lausanne) daughter of Don Vincenzo Ferrara-Pignatelli, Prince of Strongoli & Nobile Francesca Pulci-Doria
A) **Alfonso de Orleans-Borbón, Duke of Galliera** (*2 Jan 1968 Santa Cruz de Teneriffe) suc. grandfather 1997
= 28 Mar 1994 Paris (dv.2001); **Véronique Goeders**

(*16 Nov 1970 Verviers) daughter of Jean-Marie Goeders & Anne-Marie Grosjeans

1) **Alonso** Juan **de Orleans-Borbón** (*17 Jul 1994 Paris)

B) **Alvaro de Orleans-Borbón** (*4 Oct 1969 Santa Cruz de Teneriffe)

= 6 Apr 2007 Wallingford, Conn.; **Alice Acosta** (*1972)

1) **Aiden de Orleans-Borbón** (*19 Jun 2009)

2) a daughter (*2017)

III) **Beatriz de Orleans-Borbón** (*2 Apr 1943 Seville)

= 25 Apr 1964 Rome (dv.1989); **Don Tomaso dei conti Farini** (16 Sep 1938 Turin – 13 Jan 2018 Milan) son of Count Antonio Farini & Silvia Bellia

A) **Don Gerardo** Alfonso **dei conti Farini** (*23 Nov 1967 Bologna)

= 2007; **Délia Mittempergher** (...) daughter of Giulio Mittempergher & Irma Burkhalter

1) **Donna Luisa dei Conti Farini** (*2008)

2) **Donna Alessandra dei Conti Farini** (...)

B) **Donna Elena** Gioia **dei conti Farini** (*20 Oct 1969 Rome)

= 19 Jun 1999 Sanlucar de Barrameda; **Joaquin Fernández de Córdoba y de Haro** (*23 Jun 1971 Tomares) son of Joaquin de Haro y Rodas & Consuelo Fernández de Córdoba y Ybarra (brother of Nicolas de Haro Fernández de Córdoba above)

1) **Claudia de Haro y Farini** (*28 Dec 2000 Madrid)

2) **Tómas de Haro y Farini** (*12 Sep 2003 Madrid)

IV) **Alvaro Jaime de Orleans-Borbón** (*1 Mar 1947 Rome)

=1 24 May 1974 Campiglione; **Donna Giovanna San Martino de San Germano** (*10 Apr 1945 Campiglione) daughter of Casimiro San Martino, Marchese di San Germano & Donna Maria Cristina Ruffo di Calabria

=2 28 Dec 2007; **Antonella Rendina** (*1969)

issue of 1st:

A) Maria del **Pilar de Orleans-Borbón** (*27 May 1975 Rome)

= Jun 2006; **Nicholas Henderson-Stewart** (*1974 Wellington, New Zealand) son of Sir David Henderson-

Stewart, 2nd Baronet & Countess Anna von der Pahlen
1) **Felix Henderson-Stewart** (*2007 Brussels)
2) **Louis Henderson-Stewart** (*2008 Brussels)
3) **Daria Henderson-Stewart** (*2009 Brussels)
4) **Xenia Henderson-Stewart** (*10 Feb 2011 Brussels)

B) **Andrea de Orleans-Borbón** (*9 Jul 1976 Rome)
= Jan 2009 London; **Anne Laure van Exter** (...)
daughter of Robert van Exter & Marie Rose Mérey de Kaposmére et Kisdovorán
1) **Inès de Orleans-Borbón** (*30 Jan 2010 London)
2) **Eugenia de Orleans-Borbón** (*7 Mar 2011 London)

C) **Alois de Orleans-Borbón** (*24 Mar 1979 Rome)
= 28 Jun 2008 Alfieri, Italy; **Guadalupe Solis Jabón** (...)
daughter of Julián Solis Gómez & Guadalupe Jabón Trujillo
1) **Alonso de Orleans-Borbón** (*23 Mar 2010 Madrid)

issue of 2nd:
D) **Eulalia** Sveva **de Orleans-Borbón** (*2006)

b. **Prince Alfonso** Maria Cristino Justo **of Orleans, Infante of Spain** (28 May 1912 Madrid – 18 Nov 1936 near Madrid) killed in action

c. **Prince Ataulfo** Carlos Isabelo Alejandro **of Orleans, Infante of Spain** (20 Oct 1913 Madrid – 8 Oct 1974 Malaga)

G. **Grand Duke Serge** Alexandrovich **of Russia** (19 Apr/1 May 1857 Tsarskoie-Selo – 4/17 Feb 1905 Moscow) assassinated
= 3/15 Jun 1884 St. Petersburg; **Princess Elisabeth** Alexandra Louise Alice (**St. Elizabeth** Feodorovna) **of Hesse and By Rhine** (1 Nov 1864 Bessingen – 17 Jul 1918 Alapaievsk) murdered by Bolsheviks; daughter of Ludwig IV, Grand Duke of Hesse and By Rhine & Princess Alice of Great Britain; canonized by the Russian Orthodox Church
no issue

H. **Grand Duke Paul** Alexandrovich **of Russia** (3 Oct 1860 Tsarskoie-Selo – 30 Jan 1919 St. Petersburg) murdered by Bolsheviks
=1 5/17 Jun 1889 St. Petersburg; ♦**Princess Alexandra** Georgeievna **of Greece** (30 Aug 1870 Corfu – 12/24 Sep 1891 Ilyinskoie) daughter of George I, King of the Hellenes & Grand

Duchess Olga of Russia
=2 (morg.) 10 Oct 1902 Leghorn; **Olga** Valerianovna **Karnovich**, cr. **Princess Paley** and Countess von Hohenfelsen (2/14 Dec 1866 St. Petersburg – 2 Nov 1929 Nice) daughter of Valerian Karnovich & Olga Meszaros; =1st Eric von Pistohlkors; cr. Countess 29 Oct 1904 (in Bavaria) and Princess 15/28 May 1915 (in Russia)
issue of 1st:
1. **Grand Duchess Maria** Pavlovna **of Russia** (6/18 Apr 1890 St. Petersburg – 13 Dec 1958 Konstanz)
=1 20 Apr/3 May 1908 St. Petersburg (dv.1914); **Prince** Carl **Vilhelm** Ludvig **of Sweden, Duke of Södermanland** (17 Jun 1847 Tullgarn – 5 Jun 1965 Stenhammer) son of Gustaf V, King of Sweden & Princess Viktoria of Baden
=2 6/19 Sep 1917 Pavlovsk (dv.1923); **Prince Serge** Mikhailovich **Poutiatin** (7/19 Dec 1893 St. Petersburg – 26 Feb 1966 Charleston, South Carolina) son of Prince Michael Poutiatin & Sofia Paltova
issue of 1st:
a. **Count** Gustaf **Lennart** Nicolaus Paul **Bernadotte af Wisborg** (formerly Prince of Sweden, Duke of Smaland) (8 May 1909 Stockholm – 21 Dec 2004 Schloss Mainau) renounced royal titles upon first marriage, cr. Count af Wisborg 2 May 1951 (in Luxembourg)
=1 11 Mar 1932 London (dv.1972); **Karin** Emma Louise **Nissvandt** (7 Jul 1911 Nora – 9 Oct 1991 Eskilstuna) daughter of Sven Nissandt & Anna Lisa Lindberg
=2 6 May 1972 Mainau; **Sonja Haunz** (7 May 1944 Litzelsteten – 21 Oct 2008 Freibourg) daughter of Wolfgang Haunz & Anna Mayr
issue of 1st:
I) **Countess Birgitta Bernadotte af Wisborg** (*3 May 1933 Stockholm)
= 16 Jun 1955 Litzelstetten (civil) & Mainau (rel); **Friedrich Straehl** (20 Nov 1922 Konstanz – 13 Sep 2011 Kreuzlingen) son of Fritz Straehl & Ida Gombert
A) **Friedrich** Lennart **Straehl** (*10 Apr 1956 Konstanz)
= 28 Jun 1986 Homburg (dv.1998); **Regula Kleger** (*24 Aug 1960 Cur) daughter of Joseph Kleger & Adelaide

Pellegrini
1) **Fiona** Regula **Straehl** (*8 Sep 1987 Frauenfeld)
2) **Florian** Frederik **Straehl** (*23 Jun 1989 Frauenfeld)
= 24 Mar 2009 Frauenfeld; **Stephanie** Daniela **Haueter** (*4 Jan 1989 Frauenfeld) daughter of Albert Haueter & Theresia Maria Bolis
a) **Zoe** Milena **Straehl** (*15 Jul 2009 Frauenfels)
b) **Eli** Loris **Straehl** (*15 Oct 2012 Frauenfels)
B) **Andreas Straehl** (*16 Jul 1957 Konstanz)
= 14 Sep 1985 Mainau (dv.2004); **Uschi** Theresia **Hefti** (*7 Aug 1958 Glarus) daughter of Kurt Hefti & Antonia Kuen
1) **Angela** Antonia Birgitta **Straehl** (*14 Dec 1986 Münsterlingen)
2) **Timo Straehl** (*13 Aug 1988 Münsterlingen)
C) Marie **Christina Straehl** (*23 Apr 1960 Konstanz)
=1 24 Sep 1983 Mainau (dv.1985); **Alexander Haessig** (*23 Feb 1948 Lucerne) son of Alwin Haessig & Rosa Lustenberger
=2 17 Mar 2000 Bern; **Ulrich Wütrich** (*5 Jan 1943 Bern) son of Fritz Wütrich & Rosa Wägli
no issue
E) **Desirée** Elisabeth **Straehl** (*20 Oct 1961 Konstanz)
=1 23 Sep 1986 Kreuzlingen (civil) & 24 Sep 1983 Mainau (rel) (dv.); **Dieter Zepf** (*4 Jan 1960 Konstanz) son of Walter Zepf & Hilda Mobius
=2 Jun 1990 Mainau (dv.1997); **Andreas Hermann** (*26 Jun 1960 Münsterlingen) son of Gebhard Hermann & Ester Häberlin
issue of 2nd (none by 1st):
1) **Alina** Svenja **Hermann** (*2 May 1990 Kreuzlingen)
2) **Nicolas Hermann** (*6 Mar 1995 Kreuzlingen)
3) **Robin Hermann** (*18 Sep 1997 Kreuzlingen)
4) **Sophia Hermann** (*22 Jan 2003 Kreuzlingen)
E) **Stephan Straehl** (*13 Jul 1964 Konstanz)
II) **Countess Marie Louise Bernadotte af Wisborg** (6 Nov 1935 Stockholm – 24 May 1988 Konstanz)
= 10 Sep 1956 Litzelstetten (civil) & 11 Sep 1956 Mainau

(rel); **Rudolf Kautz** (24 Aug 1930 Eugen – 18 Oct 2007 Longboat Key, Florida) son of Adolf Kautz & Helene Ruh

A) **Henrik** Adolf **Kautz** (*16 Sep 1957 Konstanz); = 24 Apr 1983 Konstanz (dv.); **Kerstin** Sabine **Janke** (*4 Feb 1957 Berlin) daughter of Ehard Janke & Charlotte Romanowicz

1) **Lennart** Rudolf Erhard **Kautz** (*3 Sep 1983 Münsterlingen)

2) **Bennet** Henrik Marian **Kautz** (*29 Jul 1985 Münsterlingen)

B) **Karin** Marie-Helene **Kautz** (*13 Oct 1958 Konstanz) = 29 Aug 1992 Konstanz; **Walther Fritz** (* Jul 1958 Konstanz)

1) **Björn Fritz** (*Apr 1993 Konstanz)

2) **Louisa** Marie **Fritz** (*Jan 1996 Konstanz)

3) **Astrid Fritz** (*1999 Konstanz)

C) **Madeleine** Cecilia **Kautz** (*23 Aug 1961 Konstanz)

III) **Count** Carl **Jan** Gustaf Vilhelm **Bernadotte af Wisborg** (*9 Jan 1941 Stockholm)

=1 3 May 1965 Törö (dv.1967); Elsa **Gunilla** Margareta **Stampe** (3 Sep 1941 Törö – 22 May 2010 Lausanne) daughter of Erik Stampe & Elsa Malgren; =2nd Robert Horst

=2 26 Jun 1967 Mainau (dv.1970); **Anna** Birgitta **Skärne** (*18 Apr 1944 Stockholm) daughter of Allan Skärne & Birgitta Strohman; =2nd Robert Looft

=3 23 Jun 1972 Konstanz (dv.1974); **Annegret** Vybke **Thomssen** (*15 Nov 1938 Bremen) daughter of Hans Thomssen & Alice Bleek; =1st Hans Drenckhahn

=4 6 Sep 1974 Diepolz (dv.1987); **Marietta** Elsa **Berg** (7 Dec 1953 Diepolz – 30 Sep 2001 Stuttgart) daughter of Albert Berg & Gisela Grossman

=5 15 Mar 1993 London (dv.2004); **Gabriele Hess** (*29 Jun 1949 Weimar) daughter of Karl Voight & Alma Hess

=6 11 Sep 2004 Forbach (dv.2011); **Christiane** Rose **GrandMontagne** (*17 Mar 1944 Rabat, Morocco) daughter of Daniel GrandMontagne & Anna Catherine Brenner; =1st Sven-Michael Wagner

=7 8 Jan 2012 Almunecar, Spain; **Gunilla** Irène **Stenfors** (*8 Apr 1957)
issue of 2nd (none by 1st):

A) **Countess Sophia** Magdalena Birgitta **Bernadotte af Wisborg** (*3 May 1968 Stockholm)
has issue by Sten **Michael Söderström** (*2 Apr 1965 Stockholm) son of Sten Söderström & Lajla Einarsson:
1) **Maria** Lovisa Birgitta **Bernadotte** (*9 Feb 1997 Stockholm)
2) **Carl-Fredrik** Allan Wilhelm **Bernadotte** (*4 Jan 1998 Stockholm)
3) Anna **Lovisa** Vendela **Bernadotte** (*17 Jul 1999 Stockholm)

issue of 3rd:

B) **Countess Cia-Rosemarie Bernadotte af Wisborg** (*30 Sep 1972 Konstanz)
= 9 Jun 2006 Konstanz; **Sven Roderburg** (*2 Feb 1972 Oberlausitz) son of Hans Roderburg & Erika ...
1) **Nele** Frederike **Roderburg** (*11 Nov 2006 Konstanz)
2) **Maximilian** Lennart **Roderburg** (*13 Aug 2009 Konstanz)

issue of 4th:

C) **Count Alexander** Wilhelm **Bernadotte af Wisborg** (*25 Mar 1977 Konstanz)
= 15 May 2003 Stetten (civil) & 20 Sep 2003 Mainau (rel); **Carina** Beate **König** (*5 Dec 1981 Würzburg) daughter of Richard König & Angelika Hack
1) **Countess Desirée** Maritta **Bernadotte af Wisborg** (*4 Nov 2006 Sigmaringen)
2) **Countess Amelia** Anastasia **Bernadotte af Wisborg** (*Oct 2010 Glashütte)
3) **Countess Maxima** Victoria **Bernadotte af Wisborg** (*2015)

D) **Count Stefan** Albert **Bernadotte af Wisborg** (*4 Nov 1980 Konstanz)

issue of 5th (by adoption, his step-daughter) (none by others):

E) **Angela Gräfin Bernadotte af Wisborg** (*1 Jan 1967

Weimar) née Hess; adopted 1994
has issue by ...:
1) **Falk** Norman **Graf Bernadotte af Wisborg** (*29 Jan 1998 Offenbach am Main)

IV) **Countess** Karin **Cecilia Bernadotte af Wisborg** (*9 Apr 1944 Stockholm)
= 31 Mar 1967 Konstanz (dv.1974); **Hansjörg Baenkler** (*24 Sep 1939 Konstanz) son of Willy Baenkler & Hilde Schrott
no issue

issue of 2nd:

V) **Countess Bettina Bernadotte af Wisborg** (*12 Mar 1974 Schwerzingen)
= 2 Aug 2004 Mariefred (civil) & 29 Oct 2004 Mainau (rel); **Philipp Haug** (*22 Oct 1972 Lindau) son of Ludwig Haug & Ilse Deufel
A) **Emil** Gustaf **Haug** (*19 Jul 2005 Konstanz)
B) **Linnea** Elin **Haug** (*31 Dec 2006 Konstanz)

VI) **Count Björn** Wilhelm **Bernadotte af Wisborg** (*13 Jun 1975 Scherzingen)
= 25 Apr (civil) & 7 May (rel) 2009 Mainau; **Sandra Angerer** (*12 Mar 1977 St.Gallen) daughter of Hans Angerer & Maria Carla Moser
issue ?

VII) **Countess Catherina Bernadotte af Wisborg** (*11 Apr 1977 Scherzingen)
= 30 Jun (civil) & 7 Jul (rel) 2007 Mainau; **Romuald Ruffing** (*8 Aug 1966 Saarbrücken) son of Franz-Josef Ruffing & Ingrid Seidl
issue ?

VIII) **Count Christian** Wolfgang **Bernadotte af Wisborg** (*24 May 1979 Scherzingen)
= 22 May 2010 Mainau; **Christine Stoltmann** (*7 Nov 1977 Duderstadt) daughter of Ronald Stoltmann & Iris Fricke
A) **Count Maximilian** Benedikt **Bernadotte af Wisborg** (*10 Aug 2010 Konstanz)

IX) **Countess Diana Bernadotte af Wisborg** (*18 Apr 1982

Scherzingen)
=1 27 Sep 2003 Mainau (dv.2007); **Bernd Grawe** (*12 Mar 1966 Konstanz)
=2 8 Aug 2016 Konstanz (civil) & 13 Jan 2017 Mainau (rel.); **Stefan Dedek** (*18 Apr 1989)
issue of 1st (none by 2nd):
A) **Paulina** Marie **Grawe** (*13 Feb 2004)
Countess Diana has additional issue:
B) **Eric** Hagen Lennart **Bernadotte** (*17 Aug 2010 Kempton)
issue of 2nd:
b. **Prince Roman** Sergeievich **Poutiatin** (17 Jul 1918 St. Petersburg – 29 Jul 1919 Bucharest)
2. **Grand Duke Dmitri** Pavlovich **of Russia** (6/18 Sep 1891 Ilyinskoie – 5 May 1942 Davos)
= (morg.) 21 Nov 1926 Biarritz (dv.1937); Ann **Audrey Emery**, cr. **Princess Ilyinskya** (4 Jan 1904 New York – 25 Nov 1971 Palm Beach, Florida) daughter of Johan Josias Emery & Lela Alexander; cr. Princess 1926; =2nd Prince Dmitri Djordjadze
a. **Prince Paul** Dmitrievich **Ilyinsky** (27 Jan 1928 London – 10 Feb 2004 Palm Beach)
=1 29 Jul 1949 Honolulu (ann.1951); **Mary** Evelyn **Prince** (*Apr 1925 Memphis, Tennessee) daughter of William Prince
=2 1 Oct 1952 Palm Beach; **Angelica** Philippa **Kaufmann** (22 Mar 1932 Paris – 19 Nov 2011 Palm Beach) daughter of Philippe Kaufmann & Gloria Goodwin
issue of 2nd (none by 1st):
I) **Prince Dmitri** Pavlovich **Ilyinsky** (*1 May 1954 Palm Beach)
= 22 Sep 1979 New Haven, Connecticut; **Martha** Murray **McDowell** (*15 Jun 1952 New Haven) daughter of Ted McDowell & Phyllis Murray
A) **Princess** Catherine **Adair Ilyinsky** (*4 Aug 1981 Cincinnati, Ohio)
= 25 Jun 2011; Bradley Bissell (**Sam**) **Goodyear** (*22 Dec 1978 Los Angeles) son of Richard Goodyear & Constance Martin
1) **Louisa** Emery **Goodyear** (*2013)

B) **Princess Victoria** Bayard **Ilyinsky** (*23 Nov 1983 Cincinnati)
= 7 Aug 2013; Mbuku **Yves Binda** (*1979 Uganda)
issue ?
C) **Princess Lela** McDowell **Ilyinsky** (*26 Aug 1986 Cincinnati)

II) **Princess Paula** Pavlovna **Ilyinsky** (*18 May 1956 Palm Beach)
= 30 May 1980 Cincinnati; **Marc** Allen **Comisar** (*17 Jun 1953 Cincinnati) son of Lee Comisar & Jean Hample
A) **Alexander** Lee **Comisar** (*6 Apr 1983 Cincinnati)
B) **Makena Comisar** (20 Nov 1984 Cincinnati – 1 Aug 2002 Clermont County, Ohio) killed in a car crash

III) **Princess Anne** Pavlovna **Ilyinsky** (*1 Oct 1958 Palm Beach)
=1 9 May 1981 Henniker, New Hampshire (dv.1990); **Robin** Dale **De Young** (*25 Dec 1952 Cambridge, Massachusetts) son of Charles De Young & Glennis Finnegan
=2 18 Dec 1992 Cincinnati; **David** Wise **Glossinger** (*11 Jul 1953 Dayton, Ohio) son of Matthew Glossinger & Kathryn …
issue of 1st:
A) **Audrey De Young** (*1 Apr 1983 Cincinnati)
= 17 Jul 2010 Biddeford, Maine; **Cullin** James **Wible** (*Feb 1979 State College, Pennsylvania) son of James Wible & Sue Erb
1) **Lillian** Elizabeth Kauffmann **Wible** (*29 May 2011 Norwalk, Connecticut)
2) **Vivienne Wible** (*2014)
B) **Heather De Young** (*25 Oct 1985 Cincinnati)
issue of 2nd:
C) **Sophia Glossinger** (*5 May 1993 Cincinnati)
D) Paul **Oliver Glossinger** (*19 Sep 1994 Cincinnati)

IV) **Prince Michael** Pavlovich **Ilyinsky** (*3 Nov 1959 Palm Beach)
=1 4 Nov 1989 Cincinnati (dv.1996); **Paula Maier** (*1 Sep 1965 Cincinnati) daughter of Jack Maier & Blanche Frisch

=2 21 May 1999 (dv.2001); **Lisa** Maria **Schisler** (*17 May 1973)
=3 13 May 2010 Cincinnati; **Debra Gibson** (*20 Apr 1963 Dearborn, MI) daughter of Walter Gibson & Diana ...; =1st ... Lewis
issue of 1st (none by 2nd):
A) **Princess Alexis** Taylor **Ilyinsky** (*1 Mar 1994)

issue of 2nd:

3. **Prince Vladimir** Pavlovich **Paley** (28 Dec 1896/9 Jan 1897 Paris – 17 Jul 1918 Alapaievsk) murdered by Bolsheviks
4. **Princess Irene** Pavlovna **Paley** (21 Dec 1903 Paris – 15 Nov 1990 Biarritz)
=1 1923 (dv.); ♦**Prince Feodor of Russia** (1898 – 1968)
=2 11 Apr 1950 Biarritz; **Count Hubert de Monbrison** (15 Aug 1892 St.Avertin – 14 Apr 1971 Château de St.Roch) son of Count Henri Gaspard de Monbrison & Fanny Tyndall
issue of 1st:
see: page
issue of 2nd (born during marriage to 1st):
a. **Princess Irene** Feodorovna **Romanoff** (*7 May 1934 Fontenay-sous-Bois)
=1 23 Dec 1955 Biarritz (dv.1959); **André** Jean **Pelle** (29 Nov 1923 Biarritz – 7 Oct 1998 Biarritz) son of Lucien Pelle & Amélie Soubrian-Coste
=2 26 Dec 1962 Le Pin (dv.1975); **Victor-Marcel Soulas** (*26 Aug 1938 St. Meen-le-Grand) son of Victor Soulas & Yvonne Duval
issue of 1st:
I) **Alain Pelle** (*19 Sep 1956 Biarritz)
= 14 May 1983 Montbahus; **Pascale Deletre** (*2 Mar 1959 Villeneuve sur Lot) daughter of Philippe Deletre & Bernadette van Houcke
A) **Olivier Pelle** (*19 Jun 1984 Biarritz)
B) **Christophe Pelle** (*15 Feb 1987 Biarritz)
issue of 2nd:
II) **Joëlle Soulas** (*12 May 1966 Marseilles)
= 15 Dec 1998 Brussels; **Jean Philippe Sounard** (…)
A) **Cédric Sounard** (...)

B) **Clara Sounard** (...)

5. **Princess Natalia** Pavlovna **Paley** (5 Dec 1905 Paris – 27 Dec 1981 New York)
=1 10 Aug 1927 Paris (dv.1937); **Lucien Lelong** (11 Oct 1889 Paris – 11 May 1958 Anglet, France) son of Joseph Lelong & Valentina Lambelet; =1st Anna Audoy, =3rd Sandra Danovici
=2 8 Sep 1937 Southport, Connecticut; **John** Chapman **Wilson** (19 Aug 1899 Trenton, New Jersey – 29 Oct 1961 New York) son of James Chapman & Mary …
no issue

issue of 2nd:

I. **Prince George** Alexandrovich **Yourievsky** (30 Apr/12 May 1872 St. Petersburg – 13 Sep 1913 Marburg)
= 16 Feb 1900 Nice (dv.1908); **Countess Alexandra** Constantinovna **von Zarnekau** (10/22 May 1883 Kutais – 28 May 1957 Paris) daughter of Duke Constantin of Oldenburg & Agrafena Djaparidze, Countess von Zarnekau

1. **Prince Alexander** Georgeievich **Yourievsky** (20 Dec 1900 Nice – 29 Feb 1988 Mannedorf)
= 23 Nov 1957 Paris; **Ursula** Anne Marie **Beer de Grüneck** (30 May 1925 Flims-Grison – Mar 2001) daughter of Thomas Beer de Grüneck & Marguerite Kuschall

a. **Prince Hans-Georg Yourievsky** (*8 Dec 1961 St. Gallen)
=1 10 Oct 2003 Meilen (civil) & 24 Oct 2003 Mainau (rel) (dv.2012); **Katharina Verhagen** (*26 Apr 1964 Beerse, Belgium)
=2 30 Aug 2013 Zürich; Elikonida **Silvia Trumpp** (*1968)
no issue

J. **Princess Olga** Alexandrovna **Yourievskya** (28 Oct/9 Nov 1873 St. Petersburg – 10 Aug 1925 Wiesbaden)
= 12 May 1895 Nice; **Count George** Nikolaievich **von Merenberg** (13 Feb 1871 Wiesbaden – 31 May 1948 Wiesbaden) son of Prince Nikolaus of Nassau & Natalia Pushkina, Countess von Merenberg; he =2nd Adelphi Moran-Brambeer

1. **Count Alexander** Adolf Nikolaus **von Merenberg** (16 Sep 1896 Bonn – 27 Apr 1897 Bonn)
2. **Count Georg** Michael Alexander **von Merenberg** (16 Oct 1897 Hanover – 11 Jan 1965 Mainz)

=1 7 Jan 1926 Budapest (dv.1928); **Paulette Klovic de Gyergyö-Szent-Miklós** (…) daughter of Gustav Klovic de Gyergyö-Szent-Miklós & Princess Alinka Odescalchi
=2 27 Jul 1940 Schroda; **Elisabeth Müller-Uri** (8 Jul 1903 Wiesbaden – 20 Nov 1963 Wiesbaden) daughter of Friedrich Anton Müller & Sophie Elisabeth Burkhardt
issue of 2nd (none by 1st):
a. **Countess** Elisabeth **Clothilde von Merenberg** (*14 May 1941 Wiesbaden)
= 25 May 1965 Wiesbaden (civil) & 27 May 1965 Mainz (rel); **Enno** Martin Karl Wilhelm **von Rintelen** (9 Nov 1921 Berlin – 16 Oct 2013 Wiesbaden) son of Viktor von Rintelen & Antonie Bracht
I) **Alexander von Rintelen** (*23 Mar 1966 Wiesbaden)
II) Georg **Nicolaus von Rintelen** (*29 Jun 1970 Wiesbaden)
= 30 Jun 2007; **Olivia Minninger** (*27 Aug1969 Koln) daughter of Günther Minninger & Monika Kleineberg
A) **Julian von Rintelen** (*7 Jan 2003 Munich)
B) **Nicolai von Rintelen** (*17 Nov 2006 Munich)
III) **Gregor von Rintelen** (*13 Aug 1972 Wiesbaden)
= 2002; Christiane Mathilde (**Jane**) **Gräfin zu Benthem-Tecklenburg-Rheda-Prill** (*18 May 1973 Wiesbaden) daughter of Fiedebert Graf zu Benteim-Tecklenburg-Rheda-Prill & Rosemarie Heilhecker
A) **Frederick** Enno Christian **von Rintelen** (*11 Dec 2006)
B) **Luise von Rintelen** (*30 Jun 2009 Braine L'Alleud, Belgium)
3. **Countess Olga** Katharina Adda **von Merenberg** (3 Oct 1898 Wiesbaden – 15 Sep 1983 Bottmingen)
= 3 Nov 1923 Wiesbaden; **Count Michael** Tarielovich **Loris-Melikov** (8/21 Jun 1900 Tsarskoie-Selo – 2 Oct 1980 Bottmingen, Switzerland) son of Count Tariel Loris-Melikov & Princess Varvara Argutinskya-Dolgorukova
a. **Count Alexander** Mikhailovich **Loris-Melikoff** (*23 May 1926 Paris)
= 27 Sep 1958 Soignes; **Micheline** Celine **Prunier** (*21 Jun 1932 Liège)
I) **Countess Anna Elisabeth** Alexandrovna **Loris-Melikoff**

(*23 Jul 1959 Basel)
= 4 Nov 1983 Therwil; **Marc Moos** (*5 Feb 1953)
A) **Alain Moos** (*26 Mar 1984 Bale)
II) **Countess Dominique** Alexandrovna **Loris-Melikoff** (*23 Jun 1962 Basel)
III) **Countess Nathalie** Alexandrovna **Loris-Melikoff** (*28 Dec 1962 Basel)
= 9 Oct 1996 Kussnacht; **Johan Dierbach** (*12 Jan 1963 Stockholm)
A) **Sophie Dierbach** (*23 Feb 1997 Zurich)
IV) **Count Michel** Alexandrovich **Loris-Melikoff** (*18 Dec 1964 Basel)

K. **Boris** Alexandrovich **Dolgoruky** (16/28 Feb – 30 Mar/11 Apr 1876 St. Petersburg)

L. **Princess Catherine** Alexandrovna **Yourievskya** (9/21 Sep 1878 St. Petersburg – 22 May 1959 North Hayling, England)
=1 31 Oct 1901 Biarritz; **Prince Alexander** Vladimirovich **Bariatinsky** (22 May/3 Jun 1870 St. Petersburg – 6 Mar 1910 Florence) son of Prince Vladimir Bariatinsky & Countess Nadejda Stenbok-Fernor
=2 6/19 Oct 1916 Yalta (dv.1922); **Prince Serge** Platonovich **Obolensky** (21 Sep/3 Oct 1890 Tsarskoie-Selo – 29 Sep 1978 Grosse Pointe, Michigan) son of Prince Platon Obolensky & Maria Narishkina; =2nd Alice Astor and =3rd Marilyn Fraser-Wall
issue of 1st (none by 2nd):
1. **Prince Andrew** Alexandrovich **Bariatinsky** (2 Aug 1902 Paris – 1944 Libya)
= 30 Oct 1925 Sceaux; **Marie Paule Jedlinska** (8 Feb 1906 Paris – 13 Feb 1971 Paris) daughter of Jules Jedlinski & Louise Protet
a. **Princess Hélène** Andree Jeanne Andreievna **Bariatinskya** (17 Jul 1927 Paris – 10 Dec 1988 Avignon)
=1 24 Jun 1959 Paris (dv.1968); **Jean-Victor Hantz** (*19 Mar 1919 Sens) son of Alphonse Hantz & Mathilde Thierry
=2 5 Jul 1969 Cairanne; **Jacques-Pierre Phoebe** (*16 May 1926 Paris) son of Henri Phoebe & Simone Derrin; =1st Georgette Cottin; =3rd Jacqueline Meyer
no issue

2. **Prince Alexander** Alexandrovich **Bariatinsky** (24 Aug 1905 Paris – 25 Dec 1992 Grants Pass, Oregon) legally change name to **Barry** 1949
= Sep 1928 (dv.1935); **Olga Massalsky** (stage name: **Lola Bori**) (10/23 Oct 1912 St. Petersburg – 25 Nov 1959 Hollywood, California) daughter of Michael Pleschkov & Vera Massalsky; she =2nd Michael Levienne
a. **Olga Levienne** (*ca.1932) adopted by step-father

II. **Grand Duchess Maria** Nikolaievna **of Russia** (6/18 Aug 1819 St. Petersburg – 9/21 Feb 1876 St. Petersburg)
=1 2/14 Jul 1839 St. Petersburg; **Maximilian** (Eugenievich) Joseph Eugène August Napoléon **de Beauharnais, Duke of Leuchtenberg** (2 Oct 1817 Munich – 20 Oct/1 Nov 1852 St. Petersburg) son of Eugène de Beauharnais, Duke of Leuchtenberg & Princess Auguste of Bavaria; suc. father as Duke (in Bavaria) 28 Mar 1835; cr. Duke (in Russia) 14 Jul 1839
=2 1854 (secretly) & 4/16 Nov 1856 St. Petersburg (publicly); **Count Gregory** Alexandrovich **Stroganov** (16/28 Jun 1823 – 6/18 Feb 1878) son of Count Alexander Stroganov & Princess Natalia Kotchoubey
issue of 1st (*Titled Prince/Princess Romanovsky, Duke/Duchess of Leuchtenberg and styled Imperial Highness after 5/17 Feb 1852*):

A. **Duchess Alexandra** Maximilianovna **of Leuchtenberg** (28 Mar/9 Apr 1840 St. Petersburg – 31 Jul/12 Aug 1843 St. Petersburg)

B. **Princess Maria** Maximilianovna **Romanovsky** etc. (4/16 Oct 1841 St. Petersburg – 16 Feb 1914 Karlsruhe)
= 30 Jan/11 Feb 1863 St. Petersburg; **Prince** Ludwig **Wilhelm** August **of Baden** (18 Dec 1829 Karlsruhe – 27 Apr 1897 Karlsruhe) son of Leopold, Grand Duke of Baden & Princess Sophie of Sweden

1. **Princess Sophie** Marie Luise Amalie Josephine **of Baden** (26 Jul 1865 Baden-Baden – 29 Nov 1939 Baden-Baden)
= 2 Jul 1889 Karlsruhe; Leopold **Friedrich II** Eduard Karl Alexander, **Duke of Anhalt** etc. (18 Aug 1856 Dessau – 21 Apr 1918 Schloss Ballenstedt) son of Friedrich I, Duke of Anhalt & Princess Antoinette of Saxe-Altenburg
no issue

2. **Maximilian** Alexander Friedrich Wilhelm, **Prince of Baden** (10 Jul 1867 Baden-Baden – 6 Nov 1929 Konstanz) suc. cousin,

Grand Duke Friedrich II, as Head of the House 9 Aug 1928
= 10 Jul 1900 Gmunden; **Princess Marie Luise** Viktoria Caroline Amalie Alexandra Auguste Friederike **of Hanover,** etc. (11 Oct 1879 Gmunden – 31 Jan 1948 Schloss Salem) daughter of Crown Prince Ernst August of Hanover & Princess Thyra of Denmark

a. **Princess Marie Alexandra** Thyra Viktoria Louise Carola Hilda **of Baden** (1 Aug 1902 Schloss Salem – 29 Jan 1944 Frankfurt) killed in an air raid
   = 17 Sep 1924 Schloss Salem; **Prince Wolfgang** Moritz **of Hesse** (6 Nov 1896 Rumpenheim – 12 Jul 1989 Kronberg) son of Friedrich Karl, Landgrave of Hesse & Princess Margarete of Prussia
   no issue

b. **Berthold** Friedrich Wilhelm Ernst August Heinrich Karl, **Margrave of Baden** etc. (24 Feb 1906 Karlsruhe – 27 Oct 1963 Spaichingen) suc. father, assuming the title Margrave, 1929
   = 15 (civil) & 17 (rel) Aug 1931 Baden-Baden; ♦**Princess Theodora of Greece** (30 May 1906 Athens – 16 Oct 1959 Büdingen) daughter of Prince Andrew of Greece and Princess Alice of Battenberg

   I) **Princess Margarita** Alice Thyra Viktoria Marie Luise Scholastica **of Baden** (14 Jul 1932 Schloss Salem – 15 Jan 2013 London)
      = 1957 (dv.); ♦**Prince Tomislav of Yugoslavia** (1928 – 2000)
      see: page

   II) **Maximilian** Andreas Friedrich Gustav Ernst August Bernhard, **Margrave of Baden** etc. (*3 Jul 1933 Schloss Salem) suc. father 1963
      = 23 Sep 1966 Salem (civil) & 30 Sep 1966 Schloss Persenbeug (rel); **Archduchess Valerie** Isabella Maria Anne Alfonsa Desiderata Birgitte Sophie Thaomasa Huberta Josepha Ignatia **of Austria**, Princess of Tuscany, etc. (*23 May 1941 Vienna) daughter of Archduke Hubert Salvator of Austria & Princess Rosemary of Salm and Salm-Salm

A) **Princess Marie Louise** Elisabeth Mathilde Theodora Cecilie Sarah Charlotte **of Baden** (*3 Jul 1969 Schloss Salem)
= 15 (civil) & 29 (rel) Jul 1999 Schloss Salem; **Richard** Dudley **Baker** (*30 Mar 1936 Biddefors, Maine) son of Harold Baker & Elizabeth Dudley
1) **Sofia Baker** (*30 Mar 2001 Alamosa, Colorado)

B) **Hereditary Prince Bernhard** Max Friedrich August Gustav Louis Kraft **of Baden** (*27 May 1970 Schloss Salem)
= 22 (civil) & 23 (rel) Jun 2001 Salem; **Stephanie** Anne **Kaul** (*27 Jun 1966 Uelzen) daughter of Christian Kaul
1) **Prince Leopold** Bernhard Max Michael Ernst-August Friedrich Guillaume **of Baden** (*18 May 2002 Ravensburg)
2) **Prince Friedrich** Bernhard Leopold Christian Berthold Christoph **of Baden** (*9 Mar 2004 Ravensburg)
3) **Prince Karl-Wilhelm** Bernhard Max Alexander Ernst-August Heinrich-Donatus Mathias **of Baden** (*11 Feb 2006 Ravensburg)

C) **Prince Leopold** Max Christian Ludwig Clemens Hubert **of Baden** (*1 Oct 1971 Schloss Salem)

D) **Prince Michael** Max Andreas **of Baden** (*11 Mar 1976 Karlsruhe)
= 4 Jul 2015 Salem; **Christina Höhne** (*ca.1977) daughter of Claus Höhne & Herlinde Geiger
issue ?

III) **Prince Ludwig** Wilhelm Georg Ernst Christoph **of Baden** (*16 Mar 1937 Karlsruhe)
= 21 Sep 1967 Salem (civil) & 21 Oct 1967 Wald (rel); **Princess** Anne Maria (**Marianne**) Henriette Eleonora Gobertina **of Auersperg** (*15 Dec 1943 Zseliz) daughter of Prince Karl of Auersperg & Countess Henriette von Meran

A) **Princess Sophie** Thyra Josephine Georgine Henriette **of Baden** (*8 Jul 1975 Heidelberg)

B) **Prince Bernhard** Ernst August Emich Rainer **of Baden** (*8 Oct 1976 Heidelberg)

C) **Princess Aglaë** Margareta Tatiana Mary **of Baden** (*3 Mar 1981 Heidelberg)

C. **Prince Nicholas** Maximilianovich **Romanovsky, Duke of Leuchtenberg** (23 Jul/4 Aug 1846 Sergeievskya Dascha – 6 Jan 1891 Paris) suc. father 1852
= (morg.) 5/17 Jul 1868 St. Petersburg; **Nadejda** Sergeievna **Annenkova**, cr. **Countess de Beauharnais** 20Jan/1 Feb 1879 (5/17 Jul 1840 St. Petersburg – 25 May/6 Jun 1891 St. Petersburg) daughter of Serge Annenkov & Catharina Shidlovskya; =1st Vladimir Akinfov
Issue is surnamed de Beauharnais was cr. Duke/Duchess von Leuchtenberg (Serene Highness) 11/23 Nov 1890:

1. **Duke Nicholas** Nikolaievich **de Beauharnais von Leuchtenberg** (17 Oct 1868 Geneva – 2 Mar 1928 Ruth, France)
= 24 Apr/6 May 1894 St. Petersburg; **Countess Maria** Nikolaievna **Grabbé** (11/23 Nov 1869 Tsarskoie-Selo – 24 Oct 1948 Orange, France) daughter of Count Nicholas Grabbé & Countess Alexandra Orlova-Denisova

a. **Duchess Alexandra** Nikolaievna **de Beauharnais von Leuchtenberg** (1/13 Mar 1895 St. Petersburg – 19 Dec 1960 Beaulieu)
=1 12/25 Sep 1916 St. Petersburg (dv.); **Prince Levan** Petrovich **Melikov** (3/15 Feb 1893 – 26 Jan 1928 New York) son of Prince Peter Melikov & Baroness Anna Ostern-Sachen
=2 12 Jul 1922 Paris; **Nicholas** Ivanovich **Terestchenko** (31Jul/12 Aug 1895 Kiev – 19 Oct 1926 St. Cloud) son of Ivan Terestchenko
no issue

b. **Duke Nikolaus** Nikolaievich **de Beauharnais von Leuchtenberg** (29 Jul/10 Aug 1896 Gori – 5 May 1937 Munich)
=1 8 Sep 1919 Novotcherkask; **Olga** Nikolaievna **Fomina** (17/29 Aug 1898 St. Petersburg – 2 Sep 1921 Istanbul) daughter of Nicholas Fomine
=2 3 Nov 1928 Munich; **Elisabeth Himmler-Müller** (31 Jul 1906 Tutzing – 27 Aug 1999 Tutzing) daughter of Georg Himmler & Marianne Müller
issue of 2nd (none by 1st):

I) **Duchess Eugenia** Elisabeth **de Beauharnais von Leuchtenberg** (18 May 1929 Munich – 2 May 2006 Andernach)
= 18 Nov 1958 Bonn; **Martin vom Bruch** (10 Jun 1911 Pawesin – 6 May 1988 Remagen) son of Karl vom Bruch & Wilhelmine Schewe
A) **Irene** Alexandra **vom Bruch** (*17 Dec 1959 Bonn)
II) **Duke Nicolaus** Alexander Fritz **de Beauharnais von Leuchtenberg** (*12 Oct 1933 Munich)
= 24 Aug 1962 Oberkirchen (dv.1985); **Anne** Christine **Bügge** (*12 Dec 1936 Stettin) daughter of Gustav Bügge & Dorothea Arnold
A) **Duke Nicolaus** Maximilian **de Beauharnais von Leuchtenberg** (20 Jan 1963 Bonn - 8 Dec 2002 St. Augustin)
B) **Duke Constantin** Alexander Peter **de Beauharnais von Leuchtenberg** (*25 Jun 1965 Bonn)
c. **Duchess Nadejda** Nikolaievna **de Beauharnais von Leuchtenberg** (21 Jul/2 Aug 1898 Gori – 2 Feb 1962 Salinas, California)
= 1929 Surabaya, Java (dv.1938); **Alexander** Yakovich **Mogilevsky** (27 Jan/8 Feb 1885 Odessa – 7 Mar 1953 Tokyo) son of Yakov Mogilevsky & Irina Serebriakova
I) **Michael** de Beauharnais **Moglilevsky** (*24 Sep 1929 Bandung, Java)
= 30 Jun 1953 Winslow, Maine; **Joan Russell** (*15 Jan 1931 Waterville, Maine) daughter of Clyde Russell & Doris Garland
A) **Michelle** Mikhailovna **Mogilevsky** (*29 Jan 1956 Spokane, Washington)
=1 28 Dec 1977 Titusville, Florida (dv.1979); **Douglas Mock** (*7 Apr 1955 Chicago) son of Howard Mock & Dorothy Klinckman
=2 7 Jun 1980 Winter Park, Florida; **Jeffre** Mathew **Harrison** (20 Aug 1953 Albany, Georgia – 22 Aug 2014 Morganton, Georgia) son of Edward Harrison & Patricia Wood
1) **Russell** Neil **Harrison** (*13 Jan 1985 Winter Park)

2) **Benjamin** Mathew **Harrison** (*7 Jan 1986 Winter Park)

B) **Anton** de Beauharnais **Mogilevsky** (*14 Feb 1960 Ithaca, New York)
=1 20 Aug 1983 Orange Co. Florida (dv.1988); **Susan** Katherine **Westra** (...)
=2 22 Apr 1995 Tallahassee, Florida; **Holly** Jill **Smith** (5 Oct1969 Delray Beach, Florida – 25 May 2014) daughter of Larry Smith & Nancy Smith
=3 7 Jan 2017 Maui, Hawaii; **Victoria Mewborn** (*ca.1961) daughter of William Mewborn & Rosemary Albritton
no issue

C) **Andre** Jon **Mogilevsky** (*1 Aug 1962 Waterville)
= 1998; **Kimberly** Blake **Potter** (*1970)

1) **Natalya** Morgen de Beauharnais **Mogilevsky** (*2000)

2) **Etienne** Isabelle de Beauharnais **Mogilevsky** (*2003)

d. **Duke Maximilian** Nikolaievich **of Leuchtenberg** (26 Mar/8 Apr 1900 St. Petersburg – 10 Jan 1906 Schloss Seeon, Bavaria)

e. **Duke Serge** Nikolaievich **de Beauharnais von Leuchtenberg** (24 Jun/7 Jul 1903 St. Petersburg – 27 Jun 1966 Monterey, California)
=1 27 Oct 1925 Nice (dv.1938); **Anna** Alexandrovna **Naumova** (3/16 Mar 1900 Foros, Crimea – 26 Apr 1993 Philadelphia) daughter of Alexander Naumov & Anna Ushakova
=2 8 Mar 1939 Leipzig (civil) & 17 Apr 1939 Vevey (rel) (dv.1942); **Kira** Nikolaievna **Volkova** (*3/16 Jan 1915 St. Petersburg) daughter of Nicholas Volkov & Anna Vassilieva
=3 23 Jul 1945 Munich; **Olga** Sergeievna **Wickberg** (15 Nov 1926 Zgourovskya – 19 Nov 2013 Monterey, California) daughter of Serge Wickberg & Nina Wickberg
issue of 1st:

I) **Duchess Maria** Sergeievna **de Beauharnais von Leuchtenberg** (1 Sep 1926 Nice – 28 Jun 2005 Philadelphia)
= 7 Aug 1949 Lennox, Massachusetts; **Joseph de Pasquale** (7 Oct 1919 Philadelphia – 22 Jun 2015) son of Horace de

Pasquale & Rosa Lanza

A) **Maria Alexandra de Pasquale** (*6 Aug 1950 Pittsfield, Mass.)
= 30 Oct 1988 Morgantown, Penn.; **Scott** Michael **Jennings** (*2 Oct 1957 Harrisburg, Penn.) son of Sheldon Potteiger & Bernice Gingrich-Jennings
1) **Andrew** Michael **de Pasquale-Jennings** (*16 May 1989 Philadelphia)

B) **Elizabeth** Ann **de Pasquale** (*16 Jan 1952 Boston)
= 22 Nov 1982 Birdsboro, Penn. (dv.); **Steven** Carl **Giordano** (*7 Aug 1952 Englewood, New Jersey) son of Carl Giordano & Joan Wilson
1) **Matthew** Steven **Giordano** (*10 May 1983 Reading, Penn.)
2) **Melissa** Ann **Giordano** (*26 Jun 1986 Reading)

C) **Joseph** Serge **de Pasquale** (3 Jul 1956 Pittsfield – 1 Dec 2000 Belmont Hills, Penn.) (twin)
= 3 Aug 1985 Narbeth, Penn. (dv.1991); **Kerr** Alicia **Gallagher** (*30 Mar 1965) daughter of James Gallagher & Elizabeth Brogan
1) **Joseph** Serge Horace **de Pasquale** (*20 Jan 1986 Bryn Mawr, Penn.)
2) **Elizabeth** Maria **de Pasquale** (*10 Jul 1987 Bryn Mawr)
3) John **Alexander de Pasquale** (*7 Jan 1992 Bryn Mawr)
Joseph de Pasquale has additional issue by **Karen Carr** (…):
4) **Alyssa** Kalani **de Pasquale** (*21 Nov 1992 Reading)

D) **Charles** Nicholas **de Pasquale** (*3 Jul 1956 Boston) (twin)
= 30 Aug 1986 Bryn Mawr; **Cynthia** Louise **Scartozzi** (*11 Feb 1958 Bryn Mawr) daughter of Mario Scartozzi & Winnifried Stafford
1) **Nathalie** Rose **de Pasquale** (*12 Mar 1988 Phoenixville, Penn.)
= 30 Aug 2016; **Charles Pérez** (...)
no issue

2) **Daniel** Anthony **de Pasquale** (*7 Sep 1989 Phoenixville)
3) **Catherine** Marie **de Pasquale** (*26 Apr 1995 Phoenixville)

II) **Duchess Anna** Sergeievna **de Beauharnais von Leuchtenberg** (*5 Feb 1928 Nice)
= 18 Dec 1954 Boston; **Robert** Bayard **Stout** (*24 Aprl 1931 Middesboro, Kentucky) son of William Stout & Louise Baird

A) **Eugene** Beauharnais **Stout** (*5 Apr 1957 Rockaway, New York)
= 22 Dec 1979 Sunnyvale, California; **Patricia** Lynn **Thompson**
(*15 Feb 1959 Detroit) daughter of Thomas Thompson & Margaret Halliday

1) **Heather** Patricia **Stout** (*1 Dec 1980 San Jose, California)
= 14 Jul 2007 Los Altos, California; **Erik** Adam **Olah** (*24 Oct 1979 in Pennsylvania) son of Robert Olah & Kristie Shannon

a) **Matthew** William **Olah** (*30 Mar 2010 Mountain View, California)
b) **Luke Olah** (*Sep 2013 Mountain View)

2) **Timothy** William **Stout** (*26 Jun 1982 San Jose)
= 23 Aug 2008 Watsonville, California; **Katherine Roy** (*14 Mar 1982) daughter of Jean-Claude Roy & Linda Cantrell

a) **Jack Stout** (*2015)

3) **Katherine Stout** (*21 Feb 1985 San Jose)

III) **Duchess Olga** Sergeievna **de Beauharnais von Leuchtenberg** (25 Jun 1931 Bois-Colombes – 10 Dec 2007 Cambridge, Mass.)
= 25 Jun 1957 Brookline, Mass. (dv.1965); **Ronald** Gerald **Newburgh** (21 Feb 1926 Brookline – 30 Mar 2010 Belmont, Mass.) son of Edward Newburgh & Lillian Kurland; =1st Selma Abigadol

A) George **Alexander Newburgh** (*24 Jan 1958 Boston)
= 4 Jul 1999 Belmont, Mass.; **Tracey Spencer** (…)

1) **Gabriela Newburgh** (…)
2) **Christina Newburgh** (…)
B) **Stephanie** Anne **Newburgh** (*21 Jan 1960 Boston)
= 1991 Boston; **Edward** Patterson **Lyon** (…)
1) **Tanya** Nicolette **Lyon** (*6 Jan 1993 Newton, Mass.)
2) **Curtis** James **Lyon** (*7 May 1995 Newton)
IV) **Duchess Natalia** Sergeievna **de Beauharnais von Leuchtenberg** (*28 Feb 1934 Colombes)
= 12 Oct 1968 Lennox; **Malcolm** Baker **Bowers** (1 Sep 1933 Dallas, Texas – 13 Jan 2008 Branford, Connecticut) son of Malcolm Bowers & Virginia Lovejoy
A) **Alexandra** Anna **Bowers** (*11 Dec 1970)
B) **Nadia** Lovejoy **Bowers** (*22 Jul 1973)
= 21 Jun 2015; **Corey Stoll** (*14 Mar 1976 Yew York City) son of Stephen Stoll & Jusith ...
1) **Nikolai Stoll** (*Oct 2015)
issue of 3rd (none by 2nd):
V) **Duke Serge** Sergeievich **de Beauharnais von Leuchtenberg** (27 Nov 1955 Monterey – 17 Jan 2000 Monterey)
VI) **Duchess** Elizabeth (**Lisa**) Sergeievna **de Beauharnais von Leuchtenberg** (*25 Sep 1957 Monterey)
= 5 Oct 1975 Pacific Grove, California; **John** Howard **Craft** (*21 Nov 1954 Iowa City, Iowa) son of Daniel Craft & Mary Thomas
A) **Tasha** Nicole **Craft** (*13 Jun 1981 Pacific Grove)
= Jun 2001 Carmel, California; **Anthony d'Andrea** (…)
1) a daughter (*ca.2013)
B) **Nicholas** James **Craft** (*19 May 1983 Pacific Grove)
C) **Jonathan** Daniel **Craft** (*4 Feb 1986 Pacific Grove)
D) **Andrew** Casey **Craft** (*18 Oct 1988 Pacific Grove)
c. **Duke Michael** Nikolaievich **de Beauharnais von Leuchtenberg** (17 Feb/2 Mar 1905 St. Petersburg – 9 Feb 1928 Orange, France)
d. **Duchess Maria** Nikolaievna **de Beauharnais von Leuchtenberg** (21 May/3 Jun 1907 St. Petersburg – 6 Dec 1992 São Paulo, Brazil)
= 19 May 1929 Paris; **Count Nicholas** Dmitrievich **von**

Mengden, Baron von Altenwogen (1/13 Apr 1899 St. Petersburg – 16 Apr 1973 São Paulo) son of Count Dmitri bon Mengden, etc. & Sofia Atapova
no issue

2. **Duke George** Nikolaievich **de Beauharnais von Leuchtenberg** (10 Dec 1872 Rome – 9 Aug 1929 Schloss Seeon)
= 23 Apr/5 May 1895 St. Petersburg; **Princess Olga** Nikolaievna **Repnina-Volkonskya** (9/21 Aug 1872 Jagatine – 27 Apr 1953 Schloss Seeon) daughter of Prince Nicholas Repnin & Princess Sofia Volkonskya

a. **Duchess Elena** Georgeievna **de Beauharnais von Leuchtenberg** (2/14 May 1896 St. Petersburg – 15 Apr 1977 Paris)
= 6 Jun 1920 Zagreb; **Arkady** Constantinovich **Ugritchitch-Trebinsky** (10/22 Apr 1897 Inkliev – 10 Mar 1982 Boston) son of Constantine Ugritchitch-Trebinsky & Olga Markevich

I) **Nina** Arkadievna **Ugritchitch-Trebinskya** (*15 Jan 1925 Paris)
= 18 Nov 1950 New York (dv.1965); **Robert** Wythe **Cannaday Jr.** (4 May 1924 Floyd, Virginia – 4 Oct 1981 Boston) son of Robert Cannaday Sr. & Nena Hale

A) **Robert** Wythe **Cannaday III** (23 Dec 1955 Washington, DC – 24 Jun 2016)
=1 29 Dec 1973 (dv.1986); **Lisa Waldron** (*28 Sep 1955 Philadelphia) =2nd ... Murphy
=2 3 Jul 1989; **Shawnna** Marie **O'Connell** (*4 Dec 1959 Philadelphia) daughter of William O'Connell & Agnes Connolly
issue of 1st:

1) **Robert** Wythe **Cannaday IV** (*10 Aug 1974 Camp Hill, Penn.)
= ...; **Michelle Varquez** (*10 Jul 1977)
issue ?

2) **Sean** Michael **Cannaday** (*20 Oct 1975 Camp Hill)
= ...; **Michelle DiBuono** (...) daughter of Tony DiBuono & Janet Dilks

a) **Natalie Cannaday** (...)

3) James (**Jamie**) Ryan **Cannaday** (*23 Sep 1976 Camp

Hill)
=1 ...; **Teyona Doyle** (*2 Jul 1977)
=2 13 Jan 2015; **Caitlin Harvey** (...)
issue of 1st:
a) **Marcedes Cannaday** (*ca.1997)
b) **Kaleb Cannaday** (*2002)
issue of 2nd:
c) **Jakob Cannaday** (*12 Jul 2012)
4) **Tara** Lynn **Cannaday** (*15 Jan 1980 Vorhees, Penn.)
= 17 May 2013; **Melissa Scates** (...)
a) **Livie Cannaday** (...) triplet
b) **Henry Cannaday** (...) triplet
c) a son (...) triplet
5) **Lauren** Therese **Cannaday** (*21 Feb 1983 Vorhees)
= 22 Dec 2002; **Kurtis Hendrickson** (...)
a) **Kurtis Hendrickson Jr.** (...)
b) **Tyler Hendrickson** (...)
c) **Ethan Hendrickson** (...)
issue of 2nd:
6) **Caitlyn Cannaday** (*ca.1992)
has issue by ...
a) **Luna Cannaday** (*Feb 2015)
7) **Erin Cannaday** (ca.1992)
issue by adoption:
B) **Helen** Nina **Cannaday** (*20 Jun 1960 Saigon [now Ho Chi Ming City], Vietnam)
= ...; **... Cloud** (...)
issue ?
b. **Duke Dmitri** Georgeievich **de Beauharnais von Leuchtenberg** (18/30 Apr 1898 St. Petersburg – 25 Dec 1972 St.Saveur-des-Montagnes, Quebec)
= 13 May 1921 Rome; **Catherina** Alexandrovna **Arapova** (25 Dec 1899/6 Jan 1900 Simbirsk – 8 Aug 1991 Spring Valley) daughter of Alexander Arapov & Anna Panchieliseva; she =1st Prince Boris Chavchavadze
I) **Duchess Elena** Dmitrievna **de Beauharnais von Leuchtenberg** (30 May 1922 Munich – 10 Nov 2013 Bussy, France)

II) **Duke George** Dmitrievich **de Beauharnais von Leuchtenberg** (11 Jan 1927 Munich – 21 Jan 1963 St.Saveur-des-Montagnes)

c. **Duchess Natalia** Georgeievna **de Beauharnais von Leuchtenberg** (16/29 May 1900 St. Petersburg – 1 Aug 1995 San Bernardino, California)
= 15 Oct 1924 Schloss Seeon; **Baron Vladimir** Feodorovich **Meller-Zakomelsky** (9/21 Jul 1894 Koltyshevsky – 5 Jun 1962 Fontana, California) son of Baron Feodor Meller-Zakomelsky & Olga Filosofova
no issue

d. **Duchess Tamara** Georgeievna **de Beauharnais von Leuchtenberg** (1/14 Feb 1902 St. Petersburg – 1 Feb 1999 Toulon)
= 25 Feb 1933 Toulon; **Constantine** Grigorievich **Karanfilov** (19 Dec 1904/1 Jan 1905 Sebastopol – 15 Apr 1978 Aubinge) son of Gregory Karanfilov & Melanie Kishinskya

I) **Tatiana** Constantinovna **Karanfiloff** (10 Aug 1934 Toulon – 24 Apr 2015 Lyon)
= 16 Feb 1958 Paris; **Serge** Sergeievich **Wsevolojsky** (*9 Sep 1926 Neuilly) son of Serge Vsevolojsky & Maria Maltzova

A) **Serge** Sergeievich **Wsevolojsky** (*3 Jan 1959 Paris)
= 15 May 1982 Aix (civil) & 23 May 1982 Paris (rel); **Xenia** Sviatoslavna **Tomachevskya** (*8 Jan 1961) daughter of Sviatoslav Tomachevshy & Catherina Gormina
issue ?

B) **André** Sergeievna **Wsevolojsky** (*21 Oct 1962 Aix)
= ...; **Sibille Grappin** (...)

1) **Virgil Wesvolojsky** (...)

2) **Ludmilla Wsevolojsky** (...)

C) **Marina** Sergeievna **Wsevolojsky** (*20 Jul 1965 Toulon)

D) **Xenia** Sergeievna **Wsevolojsky** (*11 Jan 1967 Aix)

II) **Marina** Constantinovna **Karanfiloff** (1 Dec 1937 Toulon – 3 Feb 1950 Toulon)

III) **Natalia** Constantinovna **Karanfiloff** (*28 Oct 1942 Toulon)

= 28 Aug 1968 Ajaccio; **Roche Barnato** (*22 Oct 1931 Ravenna)
A) **Jean** Patrice **Barnato** (*9 Aug 1969 Ajaccio)
B) **Thiery Barnato** (*12 Jul 1973 Ajaccio)

e. **Duke Andrew** Georgeievich **de Beauharnais von Leuchtenberg** (25 Jun/8 Jul 1903 St. Petersburg – Feb 1919 Narva, Estonia) killed in action

f. **Duke Constantine** Georgeievich **de Beauharnais von Leuchtenberg** (6/19 May 1905 St. Petersburg – 16 Dec 1983 Ottawa)
= 20 Sep 1929 Schloss Seeon; **Princess Daria** Alexeievna **Obolenskya** (29 Jun/12 Jul 1903 Kaluga – 7 Jul 1982 Ottawa) daughter of Prince Alexei Obolensky & Princess Elizabeth Saltykova
I) **Duchess Xenia** Constantinovna **de Beauharnais von Leuchtenberg** (*20 Jun 1930 Traunstein)
= 12 Jul 1950 Montreal; **Count Dmitri** Yurievich **Grabbé** (23 Jul 1927 Sremski Karlovci, Serbia – 2 Mar 2011 Hershey, Penn.) son of Count Yuri Grabbé & Varvara Yarzhembskya
A) **Count Michael** Dmitrievich **Grabbé** (*7 Mar 1951 Sea Cliff, New York)
= ...; **Nina** Louise **Nail** (*20 Nov 1955)
1) **Countess Megan Grabbé** (*1986)
= 28 Jun 2014 Brownsburg, Indiana; **Andrew Strain** (...)
issue ?
B) **Countess Nina** Dmitrievna **Grabbé** (*12 Oct 1952 Sea Cliff)
=1 18 May 1975 Richmond, Maine (dv.1980); **John Eldredge** (*3 Apr 1949 Wiesbaden)
=2 1984; **Dmitri** Vladimirovich **Shishkoff** (*1958) son of Vladimir Shishkov
issue of 2nd (none by 1st):
1) **Theodore** Dmitrievich **Shishkoff** (*1989) (twin)
2) **Alexandra** Dmitrievna **Shishkoff** (*1989) (twin)
= 6 May 2017; **Andrew Thompson** (...)
issue ?

3) **Nicholas** Dmitrievich **Shishkoff** (*1995)
C) **Count Paul** Dmitrievich **Grabbé** (*7 Mar 1957 Sea Cliff)
= 2008; **Katherine Penchuck** (*Sep 1961)
no issue
D) **Count Alexis** Dmitrievich **Grabbé** (*4 Mar 1961 Sea Cliff)
= ...; **Edith Sirley** (*22 Jan 1961)
1) **Count Patrick Grabbé** (*1991)
2) **Count Kevin Grabbé** (*1994)
E) **Countess Xenia** Dmitrievna **Grabbé** (*16 Feb 1963 Sea Cliff)
= 1989; **Alexander Levitsky** (…)
1) **Paul** Alexandrovich **Levitsky** (*1991)
2) **Daria** Alexandrovna **Levitsky** (*1994)
F) **Countess Maria** Dmitrievna **Grabbé** (*7 Mar 1965 Sea Cliff) (twin)
= 1994; **Richard Melody** (…) son of ... Melogy & Carol Daniels
no issue
G) **Countess Olga** Dmitrievna **Grabbé** (*7 Mar 1965 Sea Cliff) (twin)
= 12 Aug 1990; **Dana Dewey** (…)
1) **Andrew Dewey** (*11 Dec 1993)
2) **Benjamin Dewey** (*3 Feb 1997)
3) **Katherine Dewey** (*29 Jan 2000)
II) **Duchess Olga** Constantinovna **de Beauharnais von Leuchtenberg** (*24 Apr 1934 Schloss Seeon)
= 15 Jun 1952 Sea Cliff; **Oleg** Evgenievich **Gaydeburoff** (27 Feb 1922 Athens – 13 Aug 2011 Glen Clove, NY) son of Eugene Gaydeburov & Irina Makeieva
A) **George** Olegovich **Gaydeburoff** (30 Mar 1955 Manhasset, New York – 1 Jun 1976 Jordanville, New York)
B) **Nina** Olegovna **Gaydeburoff** (*29 Apr 1957 Manhasset)
= ...; **Michael Clark** (...)
issue ?
D. **Princess Eugenia** Maximilianovna **Romanovskya** etc. (20 Mar/1

Apr 1845 St. Petersburg – 4 May 1925 Biarritz)
= 7/19 Aug 1868 St. Petersburg; **Duke Alexander** (Petrovich) Friedrich Constantin **of Oldenburg** (21 May/2 Jun 1844 St. Petersburg - 6 Sep 1932 Biarritz) son of Duke Peter of Oldenburg & Princess Therese of Nassau

1. **Duke Peter** Friedrich Georg (Alexandrovich) **of Oldenburg** (9/21 Nov 1868 St. Petersburg – 11 Mar 1924 Antibes)
=1 27 Jul/9 Aug 1901 Gatchina (dv.1916); **♦Grand Duchess Olga** Alexandrovna **of Russia** (1/13 Jun 1882 Peterhof – 24 Nov 1960 Toronto) daughter of Alexander III, Emperor of Russia & Princess Dagmar of Denmark; =2nd Nicholas Kulikovsky
=2 (morg.) 3 May 1922 Biarritz; **Olga** Vladimirovna **Ratkova-Rognova** (20 Oct/1 Nov 1878 St. Petersburg – 7 Mar 1953 Sidi-Abdallah, Morocco); daughter of Vladimir Ratkov-Rognov
no issue

E. **Prince Eugene** Maximilianovich **Romanovsky, Duke of Leuchtenberg** (27 Jan/8 Feb 1847 St. Petersburg – 18/31 Aug 1901 St. Petersburg) suc. brother 1890/1891
=1 (morg.) 20 Jan 1869 Florence; **Daria** Constantinovna **Opotchina**, cr. **Countess de Beauharnais** (7/19 Mar 1845 St. Petersburg – 7/19 Mar 1870 St. Petersburg) daughter of Constantin Opotchine & Vera Skobeleva; cr. Countess 8/20 Jan 1869
=2 (morg.) 3/15 Apr 1878 St. Petersburg; **Zenaide** Dmitrievna **Skobeleva**, cr. **Countess de Beauharnais, Duchess of Leuchtenberg** (30 May/11 Jun 1856 – 16/28 Jun 1899 St. Petersburg) daughter of Dmitri Skobelev & Olga Poltavseva; cr. Countess 2/14 Jul 1878 and Duchess (ad personam) 16/28 Aug 1889
issue of 1st (none by 2nd):

1. **Countess Daria** Evgeneievna **de Beauharnais** (7/19 Mar 1870 St. Petersburg – 4 Nov 1937 St. Petersburg) murdered by the Communists
=1 7 Sep 1893 Baden-Baden (dv.1911); **Prince Leon** Mikhailovich **Kotchoubey** (23 Jul 1862 Paris – 9 May 1927 Paris) son of Prince Michael Kotchoubey & Eugènie Bressant
=2 9/22 Dec 1911 St. Petersburg; **Baron Vladimir** Evgeneievich **von Graevenitz** (31 Oct/12 Nov 1872 Wierny, Turkestan – 24

May 1916 Helsinki, Finland) son of Baron Eugene von Graevenitz & Olga von Henning
=3 (in Russia, after the Revolution); **Viktor Markezetti** (… - 15 Jan 1938 St. Petersburg) murdered by the Communists
issue of 1st (none by others):
a. **Prince Eugene** Leonovich **Kotchoubey de Beauharnais** (12/24 Jul 1894 Peterhof – 6 Nov 1951 Paris) legally changed name in France
= 30 Aug 1917 Victoria, British Columbia; **Helen** Geraldine **Pearce** (23 Jul 1898 Redhouse, South Africa – 21 Jun 1980 Paris) daughter of Henry Pearce & Lily Gould
I) **Princess Daria Eugenia** Josephine **Kotchoubey de Beauharnais** (4 Jun 1918 Victoria – 5 Jan 1989 Paris)
=1 13 May 1939 Paris (dv.); **Georges Snopko** (2/14 Nov 1895 Vladimir – 1975) son of Arsene Snopko & Katarina …
=2 16 Nov 1961 Nantua; **George Bataille** (10 Sep 1897 Billom – 9 Jul 1962 Paris) son of Aristide Bataille & Antoinette Tornardre
issue of 1st:
A) **Catherine Sopko** (28 Apr 1941 Neuilly – 22 Jul 1990 Paris)
=1 23 Nov 1963 Paris (dv.1970); **Marcel Moyazer** (*27 Nov 1939 St.Étienne)
=2 12 Dec 1975 Paris; **Michel Brasier** (10 Sep 1946 Colombes – 1979)
no issue
issue of 2nd:
B) **Julie Bataille** (*1 Dec 1949 Geneva)
= 4 Dec 1982 Paris (dv.1995); **Michel Bellu** (*24 Feb 1942 Sartrouville)
1) **Marc** Candide Theodore **Bellu** (*18 Nov 1981)
II) **Princess Nathalie** Josephine Marianne **Kotchoubey de Beauharnais** (*19 May 1923 Eltham, Kent)
= 13 May 1955 London; **André Laguerre** (21 Feb 1915 Ottery, Kent – 18 Jan 1979 New York) son of Léon Laguerre & Dorothy Grey
A) **Michele Laguerre** (*1 Jun 1956 New York)
has issue by **Jean-Michel Faustin** (…):

1) **Matthieu Faustin** (*20 Oct 1998 Paris)
B) **Claudine** Josephine **Laguerre** (*13 Jul 1964 New York)
III) **Princess Hélène** Josephine **Kotchoubey de Beauharnais** (5 Apr 1928 Paris – 20 Jan 1980 Ponthévard)
= 2 Dec 1947 Paris; **Pierre Pellegrino** (17 Jan 1917 Cannes – 27 Jul 1995 Paris) son of Jacques Pellegrino & Elisabeth Torsello
A) **Elizabeth Pellegrino** (*18 Jul 1948 Boulogne)
=1 9 Oct 1971 Ponthévard (dv.1976); **Fabrice Jordan** (*9 Mar 1945 Paris) son of Didier Jordan & Genevieve Binet
=2 12 Jun 1982 Suresnes; **Jérôme** Henri **Charrey** (*13 Feb 1947 Paris) son of Pierre-Albert Charrey & Jacqueline-Suzanne Chauvin
issue of 1st:
1) **Alexia** Helene **Jordan** (*29 Aug 1973 Versailles)
= 19 May 2007 Lausanne; **Nicolas de Skowronski** (*4 Sep 1973) son of Marc de Skowronski & Claude de Riedmaten
a) **Victoria** Noémie Marie **de Skowronski** (*21 Oct 2008 Geneva)
b) **Roman de Skowronski** (*20 May 2010 Zurich)
c) **Adrien de Skowronski** (...)
issue of 2nd:
2) **Eric** Jean **Charrey** (*9 Oct 1982 Paris)
= 27 Mar 2010; **Marie Bigot Chardronnet** (*12 Aug 1980)
a) **Alexandre Charrey** (*Jan 2012)
3) **Noémie Charrey** (*19 Dec 1984 Paris)
= 8 Jun 2013; **Boris** Pierre **Minet** (...)
issue ?
B) **Eugénie Pellegrino** (*27 Apr 1955 Paris)
= 1 Dec 1979 Ponthévard (dv.2001); **Jean-François Charrey** (*1 Aug 1945 Boulogne) son of Pierre-Albert Charrey & Jacqueline-Suzanne Chauvin
1) **Melanie** Josephine **Charrey** (*1 Dec 1980 Paris)
= 2 Sep 2006 Asnières; **Nicolas Chambard-Sablier** (*2 Jun 1981) son of Bertrand Chambard-Sablier &

Patricia Forey
a) **Maximilien** Nicolas **Chambard-Sablier** (*20 Aug 2008 Neuilly)
b) a daughter (*ca.2011)
2) **Edouard** Pierre **Charrey** (*12 May 1982 Suresnes)
C) **Alexandra Pellegrino** (29 – 30 Apr 1958 Paris)
IV) **Princess Hortense** Stephanie **Kotchoubey de Beauharnais** (2 Jan 1935 Paris – 28 Feb 1994 Melbourne, Australia)
= 18 Mar 1958 Heidelberg; **Gerhard Murjahr** (*10 Oct 1928 Mannheim) son of Ernst Murjahr & Anna-Maria Finzer
A) **Daria** Alexandra **Murjahr** (*29 Jan 1967 Berlin)
= 16 Jun 1995 Wilnsdorf; **Alexandros Silvestros** (*15 Dec 1964 Athens)
1) **Nikolaos Silvestros** (*17 Jan 1996 Wilnsdorf)
2) **Michael Silvestros** (*22 Mar 2001)
B) **Sonia Murjahr** (*8 Jul 1970 Berlin)
b. (Princess Natalia) **Mother Sofia** Leonovna **Kotchoubey** (18 Oct 1899 Wiesbaden - 1979)
F. **Prince Serge** Maximilianovich **Romanovsky** etc. (8/20 Dec 1849 St. Petersburg – 12/24 Oct 1877 Rutchuk)
G. **Prince George** Maximilianovich **Romanovsky, Duke of Leuchtenberg** (17/29 Feb 1852 St. Petersburg – 3 May 1912 Paris) suc. brother 1901
=1 2 May 1879 Stuttgart; **Duchess Therese** Friederike Olga **of Oldenburg** (18/30 Mar 1852 St. Petersburg – 7/19 Apr 1883 St. Petersburg) daughter of Duke Peter of Oldenburg & Princess Therese of Nassau
=2 16/28 Aug 1889 Peterhof (dv.1906); **Princess Anastasia** Nikolaievna **of Montenegro** (23 Dec 1867 Cetinje – 15 Nov 1935 Cap d'Antibes) daughter of Nicholas I, King of Montenegro & Milena Vukotic; =1st ♦Grand Duke Nicholas of Russia
issue of 1st:
1. **Prince Alexander** Georgeievich **Romanovsky, Duke of Leuchtenberg** (1/13 Nov 1881 St. Petersburg – 26 Sep 1942 Salies) suc. father 1912
= (morg.) 9/22 Apr 1917 St. Petersburg; **Nadejda** Nikolaievna

Caralli (3/15 Jul 1883 St. Petersburg – 9 Feb 1964 Salies) daughter of Nicholas Caralli & Maria Gorovich; =1st … Scheiffer, and =2nd … Ignatev
no issue
issue of 2nd:
2. **Prince Serge** Georgeievich **Romanovsky, Duke of Leuchtenberg** (4/16 Jul 1890 Peterhof – 7 Jan 1974 Rome) suc. brother 1942; upon his death the Imperial line of Leuchtenberg became extinct
3. **Princess Elena** Georgeievna **Romanovskya** etc. (15 Jan 1892 Nice – 6 Feb 1970 Rome)
= 6/18 Jul 1917 Yalta; **Count Stefan** Eugenusz Maria **Tyszkiewicz** (24 Nov 1894 Warsaw – 1 Feb 1974 London) son of Count Ladyslaw Tyszkiewicz & Princess Maria-Kryztyna Lubomirska
a. **Countess Natalya** Roza Maria **Tyszkiewicz** (*16 Jan 1921 Warsaw)
issue of 2nd:
H. **Countess Sofia** Grigorievna **Stroganova** (17/29 Jan 1861 St. Petersburg – 16/29 Jan 1908 Tsarskoie-Selo)
=1 26 Dec 1878/7 Jan 1879 St. Petersburg; **Vladimir** Alexeievich **Cheremetev** (4/16 May 1847 Moscow – 5/17 Feb 1893 St. Petersburg) son of Alexei Cheremetev
=2 1896 St. Petersburg; **Gregory** Nikitich **Milachevich** (… – 1918 Sebastopol) murdered by Bolsheviks; son of Nikita Milachevich
issue of 1st (none by 2nd):
1. **Serge** Vladimirovich **Cheremetev** (24 Dec 1879/5 Jan 1880 St. Petersburg – 17 Mar 1968 Rome)
=1 11/24 Jan 1907 St. Petersburg (dv.); **Countess Alexandra** Alexandrovna **Cheremeteva** (21 Mar/2 Apr 1886 Ulianka – 9 Dec 1944 St. Maurice) daughter of Count Alexander Cheremetev & Countess Maria Heyden
=2 15 Feb 1939 Paris; **Stella** Ellis **Webber** (1 Feb 1888 Chicago – 15 Jan 1969 Rome) daughter of Charles Webber
issue of 1st (none by 2nd):
a. **Nikita** Sergeievich **Cheremetev** (26 Jan/8 Feb 1908 St. Petersburg – 15 May 1981 Brevard Co. Florida)
= 3 Nov 1935; **Catherine Vandoro** (11/24 Nov 1915 Yalta –

5 Apr 2009 Famouth, Antigua) daughter of Lucas Vandoro

I) **Maria** Nikitichna **Cheremeteff** (*7 Feb 1937 Athens)
=1 1 Nov 1959 London (dv.); **Brandon** Hambright **Grove** (8 Apr 1929 Chicago – 20 May 2016 Washington) son of Brandon Grove & Helen Gasparska; =2nd Mariana Moran
=2 ...; **Robert** Gordon **Abernethy** (*5 Nov 1927 Geneva) son of Robert Abernethy & Lois ...; =1st Jean Montgomery
issue of 1st:
A) **John** Cheremeteff **Grove** (*4 Mar 1963 Washington, DC)
= …; **Hannah Hero Wood** (…)
issue ?
B) **Catherine** Cheremeteff **Grove** (*21 Mar 1964 New Delhi, India)
= 24 Jun 1995 Washington DC; **Paul** Wayne **Jones** (…)
1) **Aleksandra** Cheremeteff **Jones** (...)
2) **Hale** Grove **Jones** (...)
C) **Paul** Cheremeteff **Grove** (*17 May 1965 Washington, DC)
= …; **Martha Merselis** (…)
1) **Samuel Grove** (...)
D) **Mark** Cheremeteff **Grove** (*15 Sep 1970 Washington, DC)
issue of 2nd:
E) a daughter
F) a daugher

II) **Vladimir** Nikitich **Cheremeteff** (*29 Jun 1938 Pirea, Greece)
=1 1964 Norwich, Norfolk; **Gillian Sadler** (...)
=2 Sep 1986 Plymouth, Devon; **Mary Scullin** (...)
issue of 1st (none by 2nd):
A) **Nikita** Vladimirovich **Cheremeteff** (*1965 London)[5]

---

[5] Nikita has been married and has children. However, he has insisted they not be included in this book, despite the information being readily available on the internet.

B) **Nathalie** Vladimirovna **Cheremteff** (*... Belgium)
= ...; **Matthew** Hubert **Phillips** (...)
1) **Tatiana Phillips** (*30 May 2002 San Diego)
2) **Luke Phillips** (*24 Mar 2005 Belgium)
III) **Serge** Nikitich **Cheremeteff** (*11 Oct 1943 Athens)
IV) **Alexandra** Nikitichna **Cheremeteff** (*14 Oct 1949 Limrassol, Cyprus)
= ... (dv.1983); **Douglas** Norman **Crotwell** (19 Feb 1939 Sandhill, Miss. – 11 Aig 2003 Palm Bay, Florida) son of Woodrow Crotwell & Annie Bustin; =2nd Mary Wheelin
A) **Steven** Woodrow **Crotwell** (*1969)
= ...; **Jaclyn** Lydia **Baldridge** (*ca.1970) daughter of ... Baldridge & Jacqueline Cockrell
1) **Cassidy Crotwell** (*ca.1995)
2) **Carly Crotwell** (ca.1999)
3) **James Crotwell** (*2003)
B) **Michael** Alexander **Crotwell** (*1976)
= ...
1) **Kamren Crotwell** (*ca.2000)
2. **Sofia** Vladimirovna **Cheremeteva** (29 Oct/10 Nov 1888 St. Petersburg – Dec 1956 Rome)
= 21 Jan/3 Feb 1902 Tiblisi; **Dmitri** Vladimirovich **von Daehn** (25 Aug/6 Sep 1874 Lagodekhi, Caucasus – 4 Sep 1937 Rome) son of Vladimir von Daehn & Princess Nina Swiatpol-Mirska
issue by adoption:
1. **Alexander** Dmitrievich **von Daehn** (10/23 Nov 1908 Peterhof – May 1979 New York) rumored to be the natural child of Grand Duke Sergei Mikhailovich and Countess Barbara Vorontzova-Daskova
= 27 Jan 1935 Rome (dv.1948); **Olga** Yurievna **Toubnikova** (30 Jan 1910 Rome – 2 Dec 1994 Chicago) daughter of Yuri Toubnikov & Olga Galabova
no issue
III. **Grand Duchess Olga** Nikolaievna **of Russia** (30 Aug/11 Sep 1822 St. Petersburg – 30 Oct 1892 Friedrichshafen)
= 1/13 Jul 1846 Peterhof; **Karl I** Friedrich Alexander, **King of Württemberg** (6 Mar 1823 Stuttgart – 6 Oct 1891 Stuttgart) son of Wilhelm I, King of Württemberg & Duchess Pauline of Württemberg ;

suc. father 25 Jun 1864
no issue

IV. **Grand Duchess Alexandra** Nikolaievna **of Russia** (12/24 Jun 1825 St. Petersburg – 29 Jul/10 Aug 1844 Tsarskoie-Selo)
= 16/28 Jan 1844 St. Petersburg; **Landgrave Friedrich** Wilhelm Georg Adolf **of Hesse-Cassel** (later **Landgrave of Hesse**) (26 Nov 1830 Cassel – 14 Oct 1884 Frankfurt) son of Landgrave Wilhelm of Hesse-Cassel & Princess Charlotte of Denmark; suc. second cousin, Elector Friedrich Wilhelm, as Landgrave of Hesse 6 Jan 1875

V. **Grand Duke Constantine** Nikolaievich **of Russia** (9/21 Sep 1827 St. Petersburg – 13/25 Jan 1892 Pavlovsk)
= 30 Aug/11 Sep 1848 St. Petersburg; **Princess Alexandra** (Josipovna) Friedeirke Henriette Pauline Mariane Elisabeth **of Saxe-Altenburg** (8 Jul 1830 Altenburg – 23 Jun/6 Jul 1911 St. Petersburg) daughter of Joseph, Duke of Saxe-Altenburg & Duchess Amalie of Württemberg

A. **Grand Duke Nicholas** Constantinovich **of Russia** (2/14 Jul 1850 St. Petersburg – 2/14 Jan 1918 Tashkent, Uzbekistan)
= (morg.) 3/15 Feb 1878 Berdy, Uzbekistan; **Nadejda** Alexandrovna **von Dreyer** (1861 Tashkent – 1929 St. Petersburg) daughter of Alexander von Dreyer & Sofia Opanovskya; assumed surname Iskander upon marriage for herself and her children.

1. **Artemi** Nikolaievich **Iskander** (1883 Tashkent – 1919) killed in action

2. **Alexander** Nikolaievich **Iskander** (3/15 Nov 1889 Tashkent – 16 Jan 1957 Grasse, France)
=1 23 Apr/5 May 1912 Tashkent (dv.); **Olga** Josipovna **Rogovskya** (1893 – …) daughter of Joseph Rogovsky; =2nd Nicholas Alexandrosov
=2 11 Oct 1930 Paris; **Natalia** Constantinovna **Khanykova** (18/30 Dec 1893 St. Petersburg – 20 Apr 1992 Nice) daughter of Constantine Khanykov & Natalia Markova
issue of 1st (none by 2nd) adopted by step-father:

a. **Cyril** Nikolaievich **Alexandrosov** (22 Nov/5 Dec 1914 Tashkent – 1992 Moscow)

b. **Natalia** Nikolaievna **Alexandrosova** (28 Jan/10 Feb 1916 Tashkent – 24 Jul 1999 Moscow)
= (dv.); **Nikolai** Vladimirovich **Dostal** (1909 Saratov – 22 Apr

1959) son of Vladimir Dostal
no issue

Grand Duke Nicholas had additional issue by **Daria** Elisseievna **Chassovitine** (1879 - …):

3. **Daria** Nikolaievna **Chassovitine** (1895 Tashkent – 1966 Moscow)
4. **Sviatoslav** Nikolaievich **Chassovitine** (1896 Tashkent – Jan 1919 Tashkent)
5. **Nicholas** Nikolaievich **Chassovitine** (1897 – 1921) killed in an accident

B. **Grand Duchess Olga** Constantinovna **of Russia** (22 Aug/3 Sep 1851 Pavlovsk – 18 Feb 1926 Pau)
= 15/27 Oct 1867 St. Petersburg; **George I, King of the Hellenes** (né Prince Christian Wilhelm Ferdinand Adolf Georg of Denmark) (24 Dec 1845 Copenhagen – 18 Mar 1913 Salonika) assassinated; son of Christian IX, King of Denmark & Princess Luise of Hesse-Cassel; elected King of the Hellenes 5 Jun 1863

1. **Constantine I, King of the Hellenes** (2 Aug 1868 Athens – 11 Jan 1923 Palermo) suc. father 1913, deposed 11 Jun 1917, restored 17 Dec 1920; abdicated 22 Sep 1922
= 27 Oct 1889 Athens; **Princess Sophie** Ulrike Alice **of Prussia** (14 Jun 1870 Potsdam – 13 Jan 1932 Frankfurt) daughter of Friedrich III, German Emperor & Princess Victoria of Great Britain

a. **George II, King of the Hellenes** (19 Jul 1890 Tatoi – 1 Apr 1947 Athens) suc. father 1922; deposed 24 Mar 1924; restored 3 Nov 1935; deposed 23 Apr 1941; restored 28 Sep 1946
= 27 Feb 1921 Bucharest (dv.1935); ♦**Princess Elizabeth** Charlotte Josephine Alexandra Victoria **of Romania** (12 Oct 1894 Pelesch Castle – 15 Nov 1956 Cannes) daughter of Ferdinand, King of Romania & Princess Marie of Edinburgh
no issue

b. **Alexander, King of the Hellenes** (1 Aug 1893 Tatoi – 25 Oct 1920 Athens) suc. father 1917
= 4 Nov 1919 Athens; **Aspasia Manos** (4 Sep 1896 Athens – 7 Aug 1972 Venice) daughter of Petros Manos & Maria Argyropoulos

I) **Princess Alexandra of Greece** (25 Mar 1921 Tatoi – 30 Jan

1993 Burges Hill, England)
= 1944; ♦**Peter II, King of Yugoslavia** (1923 – 1970)
see: page

c. **Princess Helen of Greece** (3 May 1896 Athens – 28 Nov 1982 Lausanne)
= 1921 (dv.1928); ♦**Crown Prince Carol (later King Carol II) of Romania** (1893 – 1953)
see: page

d. **Paul, King of the Hellenes** (14 Dec 1901 Tatoi – 6 Mar 1964 Athens) suc. brother, George II, 1947
= 9 Jan 1938 Athens; **Princess Friederike** Luise Thyra Viktoria Margarete Sophie Olga Cecilie Isabelle Christa **of Hanover** etc. (18 Aug 1917 Blankenburg – 6 Feb 1981 Madrid) daughter of Ernst August, Duke of Brunswick & Princess Viktoria Luise of Prussia

I) **Princess Sophia of Greece** (*2 Nov 1938 Psychiko)
= 14 May 1962 Athens; **Juan Carlos** Alfonso Victor Maria, **King of Spain** etc. (*5 Jan 1938 Rome) son of Infante Juan of Spain, Count de Barcelona & Princess Maria de las Mercedes of the Two Sicilies; declared King upon death Francisco Franco 22 Nov 1975; abdicated 18 Jun 2014

A) **Infanta Elena** Maria Isabella Dominica **of Spain, Duchess of Lugo** (*20 Dec 1963 Madrid)
= 18 Mar 1995 Sevilla (dv.2010); **Jaime de Marichalar y Saenz de Tejada** (*7 Apr 1963 Pamplona) son of Amalio de Marichalar y Bruguera, Count de Ripalda & Maria Concepción Saenz de Tejada y Fernandez de Bododilla

1) Felipe Juan **Froilán** de Todos los Santos **de Marichalar de Borbón** (*17 Jul 1998 Madrid)

2) **Victoria** Federica **de Marichalar de Borbón** (*9 Feb 2000 Madrid)

B) **Infanta Cristina** Frederika Victoria Antonia **of Spain** (formerly Duchess of Palma de Mallorca) (*13 Jun 1965 Madrid) cr. Duchess 1997; deprived of title 2015
= 4 Oct 1997 Barcelona; **Iñaki Urdangarin y Liebert** (*15 Jan 1968 Zumarraga) son of Juan Maria Urdangarin & Claire Liebert

1) **Juan** Valentin de Todos los Santos **Urdangarin de Borbón** (*29 Sep 1999 Barcelona)
2) **Pablo** Nicolas **Urdangarin de Borbón** (*6 Dec 2000 Barcelona)
3) **Miguel Urdangarin de Borbón** (*30 Apr 2002 Barcelona)
4) **Irene Urdangarin de Borbón** (*5 Jun 2005 Barcelona)

C) **Felipe VI** Juan Pablo Alfonso, **King of Spain**, etc. (*30 Jan 1968 Madrid) suc. father 2014
= 22 May 2004 Madrid; **Leticia Ortiz Rocasolano** (*15 Sep 1972 Oviedo) daughter of Jesus Ortiz Alvarez & Paloma Rocasolano Rodriguez
1) **Infanta Leonor of Spain, Princess of Asturias** (*31 Oct 2005 Madrid)
2) **Infanta Sofia of Spain** (*29 Apr 2007 Madrid)

II) **Constantine II, King of the Hellenes** (*2 Jun 1940 Psychiko) suc. father 1964; deposed 13 Dec 1967
= 18 Sep 1964 Athens; ♦**Princess Anne-Marie** Dagmar Ingrid **of Denmark** (*30 Aug 1946 Amalienborg Palace) daughter of Frederik IX, King of Denmark & Princess Ingrid of Sweden

A) **Princess Alexia of Greece** (*10 Jul 1965 Mon Repos)
= 9 Jul 1999 London; **Carlos Morales Quintana** (*31 Dec 1970 Arrecife de Lanzarote) son of Luis Miguel Morales Armas & Maria Teresa Quintana Gonzalez
1) **Arietta Morales de Grecia** (*24 Feb 2002 Barcelona)
2) **Ana-Maria Morales de Grecia** (*15 May 2003 Barcelona)
3) **Carlos Morales de Grecia** (*30 Jul 2005 Barcelona)
4) **Amelia Morales de Grecia** (*26 Oct 2007 Barcelona)

B) **Crown Prince Pavlos of Greece** (*20 May 1967 Tatoi)
= 1 (rel) & 2 (civil) Jul 1995 London; **Marie-Chantal Miller** (*17 Sep 1968 London) daughter of Robert Miller & Chantal Pesantes
1) **Princess Maria-Olympia of Greece** (*25 Jul 1996 New York)
2) **Prince Constantine-Alexios of Greece** (*29 Oct

1998 New York)

3) **Prince Achilles-Andreas of Greece** (*12 Aug 2000 New York)

4) **Prince Odysseus-Kimon of Greece** (*17 Sep 2004 London)

5) **Prince Aristidis-Stavros of Greece** (*29 Jun 2008 Los Angeles)

B) **Prince Nikolaos of Greece** (*1 Oct 1969 Rome
= 25 Aug 2010 Spetses, Greece; **Tatiana Blatnik** (*28 Aug 1980 Caracas) daughter of Ladislav Blatnik & Marie-Blanche Beierlein
no issue

C) **Princess Theodora of Greece** (*9 Jun 1983 London)

D) **Prince Philippos of Greece** (*26 Apr 1986 London)

III) **Princess Irene of Greece** (*11 May 1942 Cape Town, South Africa)

e. **Princess Irene of Greece** (13 Feb 1904 Athens – 15 Apr 1974 Florence)
= 1 Jul 1939 Florence; **Prince Aimone** Roberto Margherita Maria Giuseppe Torino **of Savoy, Duke of Aosta** (9 Mar 1900 Turin – 29 Jan 1948 Buenos Aires) son of Prince Emanuele Filiberto of Savoy, Duke of Aosta & Princess Hélène of Orleans; proclaimed King of Croatia (as Tomislav II) but never accepted 18 May 1941; suc. brother, Amadeo, 3 Mar 1942

I) **Prince Amadeo** Umberto Constantino Giorgio Paolo Elena Maria Fiorenzio Zvonimir **of Savoy, Duke of Aosta** (*27 Sep 1943 Florence) suc. father 1948
=1 22 Jul 1964 Sintra (dv.1982, ann. 1986); **Princess Claude** Marie Agnes Catherine **of France** (*11 Dec 1943 Larache, Morocco) daughter of Prince Henri of France, Count de Paris & Princess Isabelle of Orleans and Bragança; =2nd Arnoldo La Cagnina; =3rd Enrico Gandolfi
=2 30 Mar 1987 Palermo; **Marchessa Silvia Paterno di Spedalotto** (*31 Dec 1953 Palermo) daughter of Vincenzo Paterno di Spedalotto, Marchese di Regiovanni & Rosanna Bellardo Ferraris di Celle
issue of 1st (none by 2nd):

A) **Princess Bianca** Irene Olga Elena Isabella Fiorenza Maria **of Savoy** (*2 Apr 1966 Florence)
= 11 Sep 1988 Il Borro; **Count Gilberto Arrivabene Valenti Gonzaga** (*5 Jul 1961 Rome) son of Count Leonardo Arrivabene Valenti Gonzaga & Maria della Grazia dei conti di Brandolini d'Adda
1) **Viola** Moreschina Nuschi Adec Nicoletta Maria **dei conti Arrivabene Valenti Gonzaga** (*31 May 1991 Rome)
2) **Vera** Clementina Verde Aimone Elena Maria **dei conti Arrivabene Valenti Gonzaga** (*18 Aug 1993 Samedan)
3) **Mafalda** Violante Giovanna Olga Maria **dei conti Arrivabene Valenti Gonzaga** (*27 Dec 1997 Conegliano)
4) **Maddalena** Esmerelda Brandolina Maria **dei conti Arrivabene Valenti Gonzaga** (*24 Apr 2000 Conegliano)
5) **Count Leonardo** Amedeo Moreschino Sai Maria **Arrivabene Valenti Gonzaga** (*5 Oct 2001 Conegliano)

B) **Prince Aimone** Umberto Emanuele Filiberto Luigi Amadeo Elena Maria Fiorenzo **of Savoy, Duke of Apulia** (*13 Oct 1967 Florence)
= 16 Sep 2008 Moscow (civil) & 27 Sep 2008 Patmos (rel.); ♦**Princess Olga of Greece** (*17 Nov 1971 Athens) daughter of Prince Michael of Greece & Marina Karella
1) **Prince Umberto of Savoy, Prince of Piedmont** (*7 Mar 2009 Paris)
2) **Primce Amadeo of Savoy, Duke of the Abruzzio** (*24 May 2011 May Paris)
3) **Princess Isabella** Vita **of Savoy** (*12 Dec 2012 Paris)

C) **Princess Mafalda** Giovanna Shams Maria Fiorenza Isabella **of Savoy** (*20 Sep 1969 Florence)
=1 8 Sep 1994 San Giustino Valdarno (dv.2000); **Don Alessandro** Francesco **Ruffo di Calabria** (*4 Nov 1964 Turin) son of Prince Fabrizio Ruffo di Calabria, Duke of

Guardia Lombarda & Maria Elisabetta Vaciago
=2 27 Apr 2001 London; **Nobile Francesco Lombardo di San Chirico** (*31 Jan 1968 Milan) son of Nobile Carlo Lombardo di San Chirico & Maria Coltelleto
issue of 2nd (none by 1st):
1) **Nobile Anna** Egizia Maria Carla Chiara Benedetta **Lombado di San Chirico** (*4 Apr 1999 Milan)
2) **Nobile Carlo** Ferrante Gennaro Antonio Francesco **Lombardo di San Chirico** (*28 Jan 2001 Milan)
3) **Nobile Elena** Maria Carlotta Claude Silvia Stefania Vittoria **Lombard di San Chirico** (*10 Mar 2003 Milan)

The Duke of Aosta has additional issue by **Kyra von Ellinghuizen**:
D) **Ginevra di Savoia** (*19 Mar 2006 Milan)

f. **Princess Katherine of Greece** (4 May 1913 Athens – 2 Oct 2007 London) renounced titles upon marriage was granted style Lady by the King of Great Britain
= 21 Apr 1947 Athens; **Richard** Campbell Andrew **Brandram** (5 Aug 1911 Buxhill, Sussex – 28 Mar 1994 Marlow) son of Richard Brandram & Maud Campbell
I) Richard **Paul** George Andrew **Brandram** (*1 Apr 1948 London)
=1 12 Feb 1975 London (dv.1993); **Jennifer** Diane **Steele** (*23 Aug 1951 Windsor) daughter of Robert Steele & Gyllian Greville-Williams; =2nd Robert Enslow
=2 19 Sep 2009 Walton d'Eivile, Warwickshire; **Kate Moreton** (*1954) daughter of Thomas Moreton & Effie Richmond; =1st John Warhurst
issue of 1st (none by 2nd):
A) **Sophie** Eila **Brandram** (*23 Jan 1981 London)
= 11 Feb 2017 Ettington, Warks.; **Humphrey** Walter **Voelcker** (*1980) son of Peter Voelcker & Alison Edwards
no issue
B) **Nicholas** George **Brandram** (*23 Apr 1982 London)
= 10 Sep 2011 London (dv.); **Katrina** Johanne **Davis** (*21 Mar 1978 London) daughter of Jim Davis &

Adriana Verhoef
no issue
C) **Alexia** Katherine **Brandram** (*6 Dec 1985 London)
= 29 Apr 2016 London; **William** John Palairet **Hicks** (*1983) son of Jeremy Hicks & Joana Palairet
no issue

2. **Prince George of Greece** (24 Jun 1869 Corfu – 25 Nov 1957 St. Cloud)
= 21 Nov 1907 (civil) & 12 Dec 1907 (rel.); **Princess Marie Napoléon** (2 Jul 1882 St. Cloud – 21 Sep 1962 Gassin) daughter of Prince Roland Napoléon & Marie Blanc

a. **Prince Peter of Greece** (3 Dec 1908 Paris – 15 Oct 1980 London)
= 9 Sep 1939 Madras; **Irina** Alexandrovna **Outchinikova** (28 Sep/11 Oct 1904 St. Petersburg – 12 Mar 1990 Paris) daughter of Alexander Outchinikov & Lydia Somilo; =1st Jean, Marquis de Mauleon
no issue

b. **Princess Eugenie of Greece** (10 Feb 1910 Paris – 13 Feb 1989 Geneva)
=1 30 May 1938 Paris (ann.1946); **Prince Dominik** Ranier Karol Hieronim Maria Nikolaj Alfons **Radziwill** (23 Jan 1911 Balice – 19 Nov 1976 Geneva) son of Prince Hieronim Radziwill & Archduchess Renata of Austria; =2nd Lida Bloodgood
=2 28 Nov 1949 Athens (dv.1965); **Prince Don Raymond** Alessandro Maria Louis Lamoral **della Torre e Tasso, Duke of Castel Duino** (16 Mar 1907 Castel Duino – 17 Mar 1986 Castel Duino) son of Prince Don Alessandro della Torre e Tasso, Duke of Castel Duino & Princess Marie de Ligne; suc. father 11 Mar 1937
issue of 1st:
I) **Princess Tatiana** Maria Renata Eugenia Elisabeth Margarethe **Radziwill** (*28 Aug 1939 Rouen)
= 24 Mar 1966 Athens; **John Henri Fruchaud** (*1 Apr 1937 Paris) son of Henri Fruchaud & Eunice McCovey
A) **Fabiola** Frederika Marina **Fruchaud** (*7 Feb 1967 Paris)
=1 26 Aug 1994 St. Tropez; **Thierry** Georges Philippe

Hermann (*20 Dec 1965 Maison Lafitte) son of Georges Hermann & Christiane Ehrstein
=2 ...; **Didier Fradin** (*1959)
issue of 1st:
1) **Tatiana Hermann** (*31 Jul 1996)
issue of 2nd:
2) **Edouard Fradin** (*2007)
B) **Alexis Fruchaud** (*25 Nov 1969 Paris)
= 2002 St. Tropez; **Natalie Chandler** (…)
1) **Thalia** Tatiana Eugenie Lily Marie **Fruchard** (*23 Jun 2008)
II) **Prince Jerzy** Andrzej Dominik Hieronim Piotr Leon **Radziwill** (4 Nov 1942 Capetown – 27 Aug 2001 Chevilly Larue)
issue of 2nd:
III) **Prince Don Carlo Alessandro** Giorgio Pietro Lucien Maria Raymond Louis Lamoral **della Torre e Tasso, Duke of Castel Duino** (*10 Feb 1952 Neuilly) suc. father 1986
= 10 Feb 1976 St. Tropez; **Véronique Lantz** (*7 Dec 1951 Paris) daughter of Lirard Lantz & Monique Rachet
A) **Prince Don Dimitri della Torre e Tasso** (*24 Nov 1977 Cannes)
= 2017; **Elinor de Pret Roose de Calesberg** (*1981) daughter of Arnoud, Count de Pret Roose de Calesberhg & Jonkvrouw Maureen Le Sergeant d'Hendecourt
1) **Prince Don Alexandre della Torre e Tasso** (*15 Oct 2017)
B) **Prince Don Maximilian della Torre e Tasso** (*22 May 1979 St. Tropez)
C) **Princess Donna Constanza della Torre e Tasso** (*7 Aug 1989)
3. **Princess Alexandra** (Georgeievna) **of Greece** (18 Aug 1870 Corfu – 21 Sep 1938 Athens)
= 1889; ♦**Grand Duke Paul of Russia** (1860 – 1919)
see: page
4. **Prince Nicholas of Greece** (22 Jan 1872 Athens – 8 Feb 1938 Athens)
= 16/29 Aug 1902 Tsarskoie-Selo; ♦**Grand Duchess Elena**

Vladimirovna **of Russia** (5/17 Jan 1882 Tsarskoie-Selo – 13 Mar 1957 Athens) daughter of Grand Duke Vladimir of Russia and Duchess Marie of Mecklenburg

a. **Princess Olga of Greece** (11 Jun 1903 Tatoi – 16 Oct 1997 Paris)
= 22 Oct 1923 Belgrade; **Prince Paul of Yugoslavia** (15/27 Apr 1893 St. Petersburg – 14 Sep 1976 Paris)son of Prince Arsen of Yugoslavia & Aurora Demidova

I) **Prince Alexander of Yugoslavia** (13 Aug 1924 White Lodge, Richmond – 12 May 2016 Paris)
=1 12 Feb 1955 Cascais, Portugal (dv.1967); **Princess Maria Pia** Elena Elisabetta Margherita Milena Mafalda Ludovica Tecla Gennara **of Savoy** (*24 Sep 1934 Naples) daughter of Umberto II, King of Italy & Princess Marie José of Belgium; =2nd Prince Michel of Bourbon-Parma
=2 2 Nov 1973 Paris; **Princess Barbara** Eleonore Marie **of Liechtenstein** (*9 Jul 1942 Mahren-Sternberg) daughter of Prince Johannes of Liechtenstein & Countess Karoline von Ledebur-Wicheln
issue of 1st:

A) **Prince Dmitri** Umberto Anton Peter Maria **of Yugoslavia** (*18 Jun 1958 Boulogne) (twin)

B) **Prince Michael** Nikola Paul George **of Yugoslavia** (*18 Jun 1958 Boulogne) (twin)

C) **Prince Serge** Wladimir Emanuel Maria **of Yugoslavia** (*11 Mar 1963 Boulogne) (twin)
=1 6 Nov 1985 Saint-Nom-la-Bretech (civil) & 30 Nov 1985 Merlinge (rel) (dv.1986); **Sofia de Toledo Gallier** (*1 Apr 1965 Boulogne) daughter of Bertrand de Toledo & Françoise Gallier; =2nd Herve de Cuniac
=2 18 Sep 2004; **Eleonore Rajneri** (*1 Aug 1967 Turin) no issue

D) **Princess Helene** Olga Lydia Tamara Maria **of Yugoslavia** (*11 Mar 1963 Boulogne) (twin)
= 12 Jan 1988 Neuilly-sur-Seine; **Thierry Gaubert** (*7 Jul 1952 Paris) son of Armand Gaubert & Marianne Perlman

1) **Milena** Maria Pia Angelique Armaule **Gaubert** (*2 Jul

1988 Neuilly)
= 12 Sep 2017 Neuilly (civil) & 7 Sep 2017 Deauville (rel.); **Jonathan Namias** (*28 Jun 1986)
no issue

2) **Anastasia** Marie-José Tania Vanessa Isabelle **Gaubert** (*22 Feb 1991 Neuilly-sur-Seine)

3) **Leopold** Umberto Armand Michel **Gaubert** (*19 Jul 1997 Neuilly-sur-Seine)

issue of 2nd:

E) **Prince Dushan** Paul **of Yugoslavia** (*25 Sep 1977 St. Gallen)

II) **Prince Nikola of Yugoslavia** (29 Jun 1928 London – 12 Apr 1954 Datchet)

III) **Princess Elizabeth of Yugoslavia** (*7 Apr 1936 Belgrade)
=1 21 Jan 1961 Manassas,Virginia (dv.1966); **Howard Oxenberg** (22 Jul 1919 New York – 25 Jun 2010)
=2 23 Sep 1969 London (dv.1978); **Neil** Roxburgh **Balfour** (*12 Aug 1944 Lima, Peru) son of Archibald Balfour & Lilian Cooper
=3 28 Feb 1987 Lima; **Manuel Ulloa Elias** (12 Nov 1922 Lima – 9 Aug 1992 Madrid)
issue of 1st:

A) **Catherine Oxenberg** (*22 Sep 1961 New York)
=1 12 Jul 1998 Beverly Hills, California (ann.1998); **Robert Evans** (*29 Jun 1930 New York City) né Robert Shapera; =1st Sharon Hugueny, =2nd Camilla Sparv, =3rd Ali MacGraw, =4th Phyllis George, =6th Leslie Anne Woodward; =7th Victoria Tucker
=2 8 May 1991 Las Vegas (dv.2015); **Casper Van Dien** (*18 Dec 1968 Ridgefield, New Jersey) son of Casper van Dien & Diane Morrow; =1st Carrie Mitchum
issue by 2nd (none by 1st):
1) **Maya Van Dien** (*20 Sep 2001 Los Angeles)
2) **Celeste** Alma **Van Dien** (*3 Oct 2003 Los Angeles)
Catherine Oxenberg has additional issue by **William** Weitz **Shaffer** (*1946 Pittsburgh, Penn.) son of William Shaffer & Jeanne Lesner:

3) **India** Rixen **Oxenberg** (*7 Jun 1991 Los Angeles)
B) **Christina Oxenberg** (*27 Dec 1962 New York)
= Jun 1986 Amman, Jordan (dv.1996); Dusan **Damien** Cary **Elwes**[6] (*10 Aug 1960 London) son of Dominic Elwes & TessaKennedy; =2nd Lewanne Collie
no issue
issue of 2nd (none by 3rd):
C) **Nicholas** Augustus **Balfour** (*6 Jun 1970 London)
= 24 May 2000 Grimbergen; **Stephanie de Brouwer** (*30 Apr 1971 Morstel) daughter of Jean-Marie de Brouwer & Veronika Denegg
1) **India** Lily Alexandra **Balfour** (*17 Oct 2002 London)
2) **Gloria** Elizabeth **Balfour** (*Nov 2005 London)
3) **Olympia** Rose **Balfour** (*20 Jun 2007 London)
b. **Princess Elizabeth of Greece** (24 May 1904 Tatoi – 11 Jan 1955 Munich)
= 9 Jan 1934 Munich (civil) & 10 Jan 1934 Schloss Seefeld (rel.); **Carl-Theodor** Klemens, **Count zu Toerring-Jettenbach** (22 Sep 1900 Winhöring – 14 May 1967 Munich) son of Hans Veit, Count zu Toerring-Jettenbach & Duchess Sophie in Bavaria; suc. father 29 Nov 1929
I) **Hans Veit** Kaspar Nikolaus, **Count zu Toerring-Jettenbach** (*11 Jan 1935 Munich) suc. father 1967
= 22 Mar (civil) & 23 Apr (rel.) 1964 Bartenstein; **Princess Henriette of Hohenlohe-Bartenstein** (*23 Aug 1938 Bartenstein) daughter of Karl, Prince of Hohenlohe-Bartenstein & Baroness Clara von Mayern-Hochberg
A) **Countess Clarissa** Beatrix Eleonore Maria **zu Toerring-Jettenbach** (*31 Mar 1965 Munich)
= 4 Jul 1999 Winhöring; **Prince Tassilo** Ferdinand **of Ratibor and Corvey, of Hohenlohe-Waldenburg-Schillingsfürst** (*23 Oct 1965 Vienna) son of Franz, Duke of Ratibor & Altgravine Isabella of Salm-Reifferscheidt-Krautheim and Dyck

---

[6] brother of actor Cary Elwes

1) **Princess Charlotte** Margita Elisabeth Marie **of Ratibor and Corvey** etc. (*20 Nov 2000 Vienna)
2) **Prince Gregor of Ratibor and Corvey** etc. (*25 Aug 2002 Vienna)
3) **Prince Vitus of Ratibor and Corvey** etc. (*29 Nov 2004 Vienna)

B) **Hereditary Count Ignaz** Maximilian Karl Veit **zu Toerring-Jettenbach** (*30 Mar 1966 Munich)
= 14 (civil) & 15 (rel.) May 2004 Milan; **Robinia** Viviana Giada **Mentasti-Granelli** (*13 Jan 1976 Milan)
1) **Countess Floriana** Antonia Carla **zu Toerring-Jettenbach** (*5 Mar 2005 Milan)
2) **Countess Georgiana** Josepha Lavinia **zu Toerring-Jettenbach** (*11 Jul 2006 Milan)
3) **Countess Elisabeth** Ricciarda Valeria **zu Toerring-Jettenbach** (*18 Jun 2008 Milan)
4) **Countess Elena** Inocentia Maria Maximiliana Isabel Rita **zu Toerring-Jettenbach** (*28 Dec 2010 Munich)
5) **Countess Maximiliana** Marina Nicola Maria-Rosa Viviana **zu Toerring-Jettenbach** (*7 Dec 2012 Munich)

C) **Count Carl Theodor** Ferdinand **zu Toerring-Jettenbach** (*17 Feb 1969 Munich)
= 28 Oct 2009; **Natasha** Alexeievna **Ivanovna** (...)
1) **Carl Albrecht Graf zu Toerring-Jettenbach** (*9 Apr 2009 Paris)
2) **Count Alexander** August **zu Toerring-Jettenbach** (*3 Aug 2011 Frankfurt)
3) **Count Lorenz zu Toerring-Jettenbach** (*11 Apr 2016)

II) **Countess Helene** Marina Elisabeth **zu Toerring-Jettenbach** (*20 May 1937 Winhöring)
= 6 Apr 1956 Munich (civil) & 10 Apr 1956 Schloss Seefeld (rel); **Archduke Ferdinand** Karl Max Franz Otto Konrad Maria Joseph Ignatius Nikolaus **of Austria** Prince of Hungary and Bohemia (6 Dec 1918 Vienna – 6 Aug 2004 Ulm) son of Archduke Maximilian of Austria & Princess Franziska of Ratibor and Corvey, of Hohenlohe-

Waldenburg-Schillingsfürst

A) **Archduchess Elisabeth** Caecilia Helen Antonia **of Austria** etc. (15 Mar 1957 Essen – 18 May 1983 Cooma, Australia)
= 9 Oct 1982 Maria Plan; **James** William **Litchfield** (*15 Nov 1956 Sydney) son of James Litchfield & Barbara Fowler
no issue

B) **Archduchess Sophie** Franziska Maria Germaine **of Austria** etc. (*19 Jan 1959 Boulogne)
= 31 Jan (civil) & 11 Feb (rel.) 1990 Salzburg; **Mariano Hugo, Prince of Windisch-Graetz** (*27 Jul 1955 Trieste) son of Maximilian, Prince of Windisch-Graetz & Maria Luisa Serra dei principi di Carafa; suc. father 1 Nov 1976

1) **Hereditary Prince Maximilian** Hugo **of Windisch-Graetz** (*4 Aug 1990 Salzburg)

2) **Prince Alexis** Ferdinando **of Windisch-Graetz** (10 Dec 1991 Rome – 9 Feb 2010 Caserta) killed in a car crash

3) **Princess Larissa** Maria Luisa Christina Maria Grazia Leontina Hellena Franziska **of Windisch-Graetz** (*11 Feb 1996 Rome)

C) **Archduke Maximilian** Heinrich Ferdinand **of Austria** etc. (*8 Feb 1961 Boulogne)
= 2 Jul 2005 Rome; Sara **Maya Al-Askari** (*6 Nov 1977 London)

1) **Archduke Nikolaus** Heinrich **of Austria** etc. (*6 Dec 2005 Madrid)

2) **Archduke Constantin of Austria** (*4 Jun 2007 Madrid)

3) **Archduchess Katharina of Austria**. etc. (*8 Nov 2010 Madrid)

c. **Princess Marina of Greece** (13 Dec 1906 Athens – 27 Aug 1968 Kensington Palace, London)
= 29 Nov 1934 London; **Prince George** Edward Alexander Edmund **of Great Britain, Duke of Kent** etc. (20 Dec 1902 Sandringham – 25 Aug 1942 Morven) son of George V, King

of the United Kingdom & Princess May of Teck; cr. Duke 12 Oct 1934

I) **Prince Edward** George Nicholas Paul Patrick **of Great Britain, 2nd Duke of Kent** etc. (*9 Oct 1935 London) suc. father 1942
= 8 Jun 1961 York; **Katherine** Lucy Mary **Worsley** (*22 Feb 1933 York) daughter of Sir William Worsley, 4th Baronet & Joyce Brunner
  A) **George** Philip Nicholas, **Earl of St. Andrews** (*26 Jun 1962 Iver)
  = 8 Jun 1988 Edinburgh; **Silvana** Palma **Tomaselli** (*26 Jun 1957 Placentia, Canada) daughter of Maximilian Tomaselli & Josiane Preschez; =1st John Paul Jones
    1) **Edward** Edmund Maximilian George, **Lord Downpatrick** (*2 Dec 1988 London)
    2) **Lady Marina** Charlotte Alexandra Katherine Helen **Windsor** (*30 Sep 1992 Cambridge)
    3) **Lady Amelia** Sophia Theodora Mary Margaret **Windsor** (*24 Aug 1995 Cambridge)
  B) **Lady Helen** Marina Lucy **Windsor** (*28 Apr 1964 Iver)
  = 18 Jul 1992 Windsor; **Timothy** Verner **Taylor** (*8 Aug 1963 Yelverton, Devonshire) son of Michael Taylor & Susan Percy
    1) **Columbus** George Donald **Taylor** (*6 Aug 1994 London)
    2) **Cassius** Edward **Taylor** (*26 Dec 1996 London)
    3) **Eloise** Olivia Katherine **Taylor** (*2 Mar 2003 London)
    4) **Estella** Olga Elizabeth **Taylor** (*21 Dec 2004 London)
  C) **Lord Nicholas** Charles Edward Jonathan **Windsor** (*27 Jul 1970 London)
  = 19 Oct 2006 London (civil) & 4 Nov 2006 Vatican City (rel); **Paola Doimi di Frankopan** (*1969) daughter of Louis Doimi de Frankopan & Ingrid Detter
    1) **Albert** Louis Philip Edward **Windsor** (*22 Sep 2007 London)
    2) **Leopold** Ernest Augustus Guelph **Windsor** (*8 Sep

2009 London)
3) **Louis** Arthur Nicholas Felix **Windsor** (*27 May 2014 London)

II) **Princess Alexandra** Helen Elizabeth Olga Cristabel **of Kent** etc. (*25 Dec 1936 London)
= 24 Aug 1963 London; **Hon. Sir Angus** James Robert Bruce **Ogilvy** (28 Sep 1928 London – 26 Dec 2004 London) son of David Ogilvy, 12th Earl of Airlie & Lady Alexandra Coke

A) **James** Robert Bruce **Ogilvy** (*29 Feb 1964 Richmond Park)
= 30 Jul 1988 London; **Julia Rawlinson** (*28 Oct 1964 Cambridge) daughter of Charles Rawlinson & Jill Wesley
1) **Flora Ogilvy** (*15 Oct 1994 London)
2) **Alexander** Charles **Ogilvy** (*12 Nov 1996 London)

B) **Marina** Victoria Alexandra **Ogilvy** (*31 Aug 1966 London)
= 2 Feb 1990 Ham Common (dv.1997); **Paul** Julian **Mowatt** (*28 Nov 1962 Hendon) son of David Mowatt & Catherine Hegarty
1) **Zenouska** May **Mowatt** (*26 May 1990 London)
2) **Christian** Alexander **Mowatt** (*4 Jun 1993 London)

III) **Prince Michael** George Charles Franklin **of Kent** etc. (*4 Jul 1942 Iver)
= 30 Jun 1978 Vienna (civil) & 29 Jul 1983 London (rel.); **Baroness Marie-Christine** Agnes Hedwig Iga **von Reibnitz** (*15 Jan 1945 Karlovy Vary, Czech Republic) daughter of Baron Günther von Reibnitz & Countess Maria Anna Szapary de Muraszombath, Szechyziget et Szapar; =1st Thomas Troubridge

A) **Lord Frederick** Michael George David Louis **Windsor** (*6 Apr 1979 London)
= 12 Sep 2009 Hampton Court Palace; **Sophie Winkelman** (*5 Aug 1980 London) daughter of Barry Winkelman & Cindy Macdonald
1) **Maud** Elizabeth Daphne Marina **Windsor** (*15 Aug 2013 Los Angeles)
2) **Isabella** Alexandra Mary **Windsor** (*16 Jan 2016)

B) **Lady Gabriella** Marina Alexandra Ophelia **Windsor** (*23 Apr 1981 London)

5. **Princess Marie of Greece** (3 Mar 1876 Athens – 14 Dec 1940 Athens)
   =1 1900; ♦**Grand Duke George of Russia** (1863 – 1919)
   =2 16 Dec 1922 Wiesbaden; **Pericles Joannides** (1 Nov 1881 – 7 Feb 1965)
   issue of 1st (none by 2nd):
   see: page
6. **Princess Olga of Greece** (7 Apr – 2 Nov 1880 Athens)
7. **Prince Andrew of Greece** (2 Feb 1882 Athens – 3 Dec 1944 Monte Carlo)
   = 7 Oct 1903 Darmstadt; **Princess** Victoria **Alice** Elisabeth Julie Maria **of Battenberg** (25 Feb 1885 Windsor Castle – 5 Dec 1969 Buckingham Palace) daughter of Prince Louis of Battenberg (later 1st Marquess of Milford Haven) & Princess Victoria of Hesse and By Rhine

   a. **Princess Margarita of Greece** (18 Apr 1905 Athens – 24 Apr 1981 Bad Wiesse)
   = 1931; ♦**Gottfried, Prince of Hohenlohe-Langenburg** (1897 – 1960)
   see: page

   b. **Princess Theodora of Greece** (30 May 1906 Athens – 16 Oct 1969 Konstanz)
   = 1931; ♦**Berthold, Margrave of Baden** (1906 – 1963)
   see: page

   c. **Princess Cecilie of Greece** (22 Jun 1911 Tatoi – 16 Nov 1937 Steene) killed in a plane crash with husband and sons
   = 2 Feb 1931 Darmstadt; (her 1st cousin) **Georg** Donatus Wilhelm Nikolaus Eduard Heinrich Karl, **Grand Duke of Hesse and By Rhine** (8 Nov 1906 Darmstadt – 16 Nov 1937 Steene) son of Ernst Ludwig, Grand Duke of Hesse and By Rhine & Princess Eleonore of Solms-Hohensolms-Lich; suc. father 9 Oct 1937

   I) **Hereditary Grand Duke Ludwig** Ernst Andreas **of Hesse and By Rhine** (25 Oct 1931 Darmstadt – 16 Nov 1937 Steene)

   II) **Prince Alexander** Georg Karl Heinrich **of Hesse and By**

Rhine (14 Apr 1933 Darmstadt – 16 Nov 1937 Steene)

III) **Princess Johanna** Marina Eleonore **of Hesse and By Rhine** (20 Sep 1936 Schloss Wolfsgarten – 16 Jun 1939 Darmstadt) adopted by her uncle, Prince Ludwig of Hesse, after her family all died in the plane crash

d. **Princess Sophie of Greece** (*26 Jun 1914 Corfu – 24 Nov 2001 Munich)

=1 13 (civil) & 15 (rel.) Dec 1930 Kronberg; **Prince Christoph** Ernst August **of Hesse** (14 May 1901 Frankfurt – 7 Oct 1943 in the Apennine Mountains) killed in a plane crash; son of Friedrich Karl, Landgrave of Hesse & Princess Margarete of Prussia

=2 23 (civil) & 24 (rel.) Apr 1946 Salem; **Prince Georg Wilhelm** Ernst August Friedrich Axel **of Hanover** etc. (25 Mar 1915 Brunswick – 8 Jan 2006 Munich) son of Ernst August, Duke of Brunswick & Princess Viktoria Luise of Prussia

issue of 1st:

I) **Princess Christina** Margarethe **of Hesse** (10 Jan 1933 Kronberg – 21 Nov 2011 Gersau)

=1 1956 (dv.); ♦**Prince Andrej of Yugoslavia** (1929 – 1990)

=2 3 Dec 1963 London (dv.1986); **Robert van Eyck** (3 May 1916 The Hague – 19 Dec 1991 Ashford, Kent) son of Pieter van Eyck & Nelly Benjamins

issue of 1st:

see: page

issue of 2nd:

C) **Helene** Sophia **van Eyck** (*25 Oct 1963 London)

= 24 Jan 1986 Hasting, East Sussex; **Roderick** Alan **Harman** (*18 Jul 1942 Chang-Chou, China) son of Douglas Harman & Gladys Gunstone; =1st Mary Clarke

1) Alexandra (**Sascha**) Sophia **Harman** (*26 Jul 1986 St.Leonard's-on-Sea, East Sussex)

2) **Pascale** Olivia **Harman** (*19 Mar 1989 St.Leonard's-on-Sea)

= 27 Aug 2016; **Richard Miles** (...)

issue ?

D) **Mark** Nicholas **van Eyck** (*16 Feb 1966 Oxford)
= 12 Jun 1992 London (dv.1998); **Joanne** Marie **Green** (*11 Oct 1961 Timaru, New Zealand) daughter of Michael Green & Joan Craig-Braun
no issue

II) **Princess Dorothea** Charlotte Karin **of Hesse** (*24 Jul 1934 Panker)
= 31 Mar 1959 Schliersee (civil) & 1 Apr 1959 Munich (rel.); **Prince Friedrich Karl** Hugo Maximilian Maria Cyrillus Felix Hubertus **of Windisch-Graetz** (7 Jul 1917 Heilingenberg – 29 May 2002 Gersau) son of Hugo, Prince of Windisch-Graetz & Princess Leontine of Fürstenberg

A) **Princess Marina** Margherita Sophia Leontina Christiana **of Windisch-Graetz** (*3 Dec 1960 Milan)
= 28 May 1988 (civil) & 15 Apr 1989 (rel.) Rome (dv.1997); **Gyula** Lajos **Jakabffy** (*14 Nov 1962 Morosvasarhely, Hungary) son of Tamás Hakabffy & Magdolina Kovacs

1) **Reka** Dorothea Sita **Jakabffy** (*17 Sep 1988 Rome)

2) **Sophia** Magdolina **Jakabby** (*27 Aug 1989 Rome)

B) **Princess Clarissa** Elisabetta Fiore **of Windisch-Graetz** (*5 Aug 1966 Erba)
= 16 Nov 1985 Alserio; **Eric** Michel Jacques **de Waele** (*6 Jan 1962 Etterbeek) son of Jean de Waele & Annemarie Ponsar

1) **Michel** Jean Henri **de Waele** (*18 May 1986 New York)
= 6 Aug 2011 Belgium; **Caroline Libbrecht** (...) daughter of Bernard Libbrecht & Yannick Anaf

a) **Raphael de Waele** (*2 Sep 2013)

b) **Lucy de Waele** (*2 May 2015)

2) **Alexandre** Federico Mark **de Waele** (*3 Jul 1987 Ghent)

3) **Mathieu** Paul Philippe **de Waele** (*16 Dec 1988 Ghent)

4) **Rubi** Jade **de Waele** (*26 Jan 1994 Ghent)

III) **Prince Karl** Adolf Andreas **of Hesse** (*26 Mar 1937 Berlin)

= 26 Mar (civil) & 18 Apr (rel) 1966 The Hague; **Countess Yvonne** Margit Valerie **Szapary de Muraszombath, Szechyziget et Sarvar** (*4 Apr 1944 Budapest) daughter of Count Bela Szapary de Muraszombath, Szechyziget et Szapar & Baroness Ulla von Richthofen

A) **Prince Christoph of Hesse** (*18 Jun 1969 Munich)

B) **Princess Irina** Verena **of Hesse** (*1 Apr 1971 Munich)
= 29 May 1999 Heusenstamm; **Alexander** Georg Maria Ernst Heinrich Istvan Ludwig Kisito Hubertus, **Count and Lord von Schönburg-Glauchau** (*15 Aug 1969 Mogidishu, Somalia) son of Joachim, Count and Lord von Schönburg-Glauchau & Countess Beatrix Széchenyi de Sárvár et Felsövidék; suc. father 29 Sep 1998

1) **Countess Marie Laetitia** Jolanta **von Schönburg-Glauchau** (*30 Jul 2001 Potsdam)

2) **Hereditary Count Maximus** Carolus Joachim Maria **von Schönburg-Glauchau** (*25 May 2003 Berlin)

3) **Count Valentin** Polykarp Josef Maria **von Schönburg-Glauchau** (*23 Feb 2005 Berlin)

IV) **Prince Rainer** Christoph Friedrich **of Hesse** (*18 Nov 1939 Kronberg)

V) **Princess Clarissa** Alice **of Hesse** (*6 Feb 1944 Kronberg)
= 20 Jul 1971 Paris (dv.1976); **Claude** Jean **Derrien** (*12 Mar 1948 Boulogne) son of Jean Derrien & Jacqueline Laine; =2nd Hendrika Koffeman
no issue
Princess Clarissa has issue:

1) **Johanna von Hessen** (*25 Aug 1980 Munich)

issue of 2nd:

VI) **Prince Welf** Ernst August Andreas Philipp Georg Wilhelm Ludwig Berthold **of Hanover** etc. (25 Jan 1947 Marienburg – 10 Jan 1981 Poona, India)
= (morg.) 23 May 1969 Munich (civil) & 25 May 1969 Essen (rel.) (dv.1979); **Wibeke van Gunsteren** (*26 Nov 1948 Lübeck) daughter of Harry van Gunsteren & Ursula Schneidt-Prunge

A) Tania **Saskia** Viktoria-Luise **Prinzessin von Hannover** (*24 Jul 1970 Duisburg)

=1 5 Jul 1990 London (dv.); **Michael** Alexander Robert **Naylor-Leyland** (14 Jul 1956 London – 16 Oct 2015 London) son of David Naylor-Leyland & Diana Lea; =1st Lucy Potts; =3rd Anna-Louise ...

=2 27 Jan 2001; **Edward** Robert James **Hooper** (*10 Apr 1966 London) son of Ivan Hooper & Carole Bridgland

issue of 1st:

1) **Jake** James **Naylor-Leyland** (*21 Sep 1993 London)

2) **Gabriel** Georg **Naylor-Leyland** (*26 Mar 1996 London)

issue of 2nd:

3) **Louis** Ivan Welf Otto **Hooper** (*4 Jun 2007)

VII) **Prince Georg** Paul Christian **of Hanover** etc. (*9 Dec 1949 Salem)

= (morg.) 15 Sep 1973 Rottach; **Victoria** Ann **Bee** (*6 Mar 1951 New York) daughter of Robert Bee & Countess Eleonore Fugger von Babenhausen

A) **Vera** Alice **Prinzessin von Hannover** (*5 Nov 1976 Munich)

= 12 Aug 2006 Aschau im Chiemgau; **Manuel Dmoch** (*20 May 1977 Barcelona) son of Norbert Dmoch & Renate Nothdurft

1) **Celina** Sophie **Dmoch** (*30 Jun 2007)

2) **Elena** Luisa **Dmoch** (*12 Sep 2009)

B) **Nora** Sophie **Prinzessin von Hannover** (*15 Jan 1979 Munich)

= 13 May 2006 Schliersee (civil) & 3 Mar 2007 Aschbach (rel.); **Christian Falk** (*4 Jan 1972 Halle an der Saale) son of Jürgen Falk & Evelyn Fest

1) **Konstantin** Georg Erik **Falk** (*18 Dec 2007)

2) **Leopold** Welf Christian **Falk** (*5 Sep 2009)

VIII) **Princess Friederike** Elisabeth Viktoria-Luise Alice Olga Theodora Helena **of Hanover** etc. (*15 Oct 1954 Salem)

= 17 Aug 1979 Vancouver, British Columbia; **Jerry** William **Cyr** (*16 Jan 1951 Port Alberni, British Columbia) son of Gordon Cyr & Emma Grandbois

A) **Julia** Emma **Cyr** (*17 Sep 1982 Vancouver)

B) **Jean-Paul** Welf **Cyr** (*6 Mar 1985 Vancouver)
=...; **Elaine Chang** (...)
1) a child (...)

e. **Prince Philip of the United Kingdom** (formerly **of Greece**), **Duke of Edinburgh** (*10 Jun 1921 Mon Repos) renounced Greek titles assuming surname Mountbatten 28 Feb 1947; cr. Duke 19 Nov 1947; cr. Prince of the United Kingdom 22 Feb 1957
= 20 Nov 1947 London; **Elizabeth II** Alexandra Mary, **Queen of the United Kingdom** etc. (*21 Apr 1926 London) daughter of George VI, King of the United Kingdom & Lady Elizabeth Bowes-Lyon; suc. father 6 Feb 1952

I) **Prince Charles** Philip Arthur George **of the United Kingdom, Prince of Wales** etc. (*14 Nov 1948 London) cr. Prince of Wales 26 Jul 1958
=1 29 Jul 1981 (dv.1996); **Lady Diana** Frances **Spencer** (1 Jul 1961 Sandringham – 31 Aug 1997 Paris) killed in a car crash; daughter of John Spencer, 8th Earl Spencer & Hon. Frances Roche
=2 9 Apr 2005 Windsor; **Camilla** Rosemary **Shand** (*17 Jul 1947 London) daughter of Bruce Shand & Hon. Rosalind Cubitt; =1st Andrew Parker Bowles
issue of 1st (none by 2nd):

A) **Prince William** Arthur Philip Louis, **Duke of Cambridge** Earl of Strathearn, Baron Carrickfergus (*21 Jun 1982 London) cr. Duke 29 Apr 2011
= 29 Apr 2011 London; **Catherine** Elizabeth **Middleton** (*9 Jan 1982 Reading) daughter of Michael Middleton & Carole Goldsmith

1) **Prince George** Alexander Louis **of Cambridge** (*22 Jul 2013 London)
2) **Princess Charlotte** Elizabeth Diana **of Cambridge** (*2 May 2015 London)
3) due Apr 2018

B) **Prince** Henry (**Harry**) Charles Albert David **of Wales** etc. (*15 Sep 1984 London)
engaged to Rachel **Meghan Markle** (*4 Aug 1981 Los Angeles) daughter of Thomas Markle & Doria Ragland;

wedding is scheduled for 19 May 2018 Windsor

IV) **Princess Anne** Elizabeth Alice Louise **of the United Kingdom, The Princess Royal** (*5 Aug 1950 London) cr. Princess Royal 12 Jun 1987

=1 14 Nov 1973 London (dv.1991); **Mark** Anthony Peter **Phillips** (*22 Sep 1948 Tetbury) son of Peter Phillips & Anne Tiarks; =2nd Sandy Pflueger

=2 12 Dec 1992 Crathie, Scotland; **Timothy** James Hamilton **Lawrence** (*2 Mar 1955 London) son of Guy Lawrence & Barbara Symons

issue of 1st (none by 2nd):

A) **Peter** Mark Andrew **Phillips** (*15 Nov 1977 London)
= 17 May 2008 Windsor; **Autumn Kelly** (*3 Aug 1978 Montreal) daughter of Brian Kelly & Kitty …

1) **Savannah Phillips** (*29 Dec 2010 Gloucester)

2) **Isla** Elizabeth **Phillips** (*29 Mar 2012 Gloucester)

B) **Zara** Anne Elizabeth **Phillips** (*15 Mar 1981 London)
= 30 Jul 2011 Edinburgh; **Michael** James **Tindall** (*18 Oct 1978 Otley) son of Philip Tindall & Linda Shepherd.

1) **Mia** Grace **Tindal** (*17 Jan 2014 Gloucester)

2) due 2018

III) **Prince Andrew** Albert Christian Edward **of the United Kingdom, Duke of York** etc. (*19 Feb 1960 London) cr. Duke 23 Jul 1986

= 23 Jul 1986 London (dv.1997); **Sarah** Margaret **Ferguson** (*15 Oct 1959 London) daughter of Ronald Ferguson & Susan Wright

A) **Princess Beatrice** Elizabeth Mary **of York** etc. (*8 Aug 1988 London)

B) **Princess Eugenie** Victoria Helena **of York** etc. (*23 Mar 1990 London)
engaged to **Jack Brooksbank** (b.3 May 1986) son of George Brooksbank & Nicola Newton; the wedding is planned for fall 2018

IV) **Prince Edward** Anthony Richard Lewis **of the United Kingdom, Earl of Wessex** etc. (*10 Mar 1964 London) cr. Earl 18 Jun 1999

= 19 Jun 1999 Windsor; **Sophie** Helen **Rhys-Jones** (*20

Jan 1965 Oxford) daughter of Christopher Rhys-Jones & Mary O'Sullivan

Although legally titled Prince/Princess of Wessex, etc., their children are styled as the children of an Earl:

A) **Lady Louise** Alice Elizabeth Mary **Mountbatten-Windsor** (*8 Nov 2003 Surrey)

B) **James** Alexander Philip Theo, **Viscount Severn** (*17 Dec 2007 Surrey)

8. **Prince Christopher of Greece** (29 Jul/10 Aug 1888 Pavlovsk – 21 Jan 1940 Athens)
=1 1 Feb 1920 Vevey; **Nancy** May **Stewart** (renamed **Anastasia** after marriage to Prince Christopher) (20 Jan 1873 Cleveland, Ohio – 29 Aug 1923 London) daughter of William Stewart; =1st George Worthington; =2nd William Bateman Leeds Sr.
=2 11 Feb 1929 Palermo; **Princess Françoise** Isabelle Louise Marie **of Orleans** (25 Dec 1902 Paris – 25 Feb 1953 Paris) daughter of Prince Jean, Duke of Guise & Princess Isabelle of Orleans
issue of 2nd (none by 1st):

a. **Prince Michael of Greece** (*7 Jan 1939 Rome)
= 7 Feb 1965 Athens; **Marina Karella** (*17 Jul 1940 Athens) daughter of Theodor Karella & Elly Chalikiopoulos

I) **Princess Alexandra of Greece** (*15 Oct 1968 Athens)
= 27 Jun 1998 Venice; **Nicolas Mirzayantz** (*1 Jan 1963 Marseilles) son of ... & Evelyn Mirzayantz

A) **Tigran Mirzayantz** (*16 Aug 2000 New York)

B) **Darius Mirzayantz** (*Apr 2002)

II) **Princess Olga of Greece** (*17 Nov 1971 Athens)
= 2008; ♦**Prince Aimone of Savoy, Duke of Apulia** (*1967)
see: page

C. **Grand Duchess Vera** Constantinovna **of Russia** (4/16 Feb 1854 St. Petersburg – 11 Apr 1912 Stuttgart)
= 8 May 1874 Stuttgart; **Duke** Wilhelm **Eugen** August Georg **of Württemberg** (20 Aug 1846 Bückeburg – 27 Jan 1877 Düsseldorf) son of Duke Eugen of Württemberg & Princess Mathilde of Schaumburg-Lippe

1. **Duke Karl Eugen of Württemberg** (8 Apr – 9 Nov 1875

Stuttgart)

2. **Duchess Elsa** Mathilde Marie **of Württemberg** (1 Mar 1876 Stuttgart – 27 May 1936 Pfaffstatt) (twin)
   = 6 May 1897 Stuttgart; **Prince** Christian **Albrecht** Gaetano Karl Wilhelm Eduard **of Schaumburg-Lippe** (24 Oct 1869 Ratiboritz – 25 Dec 1842 Linz) son of Prince Wilhelm of Schaumburg-Lippe & Princess Bathildis of Anhalt; =2nd Maria Herget
   a. **Prince** Wilhelm Eugen Georg Constantin **Maximilian of Schaumburg-Lippe** (28 Mar 1898 Wels – 4 Feb 1974 Salzburg)
      = 9 May 1933 Bad Homburg; **Helga** Clare Lee **Roderbourg** (24 Feb 1911 Cologne – 9 Jul 2005 New York) daughter of Carl Roderbourg & Claude Miller
      no issue
   b. **Prince Franz Josef** Adolf Ernst **of Schaumburg-Lippe** (1 Sep 1899 Wels – 7 Jul 1963 Cassel)
      = 29 Jan 1959 Munich; **Maria Theresia Peschel** (29 Jul 1912 Neutitscheim – 1 Mar 2002 Tauplitz, Austria) daughter of Anton Peschel & Josephine Rosemanith; =1st Erich Hermann Ritter von Wullerstorf und Urbair; =2nd Hans Heinrich von Tschirshky und Goegebdorf
      no issue
   c. **Prince Alexander** Ernst Friedrich Albrecht **of Schaumburg-Lippe** (20 Jan 1901 Wels – 26 Nov 1923 near Münderfing)
   d. **Princess Bathildis** Wera Thyra Adelheid Hermine Mathilde Mary **of Schaumburg-Lippe** (11 Nov 1903 Wels – 29 Jun 1983 Hageburg)
      = 15 Apr 1925 Simbach (civil) & 16 Apr 1925 Pfaffstt (rel.); Ernst **Wolfrad, Prince of Schaumburg-Lippe** (19 Apr 1887 Stadthagen – 15 Jun 1962 Hanover) son of Georg II, Prince of Schaumburg-Lippe & Princess Maria Anna of Saxe-Altenburg; suc. brother, Adolf II, 26 Mar 1936
      I) **Hereditary Prince** Albrecht **Georg-Wilhelm** Eugen **of Schaumburg-Lippe** (26 Jan 1926 Hagenburg – 29 Apr 1945 Nössige) killed in action
      II) Friedrich August **Philipp-Ernst** Wolrad, **Prince of Schaumburg-Lippe** (26 Jul 1928 Hagenburg – 28 Aug

2003 Bückeburg) suc. father 1962
= 3 Oct 1955 Bückeburg; **Baroness** Eva **Bonita** Viktoria Maria **von Tiele-Winkler** (*18 Nov 1927 Vallrathsruhe) daughter of Hans Werner, Count von Tiele-Winkler & Countess Elisabeth von Bassewitz

A) **Hereditary Prince** Adolf Friedrich **Georg Wilhelm** Wolrad Hans-Werner **of Schaumburg-Lippe** (17 Jul 1956 Freiburg – 31 Jul 1983 near Steinbergen)

B) Ernst August **Alexander** Christian Viktor Hubert, **Prince of Schaumburg-Lippe** (*25 Dec 1958 Düsseldorf) suc. father 2003
=1 29 Aug 1993 Bückeburg (dv.2002); **Princess Marie Louise** Ulrike Olympia **of Sayn-Wittengenstein-Berleberg** (*25 Sep 1972 Stuttgart) daughter of Prince Otto of Sayn-Wittgenstein-Berleberg & Baroness Annette von Cramm
=2 28 (civil) & 30 (rel) Jun 2007 Bückeburg; **Nadja** Anna **Zsoeks** (*20 Feb 1975 Munich)
issue of 1st:

1. **Hereditary Prince** Ernst August Alexander Wilhelm Bernhard Krafft **Heinrich Donatus of Schaumburg-Lippe** (*13 May 1994 Bückeburg)

issue of 2nd:

2. **Princess** Friederike Marie-Caroline Elisabeth Thaddea Benita Eleonore **Felipa of Schaumburg-Lippe** (*1 Dec 2008 Munich)
3. **Princess Philomena** Sylvia Huberta Amelie Juliane Vera Marie-Anna **of Schaumburg-Lippe** (*10 Jul 2011 Munich)

III) **Prince Konstantin** Carl-Eduard Ernst-August Stephan Alexander **of Schaumburg-Lippe** (22 Dec 1930 Hagenburg – 16 Apr 2008)
=1 28 Dec 1956 Hanover; **Sigrid Knape** (2 Sep 1929 Kirschberg – 20 Aug 1997 Bielefeld) daughter of Gerhard Knape & Liselotte Henning
=2 6 Nov 1998 Bielefeld; **Petra Maas** (*18 Feb 1951 Salzburg) daughter of Werner Maas & Ruth Laugwitz
issue of 1st:

A) **Prince York** Karl-Albrecht Konstantin **of Schaumburg-Lippe** (*4 Jun 1960 Bielefeld)
= 5 (civil) & 12 (rel) Sep 1986 Bielefeld; **Susanne Seidensticker** (10 Sep 1961 Bielefeld – 19 Dec 1992 Bielefeld) daughter of Gerd Seidensticker & Gisela Werner

1) **Prince Nicolai-York** Gerhard Konstantin **of Schaumburg-Lippe** (23 Apr 1989 San Diego, California – 4 Dec 2016)

B) **Princess Tatjana** Sibylle Viktoria Juliane **of Schaumburg-Lippe** (*12 Nov 1962 Bielefeld)

issue of 2nd:

C) **Prince Olivier** Konstantin Mortimer **of Schaumburg-Lippe** (*27 Mar 1988 Bielefeld)

IV) **Princess** Elsa **Viktoria Luise** Marie Barbara Elisabeth Bathildis Wera **of Schaumburg-Lippe** (*31 Jul 1940 Hagenburg)
=1 16 Dec 1966 Willing (civil) & 30 Jan 1967 Bückeburg (rel.); **Count Karl-Georg** Kurt Gustav **von Stackelberg** (19 Jul 1913 Arensburg – 28 Aug 1980 Rosenheim) son of Count Herbert von Stackelberg & Carla Menzel; =1st Clara Maria Amster
=2 27 (civil) & 28 (rel.) Jun 1983 Bückeburg; **Hans-Jürgen von Goerne** (12 Dec 1908 Allenstein – 3 Mar 2001 Munich) son of Georg von Goerne & Elisabeth Kulenkamp; =1st Princess Antoinette von Croy; =2nd Waltraut von Klutchner

issue of 1st (none by 2nd):

A) **Count Arved-Andre** Wolrad Friedrich **von Stackelberg** (*24 Jun 1967 Munich)
= 30 Dec 1999 Bad Aibling; Anna **Cristina von Trotha** (*15 Jan 1969 San Jose, Costa Rica) daughter of Hartmuth von Trotha & Ursula Tappen

1) **Count Stanislas** Andre **von Stackelberg** (*14 Aug 2000 Munich)

2) **Countess Louisa** Antonia **von Stackelberg** (*26 Jan 2006 Munich)

B) **Count Stefan** Matthias **von Stackelberg** (*29 Sep 1968 Munich)

= …; **Baroness Nathalie von und zu Mentzingen** (*30 May 1969 Stuttgart) daughter of Baron Rudolf von und zu Mentzingen & Baroness Fides von Gemmingen-Hornberg

1) **Countess Alicia** Maxima **von Stackelberg** (*15 Feb 2006)

2) **Count Kassian** Karl-Georg Stefan **von Stackelberg** (*26 Mar 2009)

2. **Duchess Olga** Alexandrine Marie **of Württemberg** (1 Mar 1876 Stuttgart – 21 Oct 1932 Ludwigsburg) (twin)
= 3 Nov 1898 Stuttgart; **Prince Maximilian** August Jaroslav Adalbert Hermann Georg **of Schaumburg-Lippe** (13 Mar 1871 Ratiboritz – 7 Apr 1904 Abbazia) son of Prince Wilhelm of Schaumburg-Lippe & Princess Bathildis of Anhalt

a. **Prince** Wilhelm **Eugen** Georg Friedrich August Albrecht **of Schaumburg-Lippe** (8 Aug 1899 Hanover – 7 Nov 1929 Caterham, Surrey)

I) **Prince Albrecht** Adolf Konstantin Ernst Nikolaus Friedrich **of Schaumburg-Lippe** (17 Oct 1900 Ludwigsburg – 20 May 1984 Eugendorf)
= 2 Sep 1930 Partenkirchen; **Baroness Walburgis von Hirschberg** (26 Mar 1906 Nuremberg – 10 Apr 1986 Eugendorf) daughter of Baron Karl von Kirschberg & Baroness Sophie von Faber
no issue by marriage
Prince Albrecht has issue by **Baroness Marie-Gabrielle** Barbara Alberta Clara Askanie Amélie **von Pfetten-Arnbach** (*10 Jun 1927 Munich) daughter of Baron Franz von Pfetten-Arnbach & Countess Amelia Verri della Bosia:

A) **Andrea zu Schaumburg-Lippe** (*19 Sep 1960 Verden)
= 4 Sep 1993 Salzburg; **Count Franz** Joseph **von Degenfeld-Schönburg** (25 Sep 1962 Heilbronn – 10 Oct 2006 Gemmingen) son of Count Christoph-Anton von Degenfeld-Schönburg & Rosalie d'Espagne de Venevelles

1) **Countess Marie** Franziska Stephanie Lily Marie Gabriele Walburgis **von Degenfeld-Schönburg** (*30 May 1994 Sinsheim)

2) **Count Anton** Nicolas Albrecht Christoph Maria **von Degenfeld-Schönburg** (*5 Mar 1996 Sinsheim)
3) **Count Johannes von Degenfeld-Schönburg** (…)
II) **Prince Bernhard of Schaumburg-Lippe** (8 Dec 1902 Ludwigsburg – 24 Jun 1903 Ludwigsburg)

D. **Grand Duke Constantine** Constantinovich **of Russia** (10/22 Aug 1858 Strelna – 2/15 Jun 1915 Pavlovsk); = 15/27 Apr 1884 St. Petersburg; **Princess Elisabeth** Auguste Marie Agnes **of Saxe-Altenburg** (renamed **Elizabeth** Mavrikevna) (25 Jan 1865 Meiningen – 24 Mar 1927 Leipzig) daughter of Prince Moritz of Saxe-Altenburg & Princess Auguste of Saxe-Meiningen

1. **Prince Ionn** Constantinovich **of Russia** (23 Jun/5 Jul 1886 Pavlovsk – 18 Jul 1918 Alapaievsk) murdered by Bolshevi
= 3 Sep 1911 Peterhof; **Princess Elena** Petrovna **of Serbia** (4 Nov 1884 Rijecka – 16 Oct 1962 Nice) daughter of Petar I, King of Serbia & Princess Zorka of Montenegro

a. **Prince Vsevolode** Ivanovich **of Russia** (7/20 Jan 1914 Pavlovsk – 18 Jun 1973 London)
=1 31 May (civil) & 1 Jun (rel.) 1939 (dv.1956); **Lady Mary Lygon** (12 Feb 1910 Malvern, Worcestershire – 27 Sep 1982 Farmingdon) daughter of William Lygon, 7th Earl of Beauchamp & Lady Lettice Grosvenor
=2 28 Mar 1956 London (dv.1961); **Emilia de Gostonyi** (14 Apr 1914 Budapest – 9 Jul 1993 Monte Carlo) daughter of Jenő de Gostonyi & Ételt Törö de Tury; =1st Robin Lyle; =2nd Michael Banker; =3rd Count Sigismund von Berchtold
=3 8 Jun 1961 London; **Valli** Elisabeth **Knust** (*4 Apr 1930 London) daughter of Cyril Knust & Dorothy Love
no issue

b. **Princess Catherine** Ivanovna **of Russia** (12/25 Jul 1915 Pavlovsk – 13 Mar 2007 Montevideo, Uruguay)
= 15 Sep 1937 Rome; **Nobile Ruggero Farace, Marchese di Villaforesta** (4 Aug 1909 London – 14 Sep 1970 Rome) son of Nobile Alfredo Farace, Marchese di Villaforesta & Caterina Fachiri

I) **Nobile Nicoletta Farace di Villaforesta** (*23 Jul 1938 Rome)
= 25 Mar 1966 Montevideo; **Alberto Grundland** (12 Jul

1931 Montevideo – 27 Dec 1984 Montevideo)
A) **Eduardo** Alberto **Grundland** (*15 Jan 1967 Montevideo)
= 12 Nov 1999 Montevideo; **Maria Esther Pita Blanco** (...)
1) **Federico Grundland Pita** (*15 Mar 2005 Montevideo)
B) **Alexandra** Gabriella **Grundland** (*19 Jul 1971 Montevideo)
= 24 Mar 2001 Montevideo; **Roberto Castro** (...) son of Roberto Castro & Gladys Padua
1) **Santiago Castro Grundland** (*15 Oct 2006 Montevideo)
II) **Nobile Fiametta Farace di Villaforesta** (*19 Feb 1942 Budapest)
=1 16 Sep 1969 New York (dv.1980); **Victor Arcelus** (*20 Feb 1935 Montevideo)
=2 1981; **Ideal** Nelson **Zanelli** (*9 Mar 1948 Montevideo)
issue of 1st:
A) **Victor** John **Arcelus** (*29 Nov 1973 New York)
= 17 Jul 1999 Lewisburg, Pennsylvania; **Julie Renner** (…)
1) **Mathias** Carlos **Arcelus** (*2006)
2) **Ekaterina** Elena **Arcelus** (*2008)
B) **Sebastian Arcelus** (*5 Nov 1976 New York
= 25 Oct 2007 in Tuscany; **Stephanie** Janette **Block** (*19 Sep 1972)
1) **Vivienne** Marie **Arcelus** (*23 Jan 2015 New York City)
issue of 2nd:
C) **Alessandro Zanelli** (*31 Jul 1984 New York)
III) **Nobile** Giovanni (**Ivan**) **Farace, Marchese di Villaforesta** (*20 Oct 1943 Rome)
= 14 Feb 1968 Montevideo; **Marie Claude Tillier-Debresse** (*24 Apr 1944 Paris) daughter of Jean Tillier-Debresse & Monique Dumont
A) **Nobile Alessandro Farace di Villaforesta** (*29 Aug 1971 Neuilly-sur-Seine)

B) **Nobile Yann Farace di Villaforesta** (*4 Oct 1974 Versailles)
= 4 Sep 2009 Paris; **Anne-Sophie Laignel** (*17 Sep 1979 Caen)
1) **Nobile Tancredi Farace di Villaforesta** (*20 Nov 2010 Paris)

2. **Prince Gabriel** Constantinovich **of Russia** (3/15 Jul 1887 Pavlovsk – 28 Feb 1955 Paris)
=1 (morg.) 9/22 Apr 1917 St. Petersburg; **Antonina** Rafailovna **Nesterovskya** (14/26 Mar 1890 St. Petersburg – 7 Mar 1950 Paris) daughter of Raphael Nesterovsky & Eudoxia …
=2 (morg.) 11 May 1951 Paris; **Princess Irina** Ivanovna **Kurakina** (22 Sep/5 Oct 1903 Andreievskoie – 17 Jan 1993 Paris) daughter of Prince Ivan Kurakine & Countess Sofia Tolstoya
no issue

3. **Princess Tatiana** Constantinovna **of Russia** (later **Mother Tamara**) (23 Jan 1890 St. Petersburg – 28 Aug 1970 Jerusalem) Abbess of the Convent of the Mount of Olives
=1 24 Aug/6 Sep 1911 Pavlovsk; **Prince Constantine** Alexandrovich **Bagration-Moukhransky** (2/14 Mar 1889 Tiblisi – 19 May/1 Jun 1915 near Yaroslav) killed in action; son of Prince Alexander Bagration-Moukhransky & Princess Marina Maourava
=2 9 Nov 1921 Geneva; **Alexander** Vassilievich **Korotchenzov** (17/29 Aug 1877 St Petersburg – 6 Feb 1922 Lausanne) son of Vassili Korotchenzov & Maria Nomikosova
issue of 1st (none by 2nd):
a. **Prince Teymourasz** Constantinovich **Bagration-Moukhransky** (8/21 Aug 1912 Pavlovsk – 10 Apr 1992 New York)
=1 27 Oct 1940 Belgrade; **Catherine** Stefanovna **Rachich** (4 Jul 1919 London – 20 Dec 1946 Paris) daughter of Stefan Rachich
=2 27 Nov 1949 New York; **Countess Irina** Sergeievna **Czernichewa-Besobrasova** (25 Sep 1926 Neuilly-sur-Seine – 9 Jul 2015 New York) daughter of Count Serge Czernichew-Besobrazov & Countess Elizabeth Cheremeteva

no issue

b. **Princess Natalia** Constantinovna **Bagration-Moukhransky** (6/19 Apr 1914 Yalta – 26 Aug 1984 London)
= 22 Apr 1944 London; **Sir Charles** Hepburn **Johnston** (11 Mar 1912 London – 23 Apr 1986 London) son of Ernest Johnston & Emma Hepburn
no issue

4. **Prince Constantine** Constantinovich **of Russia** (20 Dec 1890/1 Jan 1891 St. Petersburg – 17 Jul 1918 Alapaievsk) murdered by Bolsheviks
5. **Prince Oleg** Constantinovich **of Russia** (15/27 Nov 1892 St. Petersburg – 29 Sep/12 Oct 1914 Vilna) killed in action
6. **Prince Igor** Constantinovich **of Russia** (29 May/10 Jun 1894 Strelna – 17 Jul 1918 Alapaievsk) murdered by Bolsheviks
7. **Prince George** Constantinovich **of Russia** (24 May/6 Jun 1903 St. Petersburg – 8 Nov 1938 New York)
8. **Princess Natalia** Constantinovna **of Russia** (10/23 Mar – 10/23 May 1905 St. Petersburg)
9. **Princess Vera** Constantinovna **of Russia** (11/24 Apr 1906 Pavlovsk – 11 Jan 2001 New York)

E. **Grand Duke Dmitri** Constantinovich **of Russia** (1/13 Jun 1860 Strelna – 28 Jan 1919 St. Petersburg) murdered by Bolsheviks

F. **Grand Duke Viatcheslav** Constantinovich **of Russia** (13 Jul 1862 Warsaw – 14/27 Feb 1879 St. Petersburg)

Grand Duke Constantin Nikolaievich had additional issue by **Anna** Vassilievna **Kuznetzova** (1847 – Dec 1922 Moscow) natural daughter of Vassili Karatyguine & Tatiana Kuznetzova.

Granted the surname Kniazev 5/17 May 1883:

H. **Serge** Constantinovich **Kuznetzov** (* & + 1873 St. Petersburg)

I. **Marina** Constantinovna **Kniazeva** (26 Nov/8 Dec 1875 St. Petersburg – 8
Jun 1941 Moscow)
= 12/24 Apr 1894; **Alexander** Pavlovich **Erchov** (24 Jun/6Jul 1861 – 1920 Akhtyrka, Russia) son of Paul Erchov & Julia Popova

1. **Marina** Alexandrovna **Erchova** (10/22 Jan 1895 St. Petersburg – 22 Mar 1965 Moscow)
= …; **Nicholas** Pavlovich **Nikolaievsky** (17/29 Mar 1893 Saratov – 8 Nov 1963 Moscow) son of Paul Nikolaievsky

a. **Gleb** Nikolaievich **Nikolaievsky** (24 Mar 1927 Moscow – 5 Mar 1931 Moscow)

b. **Marina** Nikaolaievna **Nikolaievskya** (*28 Oct 1932 Moscow) = …; **Vladimir** Dmitrievich **Rogov** (23 Jun/6 Jul 1911 Gusenki – 17 Dec 1976 Moscow) son of Vladimir Rogov

I) **Marina** Vladimirovna **Rogova** (*23 Sep 1956 Moscow) = …; **Alexander** Alexandrovich **Dunaiev** (*20 Sep 1956 Vidnoie) son of Alexander Dunaiev

A) **Marina** Alexandrovna **Dunaieva** (*30 Sep 1980 Moscow)

2. **Anna** Alexandrovna **Erchova** (23 May/4 Jun 1896 Pavlovsk – 28 Nov 1978 Moscow)
= 16 Apr 1923 Moscow; **Michael** Yurievich **Arseniev** (22 Jan/3 Feb 1894 Zatishye – 1937) executed; son of Yuri Arseniev & Olga Volkova

a. **Mariana** Mikhailovna **Arsenieva** (*5 May 1925 Moscow) = …; **Eugene** Mikhailovich **Medvedkov** (14 Nov 1922 – 27 May 1984) son of Michael Medvedkov

I) **Michael** Eugeneievich **Medvedkov** (*24 Feb 1953 Istra) = …; **Vera** Yurievna **Reshetina** (*28 Mar 1952) daughter of Yuri Reshtine

A) **Serge** Mikhailovich **Medvedkov** (*20 Aug 1977 Moscow)

B) **Irina** Mikhailovna **Medvedkova** (*18 May 1982 Moscow)

II) **Olga** Eugeneievna **Medvedkova** (*5 Jul 1957 Efremov)

b. **Lev** Mikhailovich **Arseniev** (*4 Nov 1929 Skodnia) = …; **Nina** Stepanovna **Kalmykova** (*12 Sep 1934 Lobnia) daughter of Stefan Kalmykov

I) **Anna** Lvovna **Arsenieva** (*27 Dec 1959 Moscow) = …; **Igor** Victorovich **Petrov** (*2 Apr 1958 Moscow) son of Victor Petrov

A) **Anastasia** Igorievna **Petrova** (16 Mar 1981 Moscow)

B) **Vadim** Igorievich **Petrov** (*12 Dec 1985 Moscow)

II) **Andrew** Lvovich **Arseniev** (*25 Dec 1963 Moscow) = …; **Tatiana** Alexandrovna **Timofeeva** (*10 Apr 1968 Moscow) daugher of Alexander Timofeev

A) **Paul** Andreievich **Arseniev** (*26 Nov 1989 Moscow)

3. **Julia** Alexandrovina **Erchova** (1898 Moscow – 1916 Moscow)
4. **Andrew** Alexandrovich **Erchov** (27 Sep/9 Oct 1900 St. Petersburg – 12 Jun 1968 Tallinn, Estonia)
   = …; **Leonilla** Ivanovna **Sokolova** (25 Nov/8 Dec 1904 Rybinsk – 29 Oct 1976 Tallinn) daughter of Ivan Sokolov
   a. **Irina** Andreievna **Erchova** (23 Jun 1929 Rybinsk – 3 Nov 1980 Moscow)
      =…; **Yuri** Pavlovich **Kornakov** (*1 Mar 1929 Rubtzovsk) son of Paul Kornakov
      I) **Tatiana** Yurievna **Kornakova** (*8 Nov 1954 Tallinn)
         = … (dv.); **Andrew** Yurievich **Buzine** (*12 Feb 1955) son of Yuri Buzine
         A) **Constantine** Andreievich **Buzine** (*13 Feb 1978)
      II) **Paul** Yurievich **Kornakov** (*13 May 1959 Moscow)
   b. **Vadim** Andreievich **Erchov** (*20 Jan 1933 Rybinsk)
      = …; **Margarita** Nikolaievna **Elaguina** (*23 Mar 1933 St. Petersburg) daughter of Nichols Elaguine
      I) **Leonilla** Vadimovna **Erchova** (*21 Aug 1956 St. Petersburg)
         = …; **Victor** Mikhailovich **Mukhine** (*24 Nov 1957) son of Michael Mukhine
         A) **Alexander** Victorovich **Mukhine** (*9 Oct 1981 St. Petersburg)
         B) **Eugene** Victorovich **Mukhine** (*28 Jun 1988 St. Petersburg)
      II) **Andrew** Vadimovich **Erchov** (*20 Oct 1957 St. Petersburg)
         = …; **Olga** Vladimirovna **Stepanova** (*10 Jun 1960 Tomsk) daughter of Vladimir Stepanov
         A) **Vadim** Andreievich **Erchov** (*10 Jul 1980 St. Petersburg)
         B) **Tatiana** Andreievna **Erchova** (*30 Aug 1987 St. Petersburg)
5. **Elena** Alexandrovna **Erchova** (6/19 May 1902 Klev – 11 Mar 1990 Moscow) (twin)
   = …; **Vladislav** Ignatievich **Zakharievich** (Dec 1898 Simferpol – 11Mar 1990 Moscow) son of Ignatius Zakharievich
   no issue

6. **Constantine** Alexandrovich **Erchov** (6/19 May 1902 Klev – Aug 1938) murdered
= 1932 Moscow; **Princess Tatiana** Petrovna **Ouroussova** (15/28 Oct 1903 Samara – 8 Mar 1942 Kalinia) daughter of Prince Peter Ouroussov & Natalia Istomina
a. **Tatiana** Constantinovna **Erchova** (*29 Jan 1933 Moscow)
=1 27 Dec 1958 Moscow (dv.); **Anatole** Ivanovich **Volkov** (*1 Feb 1926 Malinovka) son of Ivan Volkov
=2 21 May 1966 Moscow; **Michael** Borisovich **Pavlov** (*1 Feb 1931 Priluki) son of Boris Pavlov
issue of 1st (none by 2nd):
I) **Maxim** Anatolievich **Volkov** (*17 Dec 1961 Moscow)
= …; **Natalia** Alexeievna **Alexandrov** (*31 Jan 1963 Moscow) daughter of Alexei Alexandrov
A) **Anna** Maximovna **Volkova** (*13 Feb 1990 Moscow)
7. **Tatiana** Alexandrovna **Erchov** (14/27 Mar 1904 Kiev – 25 May 1969 Moscow)
=1 … (dv.); **Serge** Ivanovich **Matveev** (1884 – 1975) son of Ivan Matveev
=2 …; **Peter** Timofeievich **Saveliev** (12/25 Apr 1904 – 17 Sep 1977 Moscow) son of Timothy Saveliev
issue of 2nd (none by 1st):
a. **Vladimir** Petrovich **Saveliev** (*12 Nov 1937 Moscow)
= …; **Tatiana** Mikhailovna **Martynova** (*14 Dec 1941) daughter of Michael Martynov
I) **Olga** Vladimirovna **Savelieva** (*11 Dec 1963)
= …; **Yuri** Nikolaievich **Moisseev** (*4 Nov 1961) son of Nicholas Moissev
A) **Paul** Yurievich **Moisseev** (*12 Mar 1988)
b. **Tatiana** Petrovna **Savelieva** (*9 Mar 1939 Moscow)
= …; **Serge** Alexandrovich **Kazachkov** (*13 Aug 1949 Susuman) son of Alexander Kazachkov
no issue
8. **Olga** Alexandrovna **Erchova** (*24 Mar/6 Apr 1913 Moscow) has issue by **Alexander …** (…):
a. **Natalia** Alexandrovna **Erchova** (*31 Aug 1945 Moscow)
= …; **Boris** Vladimirovich **Dmitriev** (*6 May 1946 Moscow) son of Vladimir Dmitriev

I) **Olga** Borisovna **Dmitrieva** (*15 Feb 1972 Moscow)
= …; **Ivan** Sergeievich **Shevtzov** (*1 Jul 1969) son of Serge Shevtzov
A) **Nicholas** Ivanovich **Shevtzov** (*16 Feb 1993 Moscow)
II) **Elena** Borisovna **Dmitrieva** (1976 Moscow – 1978 Moscow)
III) **Nikita** Borisovich **Dmitriev** (*3 Jan 1981 Moscow)
9. **Igor** Alexandrovich **Erchov** (*8/21 Dec 1914 Moscow)
= …; **Nadejda** Romanovna **Chigachkova** (*17 Sep 1912) daughter of Roman Chigachkov
a. **Oleg** Igorievich **Erchov** (*6 Apr 1938 Moscow)
= …; **Maya** Alexeivena **…** (*1 Sep 1932)
I) **Alexei** Olegovich **Erchov** (*1962 Moscow)
= …; **Larissa …** (…)
A) **Paul** Alexeievich **Erchov** (*1988)
b. **Constantine** Igorievich **Erchov** (1949 – 8 Oct 1980)
= …; **Lydia …** (…)
I) **Roman** Constantinovich **Erchov** (…)
I. **Anna** Constantinovna **Kniazeva** (4/16 Mar 1878 St. Petersburg – 18 Feb 1920 Ekaterinodar, Caucasus)
= 17/29 Apr 1898 St. Petersburg; **Nicholas Lialine** (3/15 Aug 1869 – 14 Feb 1920 Ekaterinodar) son of Nicholas Lialine & Maria Sukareva
1. **Irina Lialina** (12/24 Nov 1899 – 20 Feb 1920 Ekaterinodar) died in typhus epidemic with parents
2. **Constantine Lialine** (26 Sep/8 Oct 1901 St. Petersburg – 26 Apr 1958 Namur, Belgium) became a Benedictine monk under the name **Dom Clement**
3. Leon **(Luc) Lialine** (1/14 Jan 1909 St. Petersburg – 2 Feb 1991 Woluwé-Saint-Pierre)
= 1 Sep 1950 Mattagne-la-Grane, Belgium; Emerence (**May**) Marie Romaine **van Vyve** (*29 May 1918 Savona, Italy) daughter of Marcel van Vyve & Marie Ickx
a. **Bernard** Marie Nicolas **Lialine** (12 Oct 1953 Schaerbeek – 10 Jul 1986) killed in an accident
J. **Ishmael** Constantinovich **Kniazev** (2/14 Aug 1879 Pavlovsk – 1885)
K. **Lev** Constantinovich **Kniazev** (Apr 1883 Orianda, Crimea – 1885)

VI. **Grand Duke Nicholas** Nikolaievich **of Russia** (27 Jul/8Aug 1831 Tsarskoie-Selo – 12/25 Apr 1891 Alouka)
= 25 Jan/6 Feb 1856 St. Petersburg; **Duchess Alexandra** (Feodorovna) Friedrike Wilhelmine **of Oldenburg** (21 May/2 Jun 1838 St. Petersburg – 12/25 Apr 1900 Kiev) daughter of Duke Peter of Oldenburg & Princess Therese of Nassau

A. **Grand Duke Nicholas** Nikolaievich **of Russia** (6/18 Nov 1856 St. Petersburg – 5 Jan 1926 Cap d'Antibe, France)
= 29 Apr/12 May 1907 Yalta; **Princess Anastasia** Nikolaievna **of Montenegro** (8 Jan 1868 Centinje – 15 Nov 1935 Cap d'Antibes) daughter of Nicholas I, King of Montenegro & Milena Vukotic; =1st ♦Prince George Romanovsky
no issue

B. **Grand Duke Peter** Nikolaievich **of Russia** (10/22 Jan 1864 St. Petersburg – 16 Jun 1961 Cap d'Antibes)
= 26 Jul/7 Aug 1889 Peterhof; **Princess Militza** Nikolaievna **of Montenegro** (26 Jul 1866 Centinje – 5 Sep 1951 Alexandria, Egypt) daughter of Nicholas I, King of Montenegro & Milean Vukovic

1. **Princess Marina** Petrovna **of Russia** (11 Mar 1892 Nice – 18 May 1981 Six-Fours, England)
= 4 Mar 1927 Cap d'Antibes; **Prince Alexander** Nikolaievich **Galitzine** (13/25 Oct 1885 St. Petersburg – 24 Mar 1977 Toulon) son of Prince Nicholas Galitzine & Eugenie de Gruenberg
no issue

2. **Prince Roman** Petrovich **of Russia** (5/17 Oct 1896 Peterhof – 23 Oct 1978 Rome)
= (morg.) 16 Nov 1921 Cap d'Antibes; **Countess Prascovia** Dmitrievna **Cheremeteva** (2/15 Oct 1901 Poltava – 21 Dec 1986 Rome) daughter of Count Dmitri Cheremetev & Countess Irina Vorontzova-Dahkova
Prince Roman did not ask for, nor received a titel for his wife and children. However, his sons were generally referred to most sources, though inaccurately, as Prince Romanoff

a. (Prince) **Nicholas** Romanovich **Romanoff** (26 Sep 1922 Cap d'Antibes – 15 Sep 2014 Bolgheri, Italy))
= 21 Jan 1952 Cannes; **Countess Sveva della Gherardesca** (*15 Jul 1930 Florence) daughter of Count Walfredo della

Gherardesca & Nicoletta dei marchesi Piccolelis
(I) **Natalia** Nikolaievna **Romanoff** (*14 Dec 1952 Rome)
= 30 Apr 1973 San Vincenzo; **Giuseppe Consolo** (*6 Sep 1948 Naples) son of Enzo Consolo & Jole Gambrosier
(A) **Enzo** Manfredi **Consolo** (1 Jan 1976 Rome – 26 May 1997 Rome)
(B) **Nicoletta Consolo** (*14 May 1980 Rome) stage name: Nicoletta Romanoff
= 20 Sep 1999 Rome (dv.); **Federico Scardamiglia** (*24 Mar 1974 Rome) son of Francesco Scardamiglia & Maria-Augusta Fenoaltea
(1) **Francesco Scardamiglia** (*30 Jul 1999 Rome)
(2) **Gabriele Scardamiglia** (*21 Nov 2000 Rome)
issue by **Giorgio Pasotti** (*22 Jun 1973 Bergamo) son of Mario Pasotti:
(3) **Maria Pasotti** (*19 Jan 2010 Rome)
issue by **Federico Alverà** (...):
(4) due in 2018
(II) **Elisabetta** Nikolaievna **Romanoff** (*7 Aug 1956 Rome)
= 14 May 1982 Las Vegas (civil) & 14 May 1983 San Vincenzo (rel.); **Mauro Bonacini** (*13 Mar 1950 Salsomaggiore) son of Ernes Bonacini & Alba Massen
(A) **Niccolò Bonacini** (*4 Jan 1986 Rome)
= 26 Jun 2014 Rome; **Giorgia Napolitano** (*30 May 1984 Rome)
(1) **Sveva Bonacini** (*2016)
(B) **Sofia Bonacini** (*21 Dec 1987 Rome)
(III) **Tatiana** Nikolaievna **Romanoff** (*12 Apr 1961 Rome)
=1 2 Jul 1983 Villa Biserno (dv.1990); **Giambattista Alessandri** (*31 Dec 1958 Oslo) son of Marcello Alessandri & Ginvor Jørgensen
=2 29 Aug 1998 San Giovanni di Mariagnano; **Giancarlo Tirotti** (*1 Nov 1947 Rome) son of Carrado Tirotti & Maria Cecilia Cerri
issue of 2nd (none by 1st):
(A) **Allegra Tirotti** (*2 Sep 1992 Cattolica)
b. (Prince) **Dmitri** Romanovich **Romanoff** (15 May 1926 Cap d'Antibes – 31 Dec 2016 Copenhagen)

=1 21 Jan 1959 Copenhagen; Inge Magna **Jeanne** Mimi **von Kaufmann** (1 Jun 1936 Copenhagen – 13 May 1989 Copenhagen) daughter of Axel von Kaufmann & Inger Kerr
=2 28 Jul 1993 Kostroma, Russia; **Dorrit Reventlow** (*22 Apr 1942 Recife, Brazil) daughter of Erik Reventlow & Nina Bentie
no issue

3. **Princess Nadejda** Petrovna **of Russia** (3/15 May 1898 Dulber – 21 Apr 1988 Chantilly)
= 10/23 Apr 1917 Haraks (dv.1940); **Prince Nicholas** Vladimirovich **Orlov** (12/24 Mar 1896 St. Petersburg – 30 May 1961 New York) son of Prince Vladimir Orlov & Princess Olga Beloselskya-Belozerskya
   a. **Princess Irina** Nikolaievna **Orlova** (27 Mar 1918 Kareje – 16 Sep 1989 Villecerf)
   =1 27 Mar 1940 Rome (dv.1946); **Baron Herbert** Hans Heinrich Rene **von Waldstätten** (1 Jan 1918 Vienna – 24 Jul 1977 Vienna) son of Baron Hans von Waldstätten & Lily von Boeckmann
   =2 8 Jan 1960 The Hague; **Anthony Adama-Zylstra** (9 Jan 1902 Izendijk – 29 Apr 1982 Fontainbleau) son of Piotr Adama-Zystra & Clazina-Antoinette Freysse
   issue of 1st (none by 2nd):
      I) **Baroness Elizabeth von Waldstätten** (*7 Feb 1941 Budapest)
      = 27 Jul 1970 Red Bank, New Jersey; **Christopher** Morgan **Wynkoop** (*7 Dec 1943 Red Bank) son of Burson Wynkoop & Elizabeth Jenkins
         A) **Mark** Burson **Wynkoop** (*21 Jul 1972 Red Bank)
         = 27 Jun 1997; **Angelique Tritaris** (*17 May 1972)
            1) **Elizabeth** Morgan **Wynkoop** (*22 May 2007 Charlotteville, Virginia)
            2) **Jack** Klees **Wynkoop** (*2012)
         B) **Gregory** Alexis **Wynkoop** (*22 Dec 1975 Red Bank)
         = 27 Jun 2015; **Samatha** Rae **Promer** (*20 Sep 1993 Placer, California)
            1) **Reese** Darwin **Wynkoop** (*2015)
   Princess Irina Orlova has additional issue:
      II) **Alexis** Nicolas **Orloff** (*10 Sep 1947 Boulogne-sur-Seine)

= 12 Jun 1974 Paris; **Françoise** Jeanne **Mazocco** (*21 Jan 1950 Paris)
issue by adoption:
A) **Wladimir Orloff** (*12 Jun 1993 St. Petersburg)

b. **Princess Xenia** Nikolaievna **Orlova** (27 Mar 1921 Paris – 17 Aug 1963 Ennordres)
=1 17 Apr 1943 Avon (dv.1950); **Paul-Marcel de Montaignac de Pessotte de Bressolles** (*5 Jan 1909 Paris) son of Calixte de Montaignac de Pessotte & Marcelle Achaume
=2 14 Mar 1951 Paris; **Chevalier Jean Albert** Louis Marie **d'Almont** (27 Jul 1909 Ivoy-le-Pre – 18 May 2003 Tours) son of Chevalier Charles Louis d'Almont & Laure-Louise Grénouillet
issue of 1st:
I) **Calixte** Nicolas August **de Montaignac de Pessotte de Bressolles** (*24 Sep 1944 Boulogne)
=1 12 Mar 1972 Paris (dv.1979); **Florentine Hunter** (*13 Jul 1942 Charlotte, South Carolina)
=2 …; **Pascale Remaudière** (…)
issue by 2nd (none by 1st):
A) **Eve de Montaignac de Pessotte de Bressolles** (*1994)
Calixte Motaignac de Pessotte has additional issue by **Nicole Mouton**:
B) **Julie de Montaignac** (*1986)
C) **Marie de Montaignac** (*1988)
issue of 2nd:
II) **Marie** Isabelle Nadejda **d'Almont** (*20 Mar 1952 St. Germain)
= 4 Mar 2002 l'Echeneau; **Count Rafal** Zdislaw **Tarnowski** (*9 Sep 1937 Sucha) son of Count Juliusz Tarnowski & Countess Roza Zamoyska; =1st Mercedes Olavarria-Gomez
no issue

Grand Duke Michael had additional issue by **Catherina** Gavrilovna **Chislova** (9/21 Oct 1846 – 1/13 Dec 1889) daughter of Gabriel Chislov:
Issue was recognized and surnamed by Imperial Decree 26 Oct/8 Nov 1882:

C. **Olga** Mikolaievna **Nikolaieva** (29 May/10 Jun 1868 St. Petersburg – 31 Aug 1950 Nice)
= 17/29 Apr 1892 St. Petersburg; **Prince Michael** Mikhailovich **Cantacuzene** (1/13 Oct 1858 Jassy – 17 Sep 1927 Bordighera, Italy) son of Prince Michael Cantacuzene & Elizabeth Bonich

1. **Princess Irina** Mikhailovna **Cantacuzena** (10/22 May 1895 St. Petersburg – 27 Feb 1945 Jagstzell) killed in an air raid
=1 12 Jul Rostov (dv.1927); **Alexander** Mikhailovich **Narishkine** (22 Aug/3 Sep 1878 – 1941 Paris) son of Michael Narishkine & Natalia Karamzina
=2 24 Nov 1928 Paris; **Vladimir** Alexandrovich **Poliakov** (10/23 Dec 1901 Novocherkassk - …) son of Alexander Poliakov & Maria Grekova
issue of 2nd (none by 1st):
a. **Irene** Vladimirovna **Poliakoff** (*3 May 1929 Neuilly-sur-Seine)
= 29 Aug 1959 Ellwangen; **Karl-Heinz Krebs** (*8 Jan 1926 Ellwangen) son of Alfons Krebs & Ida Maucher
I) **Claudia Krebs** (*2 Aug 1960 Stuttgart)
II) **Cornelia Krebs** (*17 Sep 1961 Stuttgart)
2. **Princess Olga** Mikhailovna **Cantacuzena** (3/15 Feb 1899 St. Petersburg – 15 Feb 1983 Nice)

D. **Vladimir** Nikolaievich **Nikolaiev** (23 May/4 Jun 1873 Peterhof – 28 Jan 1942 Sainte-Geneviève-des-Bois)
=1 … (dv.1907); **Vera** Vladimirovna **Popova** (… - 1967) daughter of Vladimir Popov & Lydia Kraousolta
=2 1907 St. Petersburg; **Elenora Lencioni** (8/20 Dec 1885 St. Petersburg – Jul 1913 St. Petersburg) daughter of Francesco Lencioni & Olga Ducklau
=3 …; (his sister-in-law) **Olga** Dmitrievna **Zabotkina** (18/30 Jan 1871 – 1925 St. Petersburg) died in a famine; daughter of Dmitri Zabotkin & Sofia Boita; =1st Alexander Spechinsky, =2nd Alexander Kuzminsky, =3rd ♦Nicholas Nikolaiev
=4 …; (his sister-in-law) **Maria** Dmitrievna **Zabotkina** (25 Mar/6 Apr 1878 Oranienbaum – 26 Jul 1961 Sainte-Geneviève-des-Bois) daughter of Dmitri Zabotkin & Sofia Boita
issue of 1st:
1. **Vladimir** Vladimirovich **Nikolaiev** (8/20 Aug 1895 St. Petersburg – 10 Apr 1956 Toulon)

= 1916 Georgievsk; **Countess Vera** Georgievna **Seivers** (Feb 1896 – 5 Apr 1988 Toulon) daughter of Count George Sievers & Olga Danilova

a. **Vassili** Vladimirovich **Nikolaiev** (+ young)

b. **Elizabeth** Vladimirovna **Nikolaieva** (*14 Feb 1919 Poltava)

c. **George** Vladimirovich **Nikolaievich** (22 Feb 1921 Yugoslavia – 1 Aug 1974 Toulon)
= 4 Feb 1942 Toulon (dv.); **Olga** Appolonovna **Karbovskya** (*15/28 Oct 1918 Kherson) daughter of Appolon Karbovsky & Irina …
no issue

d. **Oleg** Vladimirovich **Nikolaiev** (*20 Jul 1922 Pancevo, Serbia)
= 22 Jul 1943 Toulon; **Éliane** Augustine Eienette Rolande **Villecrose** (*27 Jan 1925 Cogolin) daughter of Albert Villecrose & Léa Rousset

I) **Daniel** Paul Georges **Nicolaieff** (*28 Mar 1945 Toulon)
= 17 Sep 1969 Toulon (dv.1974); **Claire Favarel** (*10 Jan 1945 Toulouse) daughter of René Favarel & Rose Laurençon

A) **Franck** Raul René **Nicolaieff** (*29 Dec 1971 Toulon)

II) **Maxime Nicolaieff** (*9 Jul 1948 Toulon)
= 22 Jul 1978 Grasse; **Michéle Lizero** (*20 Feb 1949 Le Carnet) daughter of Auguste Lizero & Madeleine Bottero; no issue

e. **Serge** Vladimirovich **Nikolaiev** (25 Nov 1923 Pancevo - ...)
=1 23 Aug 1947 Marseilles; **Nina** Madeline **Delmont** (21 Aug 1926 Le Pouzon – 28 Oct 1953 Toulon) daughter of Victor Delmont & Lucie Doudoux
=2 23 Apr 1955 Toulon; **Irene** Borisovna **Viranovskya** (20 Apr 1926 La Seyne-sur-Mer - ...) daughter of Boris Viranovsky & Tatiana …
issue of 1st:

I) **Luc** Jean Paul **Nicolaieff** (*25 Jun 1950 Toulon)
= 2 Fen 1976 Bandol; **Hélène** Victorine Reine **Barrière** (*12 Jul 1954 Sanary-sur-Mer) daughter of Marius Barrière & Marie Poggio

A) **Nina Nicolaieff** (*28 Feb 1978 Ollioules) (twin)

B) **Céline Nicolaieff** (*28 Feb 1978 Ollioules) (twin)

issue of 2nd:

II) **Michel** Nicolas **Nicolaieff** (*18 May 1955 Toulon)
= 7 Oct 1977 Dijon; **Nicole Terrier** (*10 Oct 1955 Dijon) daughter of Roger Terrier & Paulette Adenot

A) **Alexandre Nicolaieff** (*16 Jan 1979 Toulon)

B) **Jeremy Nicolaieff** (*9 Jul 1980 Toulon)

C) **Lina Nicolaieff** (*20 Jun 1996 Toulon)

2. **Galina** Vladimirovna **Nikolaieva** (12/24 May 1897 Peterhof – 1969 Soviet Union)
= …; **Alexander** Nikolaievich **Gotovsky** (11/23 Mar 1888 – 1937 Soviet Union) murdered by the Communists; son of Nicholas Gotovsky
issue ?

3. **George** Vladimirovich **Nikolaiev** (24 July/5 Aug 1898 – 1919) killed in action

4. **Paul** Vladimirovich **Nikolaiev** (26 Jun 1901 Peterhof – 18 Oct 1969 Toulon)
= 11 Nov 1948 Paris; (his cousin and step-niece) ♦**Marina** Mikhailovna **Archenevskya** (31 Oct 1919 Novorosiisk – 17 Nov 1992 Aubais) daughter of Michael Archenevsky & Nina Nikolaieva

a. **Hélène Nicolaieff** (*19 Mar 1949 Paris)
=1 31 Mar 1974 Valvignères (dv.); **Omar Kachobi** (*1 Sep 1943 Oeud Zem, Morocco) son of Ben Omar Larbi Kachobi & Pent Massouda
=2 1 Jul 1995 Cergy-Pontoise (dv.); **Paul** Igorevich **Bondarovsky** (*25 Jul 1953 Zagorsk) son of Igor Bondarovsky & Guenreitta Machina
issue of 1st (none by 2nd):

(I) **Myriam Kachobi** (*31 Jul 1975 Pontoise)

(II) **Anice Kachobi** (*26 Apr 1977 Pontoise)

b. **Cyrille** André **Nicolaieff** (*12 Oct 1955 Paris)
has issue by **Charlotte Hannoun** (*20 Jan 1956 Paris) daughter of Claude Hounnoun & Coline Tison:

(I) **César** Kyrill Clarence Colin **Nicolaieff** (*5 Jun 1988 Nimes)

(II) **Lola Nicolaieff** (*5 Aug 1991 Nimes) (twin)

(III) **Amanda Nicolaieff** (*5 Aug 1991 Nimes) (twin)

Paul Nikolaiev has additional issue of **Rosa** Marie Emilie **Bachat** (12 Sep 1904 Thônon-les-Bains - …) daughter of Jean Bachat & Louise Lauvers:

c. **Georges** François **Nicolaieff** (*25 Sep 1931 Paris)
= 14 May 1966 Montreal; **Ginette** Hosiane Geneviève **Daher** (*28 Nov 1929 Jutigny) daughter of Ferdinand Daher & Paulette Gauthier

(I) **Philippe** Patrick **Nicolaieff** (*18 Dec 1959 Montreal)
= 7 Jan 1987 Bizard Island, Quebec; **Kathleen** Josée **Leblanc** (*5 Jul 1963 Montreal) daughter of Albert Leblanc & Julie Turcotte

(A) **Alexandra** Virginia **Nicolaieff** (*9 Oct 1991 Montreal)

(B) **Catherine** Ginette Julie **Nicolaieff** (*22 Jan 1993 Montreal)

issue of 2nd (none by others):

5. **Valentina** Vladimirovna **Nikolaieva** (29 Jun/12 Jul 1908 St. Petersburg – 19 Jun 1973 Helsinki)
= 5 Jul 1933 Helsinki; **Carli** Auguste **Timgren** (3/18 Feb 1901 Vyborg, Russia - …) son of Gosta Timgren & Agnes Ekström

a. **Carola Timgren** (*31 Jul 1934 Helsinki)
= 21 Jun 1956 Helsinki; **Berndt** Valter **Nordgren** (*25 Mar 1932 Helsinki) son of Johan Nordgren & Kerstin Boucht

I) Berndt **Michael Nordgren** (*15 Sep 1958 Helsinki)
= ...; **Leila** Maria **...** (*9 May 1958 Forssa, Finland)

A) **Sebastian** Michael **Nordgren** (*1986)

B) **Daniela** Maria **Nordgren** (*1988)

II) **Benita** Carola **Nordgren** (*30 Aug 1962 Helsinki)
has issue by **Stone Stenbacka** (*1 Mar 1956):

A) **Björn** Valter Simon **Nordgren** (*30 Sep 1991) (twin)

B) **Robert** Andreas Sigurd **Nordgren** (*30 Sep 1991) (twin)

III) **Maria** Carola **Nordgren** (*8 Sep 1964 Helsinki)

E. **Catherina** Nikolaievna **Nikolaieva** (1874 St. Petersburg – 26 Jan 1940 Belgrade)
=1 … (dv); **Nicholas** Nikolaievich **Korevo** (31 May/12 Jun St. Petersburg – 3 May 1935 Paris) son of Nicholas Korevo & Elizabeth Spiridonova
=2 5 Nov 1914; **Ivan** Alexandrovich **Persiani** (…) son of Alexander Persiani

issue of 1st (none by 2nd):
1. **Catherina** Nikolaievna **Koreva** (11/23 Feb 1895 - …)
F. **Nicholas** Nikolaievich **Nikolaiev** (4/16 Apr 1875 St. Petersburg – 27 Dec 1901/9 Jan 1902 Sergeivoie Purtin)
= …; **Olga** Dmitrievna **Zabotkina** (18/30 Jun 1871 – 1925 St. Petersburg) daughter of Dmitri Zabotkin &Sofia Boita; =1st Alexander Spechinsky, =2nd Alexander Kuzminsky, =4th ♦Vladimir Nikolaiev
1. **Olga** Nikolaievna **Nikolaieva** (11/23 Sep 1894 St. Petersburg – 28 Nov 1984 Zurich)
= 1919 Odessa; **Alexei** Dmitrievich **Kelepovsky** (16/28 Dec 1893 Kiev – 8 Jan 1966 Boulogne) son of Dmitri Kelepovsky & Nadejda Kolomeitzeva
a. **Natalia** Alexeievna **Kelepovskya** (*5 Jun 1920 Yalta)
2. **Nina** Nikolaievna **Nikolaieva** (20 May/1 Jun 1896 St. Petersburg – 14 Apr 1965 Issy-les-Moulineaux)
= 1917 St. Petersburg; **Michael** Constantinovich **Archenevsky** (1890 St. Petersburg – 1919) missing, presumed killed, in action; son of Constantine Archenevsky & Olga Markozova; =1st Natlia Adelerberg
a. **Marina** Mikhailovna **Archenevskya** (18/31 Oct 1919 Novorossiisk – 17 Nov 1992 Aubais)
=1 …; **Cyril** Borisovich **Radischev** (19 Nov 1921 Warsaw – 10 Aug 1944 Sonnenburg) killed in action; son of Boris Radischev & Sofia Mordinova
=2 1948; ♦**Paul Nikolaiev** (1901 – 1969)
issue of 1st:
I) **Kira** Kirillovna **Radischeff** (*2 Jan 1942 Paris)
= 23 Jul 1962 Boulogne; **Bernard Bester** (*19 Jan 1934 Paris) son of Samuel Bester & Chaja Goldberg
A) **Jean-Baptiste** Alexandre **Bester** (*10 Nov 1962 Boulogne)
issue of 2nd:
see: page
G. **Galina** Nikolaievna **Nikolaieva** (16/28 Jan 1877 St. Petersburg – 22 Jul/3 Aug 1878 St. Petersburg)
VII. **Grand Duke Michael** Nikolaievich **of Russia** (23/25 Oct 1832 Peterhof – 18 Dec 1909 Cannes)

= 16/28 Aug 1857 St. Petersburg; **Princess Cäcilie** Auguste **of Baden** (renamed **Olga** Feodorovna) (20 Sep 1839 Karlsruhe – 31 Mar/12 Apr 1891 Kharkov) daughter of Leopold, Grand Duke of Baden & Princess Sophie of Sweden

A. **Grand Duke Nicholas** Mikhailovich **of Russia** (14/26 Apr 1859 Tsarskoie-Selo – 30 Jan 1919 St. Petersburg) murdered by Bolsheviks

B. **Grand Duchess Anastasia** Mikhailovna **of Russia** (16/28 Jul 1860 Peterhof – 11 Mar 1922 Eze)
= 12/24 Jan 1879 St. Petersburg; **Friedrich Franz III** Paul Nikolaus Ernst Heinrich, **Grand Duke of Mecklenburg-Schwerin** (19 Mar 1851 Ludwigslust – 10 Apr 1897 Cannes) son of Friedrich Franz II, Grand Duke of Mecklenburg-Schwerin & Princess Auguste Reuss; suc. father 3 Mar 1862

1. **Duchess Alexandrine** Auguste **of Mecklenburg** (24 Dec 1879 Schwerin – 28 Dec 1952 Copenhagen)
= 26 Apr 1898 Cannes; **Christian X** Carl Frederik Albert Alexander Wilhelm, **King of Denmark** (26 Sep 1870 Charlottenlund – 20 Apr 1947 Amalienborg) son of Frederik VIII, King of Denmark & Princess Louise of Sweden; suc. father 14 May 1912; also reigned as King of Iceland 1 Dec 1918 – 17 Jun 1944

a. Christian **Frederik IX** Franz Michael Carl Valdemar Georg, **King of Denmark** (11 Mar 1899 Sorgenfri – 14 Jan 1972 Copenhagen) suc. father 1947
= 24 May 1935 Stockholm; **Princess Ingrid** Victoria Sofia Louise Margareta **of Sweden** (28 Mar 1910 Stockholm – 7 Nov 2000 Fredensborg) daughter of Gustaf VI, King of Sweden & Princess Margaret of Connaught

I) **Margarethe II** Alexandrine Thorhildur Ingrid, **Queen of Denmark** (*16 Apr 1940 Amalienborg) suc. father 1972
= 10 Jun 1967 Copenhagen; Henri (**Henrik**) Marie Jean André **de Laborde de Monpézat** (cr. **Prince of Denmark**) (*11 Jun 1934 Talence) son of André de Laborde de Monpézat & Renée Doursenot

A) **Crown Prince Frederik** Andre Henrik Christian **of Denmark** (*26 May 1968 Copenhagen)
= 14 May 2004 Copenhagen; **Mary** Elizabeth

Donaldson (*5 Feb 1972 Hobart, Tasmania) daughter of John Donaldson & Henrietta Horne

1) **Hereditary Prince Christian** Valdemar Henri John **of Denmark** (*15 Oct 2005 Copenhagen)

2) **Princess Isabella** Henrietta Ingrid Margarethe **of Denmark** (*21 Apr 2007 Copenhagen)

3) **Prince Vincent** Frederik Minik Alexander **of Denmark** (*8 Jan 2011 Copenhagen) (twin)

4) **Princess Josephine** Sophia Ivalo Mathilda **of Denmark** (*8 Jan 2011 Copenhagen) (twin)

B) **Prince Joachim** Holger Valdemar Christian **of Denmark** (*7 Jun 1969 Copenhagen)
=1 18 Nov 1995 Copenhagen (dv.2005); **Alexandra** Christina **Manley** (*30 Jun 1964 Hong Kong) daughter of Richard Manley & Christa Nowotny; cr. Countess af Frederiksborg 2005; =2nd Martin Jørgensen
=2 24 May 2008 Mogeltønder; **Marie** Agathe Odile **Cavallier** (*6 Feb 1976 Paris) daughter of Alain Cavallier & Françoise…
issue of 1st:

1) **Prince Nikolai** William Alexander Frederik **of Denmark** (*28 Aug 1999 Copenhagen)

2) **Prince Felix** Henrik Valdemar Christian **of Denmark** (*22 Jul 2002 Copenhagen)

issue of 2nd:

3) **Prince Henrik** Carl Joachim Alain **of Denmark** (*4 May 2009 Copenhagen)

4) **Princess Athena** Marguerite Françoise Marie **of Denmark** (*24 Jan 2012 Copenhagen)

II) **Princess Benedikte** Astrid Ingeborg Ingrid **of Denmark** (*29 Apr 19444 Amalienborg)
= 3 Feb 1968 Schloss Fredensborg; **Richard** Casimir Karl August Robert Konstantin, **Prince of Sayn-Wittegenstein-Berleberg** (29 Oct 1934 Giessen – 13 Mar 2017 Berleberg) son of Gustav Albrecht, Prince of Sayn-Wittgenstein-Berleberg & Margareta Fouché d'Otrante; suc. father 29 Nov 1969

A) **Gustav** Frederik Philip Richard, **Prince of Sayn-**

Wittgenstein-Berleberg (*12 Jan 1969 Frankfurt) suc. father 2017

B) **Princess Alexandra** Rosemarie Ingrid Benedikte **of Sayn-Wittgenstein-Berleberg** (*20 Nov 1970 Copenhagen)
= 6 Jun 1998 Graasten Slotskirch; **Count Jefferson-Friedrich** Volker Benjamin **von Pfeil und Klein-Ellguth** (*12 Jul 1967 Mainz) son of Count Friedrich-August von Pfeil und Klein-Ellguth & Astrid Andres

1) **Count** Friedrich **Richard** Oscar Jefferson **von Pfeil und Klein-Ellguth** (*14 Sep 1999 Copenhagen)

2) **Countess Ingrid** Alexandra Irma Astrid Benedikte **on Pfeil und Klein-Ellguth** (*16 Aug 2003 Copenhagen)

C) **Princess Nathalie** Xenia Margaretha Benedikte **of Sayn-Wittgenstein-Berleberg** (*2 May 1975 Copenhagen)
= 27 May 2010 (civil) & 18 Jun 2011 (rel.) Berleberg; **Alexander Johannsmann** (*6 Dec 1977 Gütersloh) son of Heinrich Wilhelm Johannsmann & Jutta ...

1) **Konstantin** Gustav Heinrich Richard **Johannsmann** (*24 Jul 2010 Berleberg)

III) **Princess Anne-Marie** Dagmar Ingrid **of Denmark** (*30 Aug 1946 Amalienborg)
= 1964; ♦**Constantine II, King of the Hellenes** (*1940) see: page

b. **Prince Knud** Christian Frederik Michael **of Denmark** (27 Jul 1900 Sorenfri – 14 Jun 1976 Gentofte)
= 8 Sep 1933 Schloss Fredensborg; (his first cousin) **Princess Caroline Mathilde** Louise Dagmar Christiane Maud Augusta Ingeborg Thyra Adelheid **of Denmark** (27 Apr 1912 Jaegersborghus – 12 Dec 1995 Sorgenfri) daughter of Prince Harald of Denmark & Princess Helena of Schleswig-Holstein-Sonderburg-Glücksburg

I) **Princess Elisabeth** Caroline Mathilde Alexandrine Olga Thyra Feodora Astrid Margarethe Desirée **of Denmark** (*8 May 1935 Copenhagen)

II) **Count Ingolf** Christian Frederik Knud Harald Gorm Gustav Viggo Valdemar Aage **af Rosenborg** (*17 Feb 1940

Sorgenfri) né Prince of Denmark, renounced titles and cr. Count 4 Jan 1968
=1 13 Jan 1968 Lungby; **Inge Terney** (21 Jan 1938 Copenhagen – 21 Jul 1996 Vejile) daughter of Georg Terney & Jenny Hansen
=2 7 Mar 1998 Engtved; **Sussie Hjørhoy** (*20 Feb 1950 Copenhagen) daughter of Fritz Petersen & Ruth Hjørhoy
no issue

III) **Count Christian** Frederik Franz Knud Harald Carl Oluf Gustav Georg Erik **af Rosenborg** (22 Oct 1942 Sorgenfri – 21 May 2013 Copenhagen) né Prince of Denmark, renounced titles and cr. Count 27 Feb 1971
= 27 Feb 1971 Lyngby; **Anne-Dorthe Maltofte-Nielsen** (3 Oct 1947 Copenhagen – 2 Jan 2014 Copenhagen) daughter of Villy Nielsen & Bodil Mantofte

A) **Countess Josephine** Caroline Elisabeth **af Rosenborg** (*29 Oct 1972 Frederikssund (twin)
= 3 Oct 1998 Lyngby (dv.2015); **Thomas** Christian **Schmidt** (*22 Apr 1970 Copenhagen) son of Ole Schmidt & Hedvig …

1) **Julius** Christian Emil **af Rosenborg** (*1 Dec 2001 Copenhagen)

2) **Clara** Dorthe Elisabeth **af Rosenborg** (*26 Nov 2004 Copenhagen)

has issue by **Kenneth Schmidt** (*29 Dec 1977):

3) a child (*2016)

B) **Countess Camilla** Alexandrine Kristine **af Rosenborg** (*29 Oct 1972 Frederikssund) (twin)
= 18 May 1995 Sollerød; **Mikael Rosanes** (*8 Feb 1952 Copenhagen) son of Jan Rosanes & Kristen ...;

1) **Anastasia** Claudine Amalie **af Rosenborg** (*24 Nov 1997 Gentofte)

2) **Ludwig** Christian **af Rosenborg** (*5 Jun 2000 Sonderborg Sygenhus)

3) **Leopold** Christian Ingolf **af Rosenborg** (*15 Apr 2005 Gentofte)

4) **Theodor** Christian Emanuel **af Rosenborg** (*19 Jun 2008 Gentofte)

C) **Countess Feodora** Mathilda Helena **af Rosenborg** (*27 Feb 1975 Fredrikssund)
= 31 Jul 2004 Copenhagen; **Eric** Herve Patrice **Patte** (*20 Aug 1976 Pont-a-Mousson)
1) **Caroline-Mathilde** Margarethe **af Rosenborg** (*1 Feb 2009 Copenhagen)

2. **Friedrich Franz IV** Michael, **Grand Duke of Mecklenburg-Schwerin** (9 Apr 1882 Palermo – 17 Nov 1945 Flensborg) suc. father 1897 (under Regency of uncle, Duke Albrecht, until 9 Apr 1901); abdicated 14 Nov 1918
= 7 Jun 1904 Gmunden; **Princess Alexandra** Luise Olga Elisabeth Therese Vera **of Hanover** etc. (29 Sep 1882 Gmunden – 30 Aug 1963 Glücksburg) daughter of Crown Prince Ernst August of Hanover & Princess Thyra of Denmark
a. **Hereditary Grand Duke Friedrich Franz** Michael Wilhelm Nikolaus Franz-Joseph Ernst August Hans **of Mecklenburg-Schwerin** (22 Apr 1910 Schwerin – 31 Jul 2001 Blankensee) renounced succession rights 1 Feb 1943
=1 (morg.) 11 Jun 1941 Schwerin (dv.1967); **Karin Elisabeth** Henriette Lori Gudela **von Schäper** (31 Jan 1920 Wroclaw – 26 Dec 2012 Glücksburg) daughter of Walther von Schäper & Baroness Isa von Münchhausen;
=2 (morg.) 22 Apr 1977 Glücksburg; his first wife
no issue
b. **Christian Ludwig** Ernst August Maximilian Johann Albrecht Adolf Friedrich, **Duke of Mecklenburg** (29 Sep 1912 Ludwigslust – 18 Jul 1996 Eckernförde) suc. father as Head of the House 1945
= 5 (civil) & 11 (rel) Jul 1954 Glücksburg; **Princess Barbara** Irene Adelheid Viktoria Elisabeth Bathildis **of Prussia** (2 Aug 1920 Hemmelmark – 31 May 1994 Hemmelmark) daughter of Prince Sigismund of Prussia & Princess Charlotte Agnes of Saxe-Altenburg
I) **Duchess Donata of Mecklenburg** (*11 Mar 1956 Kiel)
= 14 Aug 1987 London (civil) & 19 Sep 1987 Hemmelmark (rel.); **Alexander von Solodkoff** (*20 Jan 1951 Cologne) son of Georg von Solodkoff & Erdmuthe Tucholski
A) **Thyra von Solodkoff** (*12 Oct 1989 London)

B) **Alix von Solodkoff** (*17 Mar 1992 London)
C) **Niklot-Alexis Herzog zu Mecklenburg von Solodkoff** (*8 Dec 1994 London)
II) **Duchess Edwina of Mecklenburg** (*25 Sep 1960 Kiel)
= 20 Sep 1995 Eckernförde (civil) & 14 Oct 1995 Hemmelmark (*rel.); **Konrad** Egon Franz Maria **von Posern** (*24 Jul 1964 Innsbruck) son of Hubertus von Posern & Verena von Schuschnigg
A) Ludwig **Leopold** Bernhard Georg Maria **von Posern** (*27 Feb 1996 Eckernförde)
B) Paul **Friedrich** Christian Fabian Maria **von Posern** (*14 Jun 1997 Eckernförde)
C) **Ferdinand** Johann Albrecht Maria **von Posern** (*19 Jun 1999 Eckernförde)
c. **Duchess Olga of Mecklenburg** (27 Dec 1916 Schwerin – 4 Feb 1917 Schwerin)
d. **Duchess Thyra** Anastasia Alexandrine Marie-Louise Olga Cecilie Charlotte Elisabeth Emma **of Mecklenburg** (18 Jun 1919 Sorgenfri – 27 Sep 1981 Flensborg)
e. **Duchess Anastasia** Alexandrine Cecilie Marie Louise Wilhelmine **of Mecklenburg** (1 Nov 1922 Gelbensande – 25 Jan 1979 Hamburg)
= 1 Sep 1943 Willigrad; **Prince Friedrich Ferdinand** Karl Ernst August Wilhelm Harald Kasimir Nicola **of Schleswig-Holstein-Sonderburg-Glücksburg** (14 may 1913 Gotha – 31 May 1989 Glücksburg) son of Prince Albrecht of Schleswig-Holstein-Sonderburg-Glücksburg & Countess Ortrud zu Ysenburg und Büdingen in Meerholz
I) **Princess Elisabeth** Marie Alexandra **of Schleswig-Holstein-Sonderburg-Glücksburg** (*10 Sep 1945 Schleswig)
= 2 (civil) & 5 (rel.) Jan 1975 Glücksburg; **Prince Ferdinand-Heinrich** Karl August Hermann Gotthard **of Ysenburg and Büdingen** (19 Oct 1940 Frankfurt – 8 Mar 1989 Budingen) son of Otto Friedrich, Prince of Ysenburg and Büdingen & Princess Felizitas Reuss
A) **Prince Johann-Georg** Gerd Max Alexander Sylvester Gisbert **of Ysenburg and Büdingen** (*8 Jul 1976

Frankfurt)
= 4 (civil) & 5 (rel.) Jun 2010 Glücksburg; **Stefanie Bittner** (*5 Feb 1977 Flensburg)
1) **Princess Anna-Carolina** Sophia Dorothea Katinka Alexandra **of Ysenburg and Büdingen** (*8 Jan 2010 Frankfurt)
B) **Prince Ludwig-Ferdinand** Wittekind Heinrich Friedrich Wolfgang **of Ysenburg and Büdingen** (*6 Feb 1979 Frankfurt)
= 1 (civil) & 2 (rel.) Oct 2010 Glücksburg; **Chantal Tolle** (*7 Oct 1975 Hamburg)
no issue
II) **Princess Irene** Olga Adelheid **of Schleswig-Holstein-Sonderburg-Glücksburg** (*11 Oct 1946 Flensborg)
III) **Princess Margarethe** Friederike Luise **of Schleswig-Holstein-Sonderburg-Glücksburg** (*10 Feb 1948 Flensborg)
IV) **Princess Sibylla** Ursula Ortrud **of Schleswig-Holstein-Sonderburg-Glücksburg** (*11 Sep 1955 Flensborg)
= 24 (civil) & 25 (rel.) Oct 1980 Glücksburg; **Dieter Franz** (*26 Mar 1950 Kirchberg) son of Friedrich Franz & Renate Gerstein
A) **Friedrich** Emil **Franz** (*22 Apr 1981 Tübingen)
B) **Johann** Elisa **Franz** (*10 Mar 1983 Tübingen)
C) **Philipp** Georg **Franz** (*1 Apr 1986 Eckernförde)
3. **Duchess Cecilie** Auguste Marie **of Mecklenburg** (20 Sep 1886 Schwerin – 6 May 1954 Bad Kissingen)
= 6 Jun 1905 Berlin; **Crown Prince** Friedrich **Wilhelm** Viktor August Ernst **of Prussia** (6 May 1882 Marmorpalais – 20 Jul 1951 Hechingen) son of Wilhelm II, German Emperor & Princess Auguste Viktoria of Schleswig-Holstein-Sonderburg-Augustenburg; suc. father as Head of the House 4 Jun 1941
a. **Prince Wilhelm** Friedrich Franz Joseph Christian Olaf **of Prussia** (4 Jul 1906 Marmorpalais – 26 May 1940 Nivelles) killed in action
= 3 Jun 1933 Bonn; **Dorothea von Salviati** (10 Sep 1907 Bonn – 7 May 1972 Bonn-Bad Godesburg) daughter of Alexander von Salviati & Ella Crasemann

I) **Princess Felicitas** Cecilie Alexandrine Helene Dorothea **of Prussia** (7 Jun 1934 Bonn - 1 Aug 2009 Wohltorf)
=1 12 Sep 1958 Bonn (dv.1972); **Dinnies** Karl Friedrich **von der Osten** (*21 May 1929 Koslin) son of Karl August von der Osten & Wilhelmine von Boddion
=2 27 Oct 1972 Aumuhl; **Jörg** Hartwig **von Nostitz-Wallwitz** (*26 Sep 1937 Verden) son of Gustav-Adolf von Nostitz-Wallwitz & Renate Rachals
issue of 1st:
A) **Friederike** Thyra Marian Wilhelmine Dorothea **von der Osten** (*14 Jul 1959 Bad Bodesburg)
= 17 Aug 1984 Ismaning (civil) & 1 Sep 1984 Aumuhle (rel.); **Bernhard** Ernst Diester **von Reiche** (*26 Apr 1956 Celle) son of Hans von Reiche & Astrid-Eleonore Gartner
1) **Felicitas** Catherine Malina Johann **von Reiche** (*28 Oct 1986 Munich)
2) **Victoria** Cecilie Alexandra Josephine **von Reiche** (*19 Jan 1989 Munich)
3) **Donata** Friederike Diana Sophie **von Reiche** (*28 Jan 1992 Munich)
B) **Dinnies-Wilhelm** Karl Alexander **von der Osten** (15 Feb 1962 Bad Godesburg – 28 Jun 1989 Cologne)
C) **Hubertus** Christoph Joachim Friedrich **von der Osten** (*5 May 1964 Hamburg)
D) **Cecilie** Felicitas Katherina Sophie **von der Osten** (*23 Mar 1967 Hamburg)
= 23 Jul 1997 Lujenburg (civil) & 26 Jul 1997 Panker (rel.) (dv.2012); **Ole** Hugo **Marxen** (*10 Mar 1964 Hamburg) son of Peter Marxen & … Maak
1) **Julius** Dinnie Peter Ole **Marxen** (*17 Oct 1998 Eutin)
2) **Victor** August Hubertus Camillo **Marxen** (*14 Apr 2002 Eutin)
issue of 2nd:
E) **Diana** Renata Friederike **von Nostitz-Wallwitz** (*7 Oct 1974 Hamburg)
= 3 May 2002 Wohltorf (civil) & 13 Jul 2002 Bad Laustatt (civil); **Baron Carl-Jan von der Göltz** (*4 Aug

1968 Mannheim) son of Baron Erik von der Göltz & Barbara Vermehren
no issue

II) **Princess Christa** Friederike Alexandrine Viktoria **of Prussia** (*31 Oct 1936 Schloss Klein-Obisch)
= 24 Mar 1960 Wahlscheid (civil) & Auel (rel.); **Peter** Paul Eduard Maria Clemens Maximilian Franz von Assisi **Liebes** (18 Jan 1926 Munich – 15 May 1967 Bonn) son of Martin Liebes & Countess Clementine von Montgelas
no issue

b. **Louis Ferdinand** Viktor Eduard Albert Michael Hubertus, **Prince of Prussia** (9 Nov 1907 Marmorpalais – 25 Sep 1994 Bremen) suc. father 1951
= 2 May 1938 Potsdam (civil) & 4 May 1938 Haus Doorn (rel.); ♦**Grand Duchess Kira** Kirillovna **of Russia** (9 May 1909 Paris – 8 Sep 1967 St. Briac) daughter of Grand Duke Cyril of Russia & Princess Victoria Melita of Great Britain

I) **Prince** Louis Ferdinand **Friedrich Wilhelm** Hubertus Michael Kirill **of Prussia** (9 Feb 1939 Berlin – 29 Sep 2015 Berlin) barred from succession by father due to unapproved marriage
=1 (morg.) 22 Aug 1967 Plon (dv.1975); **Waltraut Freytag** (14 Apr 1940 Kiel – 2010) daughter of Alois Waltraut & Annemarie Rolfs
=2 (morg.) 23 Apr 1976 Bisingen (civil) & 24 Apr 1976 Burg Hohenzollern (rel) (dv.2004); **Ehrengard** Insea Elisabeth **von Reden** (*7 Jun 1943 Berlin) daughter of Günther von Reden & Ehrengard von Hülsen
=3 (morg.) 23 Mar 2004 Berlin; **Sibylle Kretschmer** (*23 Mar 1952 Berlin)
issue of 1st:

A) **Philipp** Kirill Friedrich Wilhelm Moritz Boris Tanko **Prinz von Preussen** (*23 Apr 1968 Eutin)
= 25 Jun 1994 Kiel (civil) & 2 Jul 1994 Köppelsberg (rel); **Anna** Christine **Soltau** (*2 Apr 1968 Preetz) daughter of Eggert Soltau & Annegret Graupner

1) **Paul Wilhelm** Philipp Friedrich Aloysius Johannes Mose **Prinz von Preussen** (*4 Oct 1995 Eutin)

2) **Marie Luise** Anne Philippa Helene Julie Margarethe Elisabeth **Prinzessin von Preussen** (*12 Mar 1997 Eutin)

3) **Elisabeth** Christine Philine Cecilie Annegret Salome Maria **Prinzessin von Preussen** (*16 Dec 1998 Eutin)

4) **Anna** Sophie Phila Wilhelmine Amélie Elisabeth Maria **Prinzessin von Preussen** (*26 Mar 2001 Eutin)

5) **Johanna** Amalie Kira Philippa Rose Elisabeth Maria **Prinzessin von Preussen** (*10 Sep 2002 Eutin)

6) **Thimotheus** Friedrich **Prinz von Preussen** (*9 Jun 2005 Plon)

issue of 2nd (none by 3rd):

B) **Friedrich Wilhelm** Louis Ferdinand Kirill **Prinz von Preussen** (*16 Aug 1979 Berlin)
= 30 Apr 2009 Wiesbaden; **Baroness Anna Christine von Salza und Lichenau** (*7 Aug 1981 Frankfurt) daughter of Baron Hermann von Salza und Lichtenau & Ulrike Prescher

1) **Friedrich Wilhelm Prinz von Preussen** (*2012)

C) **Viktoria Luise** Kira Ehrengard **Prinzessin von Preussen** (*2 May 1982 Berlin)
= 19 Sep (civil) & 5 Oct (rel.) 2017 Amorbach; ♦**Hereditary Prince Ferdinand** Heinrich Emich Christian Karl **of Leiningen** (*8 Aug 1982 Frankfurt) son of Andreas, Prince of Leiningen & Princess Alexandra of Hanover
no issue

D) **Joachim** Albrecht Bernhard Christian Ernst **Prinz von Preussen** (*26 Jun 1984 Berlin)

II) **Prince** Wilhelm Friedrich **Michael** Louis Ferdinand Friedrich Franz Wladimir **of Prussia** (22 Mar 1940 Berlin – 3 Apr 2014 Sindelfingen) barred from succession by father due to unapproved marriage
=1 (morg.) 23 Sep 1966 Düsseldorf (civil) & 25 Sep 1966 Bremen (rel) (dv.1982); **Jutta Jörn** (*27 Jan 1943 Gissen) daughter of Otto Jörn & Ernestine Prubenau

=2 (morg.) 23 Jun 1982 Bad Soden; **Brigitte Dallwitz-Wegner** (17 Sep 1939 Kitzbuhel – 14 Oct 2016) daughter of Hans Viktor Dallwitz-Wegner & Elisabeth Heimann
issue of 1st (none by 2nd):

A) **Micaela** Maria **Prinzessin von Preussen** (*5 Mar 1967 Berlin)
= 14 Feb 2000 Frankfurt; **Jürgen Wessolly** (*2 Feb 1961 Cologne)

1) **Maximilian Prinz von Preussen** (*17 Mar 2000 Stuttgart)

2) **Marie Charlotte Prinzessin von Preussen** (*15 Dec 2001 Stuttgart)

B) **Nataly** Alexandra Caroline **Prinzessin von Preussen** (*13 Jan 1970 Frankfurt)

III) **Princess Marie Cecilie** Kira Viktoria Louise **of Prussia** (*28 May 1942 Cadinen)
= 3 (civil) & 4 (rel) Dec 1965 Berlin (dv.1989); **Duke Friedrich August** Wilhelm Christian Ernst **of Oldenburg** (*11 Jan 1936 Rastede) son of Hereditary Grand Duke Nikolaus of Oldenburg & Princess Helene of Waldeck and Pyrmont; =2nd Countess Donata zu Castell-Rüdenhausen (widow of ♦Prince Louis Ferdinand of Prussia)

A) **Duke Paul-Wladimir** Nikolaus Louis-Ferdinand Peter Max Karl-Emich **of Oldenburg** (*16 Aug 1969 Lübeck)
= 20 Jan 2001 Bronnbach; **Maria del Pilar Méndez de Vigo y de Löwenstein** (*20 Oct 1970 Madrid) daughter of Jaime Méndez de Vigo & Princess Monika of Löwenstein-Wertheim-Rosenberg

1) **Duke Kirill** Friedrich August Jaime Cristobal Hermann Antonius Vincenz Josef Maria **of Oldenburg** (*13 Jun 2002 Berlin)

2) **Duke Carlos** Jakobus Leo Wilfreid Josef Maria **of Oldenburg** (*19 Apr 2004 Eutin)

3) **Duke Paul** Marie **of Oldenburg** (*8 Sep 2005)

4) **Duchess Maria Assunta of Oldenburg** (*21 Mar 2007)

5) **Duke Louis Ferdinand of Oldenburg** (*2012)

B) **Duchess Rixa** Marie-Alix Kira Altburg **of Oldenburg**

(*17 Sep 1970 Lübeck)
= 13 Oct 2012 Hamburg; **Stephen Sanders** (*27 Mar 1964)

C) **Duchess Bibiane** Maria Alexandra Gertrud **of Oldenburg** (*24 Jun 1974 Oldenburg)
= 22 May 2004 Merano; **Peter Dorner** (*19 Feb 1972 Wasserburg)
1) **Xenia Dorner** (*2006)
2) **Rixa** Louise Cecilie **Dorner** (*2009)
3) **Max** Wladimir **Dorner** (*2011)

IV) **Princess Kira** Auguste Viktoria Friederike **of Prussia** (27 Jun 1943 Cadinen – 10 Jan 2004 Berlin)
= 10 Sep 1973 Munich (civil) & 11 Sep 1973 Felizenzell (rel) (dv.1984); **Thomas** Frank **Liepsner** (*20 Jan 1945 St. Louis, Missouri) son of Robert Liepsner & Lorene Wonsetler

A) **Kira** Marina **Liepsner** (*22 Jan 1977 Munich)
= 5 May 2005 Berlin; **Andreas** Felix Paul **von Bismarck** (*31 Jan 1979 Munich) son of Hans von Bismarck & Cornelie von Schwerin
1) **Luise** Kira Pauline **von Bismarck** (*17 Feb 2002 Berlin)
2) **Sophie von Bismarck** (*2007)

V) **Prince Louis Ferdinand** Oskar Christian **of Prussia** (*25 Aug 1944 Golzow – 11 Jul 1977 Bremen)
= 24 May 1975 Rudenhausen; **Countess Donata** Emma **zu Castell-Rüdenhausen** (*20 Jun 1950 Rudenhausen) daughter of Siegfried, Count zu Castell-Rüdenhausen & Countess Irene zu Solms-Laubach; =2nd Duke Friedrich August of Oldenburg (ex-husband of ♦Princess Marie Cecilie of Prussia, above)

A) **Georg Friedrich** Ferdinand, **Prince of Prussia** (*10 Jun 1976 Bremen) suc. grandfather 1994
= 25 (civil) & 27 (rel.) Aug 2011 Potsdam; **Princess Sophie** Johanna Maria **of Isenburg** (*7 Mar 1978 Frankfurt) daughter of Franz, Prince of Isenburg & Countess Elisabeth von Saurma
1) **Prince Carl Friedrich of Prussia** (*20 Jan 2013

Bremen) (twin)

2) **Prince Louis Ferdinand ofPrussia** (*20 Jan 2013 Bremen) (twin)

3) **Princess Emma** Marie **of Prussia** (*2 Apr 2015 Bremen)

4) **Prince Heinrich** Albert Johann Georg **of Prussia** (*17 Nov 2016 Bremen)

B) **Princess Cornelie-Cecilie** Viktoria Irene **of Prussia** (*ph.30 Jan 1978 Bremen)

VI) **Prince Christian Sigismund** Louis Ferdinand Killian **of Prussia** (14 Mar 1946 Bad Kissingen)

= 29 Sep 1984 Damp; **Countess Nina** Helene Lydia Alexandra **zu Reventlow** (*13 Mar 1954 Kiel) daughter of Count Ludwig zu Reventlow & Nina Pryadkina

A) **Prince Christian Ludwig** Michael Friedrich Ferdinand **of Prussia** (*16 May 1986 Bremen)

B) **Princess Irina** Maria Nina Kira **of Prussia** (*4 Jul 1988 Bremen)

Prince Christian Sigismund has additional issue by **Christiane** Rose **GrandMontagne** (*17 Mar 1944 Rabat, Morocco) daughter of Daniel GrandMontagne & Anna Elisabeth Brenner; sometime wife of ♦Count Jan Bernadotte af Wisborg:

C) **Isabelle** Alexandra **GrandMontagne-Prinzessin von Preussen** (*18 Sep 1969 Sarreguemine)

VII) **Princess Xenia** Sophie Charlotte Cecilie **of Prussia** (9 Dec 1949 Bremen – 18 Jan 1992 Selendorf)

= 26 (civil) & 27 (rel) Jan 1973 Bremen (dv.1978); **Per-Edvard Lithander** (10 Sep 1945 Vasa – 9 May 2010 Gothenborg) son of Patrik Lithander & Kerstin Aurell

A) **Patrick** Edvard Christian **Lithander** (*25 Jun 1973 Bremen)

= 16 Oct 2003 Berlin (civil) & 18 Oct 2003 Kleinmachnow (rel); **Maja Flechtner** (*29 Apr 1973 Essen) daughter of Jürgen Flechtner & Bernhardine von Arnim

1) **Pius Lithander** (*1 Jan 2005 Berlin)

2) **Hugo Lithander** (*2 Aug 2006 Munich)

3) **Karl Lithander** (*26 Mar 2008 Munich)
4) **Merle Lithander** (*25 Feb 2010 Munich)
B) Wilhelm **Sebastian Lithander** (*21 Nov 1974 Bremen) = 29 May 2009 Hamburg; **Tiana Bischoff** (*1973)
1) **Steen** Edvard **Lithander** (*Feb 2010)
2) **Ebba** Viktoria **Lithander** (*13 May 2012 Hamburg)

c. **Prince Hubertus** Karl Wilhelm **of Prussia** (30 Sep 1909 Marmorpalais – 8 Apr 1950 Windhoek, South Africa)
=1 29 Jan 1941 Oels (dv.1943); **Baroness Marie-Anna** Sibylla Margaretha **von Humboldt-Dachroeden** (9 Jul 1916 Bromberg – 24 Sep 2003 Hamburg) daughter of Baron Alexander von Humboldt-Rachroeden & Katharina Daum; she =2nd Constantin Hahm
=2 5 Jun 1943 Schloss Prillwitz; **Princess Magdalene** Pauline **Reuss** (20 Aug 1920 Leipzig – 10 Oct 2009) daughter of Prince Heinrich XXXVI Reuss & Princess Hermine of Schönburg-Waldenburg
issue of 2nd (none by 1st):

I) **Princess Anastasia** Victoria Cecilia Hermine **of Prussia** (*14 Feb 1944 Brieg)
= 8 Oct 1965 Bronnbach (civil) & 8 Nov 1965 Erbach (rel.); **Alois Konstantin** Karl Eduard Joseph Johann Konrad Antonius Gerhard Georg Bernhard Pius Eusebius Maria, **Prince of Löwenstein-Wertheim-Rosenberg** (*16 Feb 1941 Würzburg) son of Karl, Prince of Löwenstein-Wertheim-Rosenberg & Carolina dei conti Rignon; suc. father 23 Aug 1990

A) **Hereditary Prince Carl Friedrich** Hubertus Georg Eduardo Paolo Nicolo Franz Alois Ignatius Hieronymous Maria **of Löwenstein-Wertheim-Rosenberg** (30 Sep 1966 Frankfurt – 24 Apr 2010)
= 8 Aug 1998 Brenken; **Baroness Stephanie** Sophie Maria Coletta **von und zu Brenken** (*21 Apr 1970 Paderborn) daughter of Baron Georg von und zu Brenken & Countess Rosa von Nostitz-Rieneck

1) **Princess Augustina** Sophia Carolina Dominique Anastasia Rosa Magdalene Kiliana Margarethe Maria **of Löwenstein-Wertheim-Rosenberg** (*8 Jul 1999

Oslo)

2) **Hereditary Prince Nicodemus** Hieronymous Alois Georg Hubertus Mario Hugo Eusebius Maria **of Löwenstein-Wertheim-Rosenberg** (*2 Aug 2001 Oslo)

3) **Prince Laurentius** Christophorus Alois Georg Andreas Benediktus Carl Hubertus Fatima Maria **of Löwenstein-Wertheim-Rosenberg** (*13 Feb 2006 Frankfurt)

4) **Princess Kiliana of Löwenstein-Wertheim-Freudenburg** (*23 May 2008)

B) **Prince Hubertus** Maximilian Gabriel Louis Franz Constantin Dominik Wunibald Maria **of Löwenstein-Wertheim-Rosenberg** (*18 Dec 1968 Frankfurt)
= 17 (civil) & 18 (rel) Sep 2010 Alsfeld; **Baroness Iris** Beatrice **von Dörnberg** (*3 May 1969 Göttingen) daughter of Baron Jürgen von Dörnberg & Beatrix von Bischoffhausen
no issue

C) **Princess Christina** Maria Johanna Caroline Magdalene Osy Cecilie Hermine Isidora Anastasia **of Löwenstein-Wertheim-Rosenberg** (*4 Apr 1974 Frankfurt)
= 1 Jun 2002 Miltenberg (civil) & 5 Oct 2002 Kleinheubach (rel); **Guido von Rohr** (*27 Sep 1969 Hanover) son of Gisilot von Rohr & Sylvia Fischer-Bühring

1) **Antonius** Gisilot Alois Christian Kajetan Maria **von Rohr** (*7 Aug 2003 London)

2) **Constantin von Rohr** (*8 Jun 2007 London)

3) **Cecilia** Marie **von Rohr** (*6 Oct 2008 London) (twin)

4) **Maria** Sylvia **von Rohr** (*6 Oct 2008 London) (twin)

D) **Prince Dominik** Wilhelm Christian Nikolaus Sturmius Antonius Charles Benedikt Felix Maria **of Löwenstein-Wertheim-Rosenberg** (*7 Mar 1983 Frankfurt)
= 12 Oct 2012; **Countess Olga** Graziella **zu Castell-Rüdenhausen** (*31 Jan 1987 Würzburg) daughter of Johann Friedrich, Count zu Castell-Rüdenhaausen & Countess Maria von Schönborn-Wiesentheid

1) **Prince Casimir** Aloys **of Löwensein-Wertheim-Rosenberg** (*2015)

II) **Princess Marie-Christine of Prussia** (18 Jul 1947 Gelnhausen – 29 May 1966 Giessen) killed in a car crash

d. **Prince Friedrich** Georg Wilhelm Christoph **of Prussia** (19 Dec 1911 Berlin – 20 Apr 1966 Reinhartshausen)
= 30 Jul 1945 Little Hadham, Hertfordshire; **Lady Brigid Guinness** (30 Jul 1920 London – 8 Mar 1995 Albury) daughter of Rupert Guinness, 2nd Earl of Iveagh & Lady Gwendolen Onslow; =2nd Anthony Ness

I) **Prince** Friedrich **Nicholas of Prussia** (*3 May 1946 London)
= (morg.) 27 Feb 1980 London (dv.2005); **Hon. Victoria** Lucinda **Mancroft** (*7 Mar 1952 London) daughter of Stormont Mancroft, 2nd Baron Mancroft & Diana Lloyd

A) **Beatrice** Victoria **von Preussen** (*10 Feb 1981 London)

B) **Florence** Jessica **von Preussen** (*28 Jul 1983 London)
= 10 May 2014 East Cpker, Som.; **Hon. James** Henry Timothy **Tollemache** (*1980) son of Timothy Tollemache, 5th Baron Tollemache & Alexandra Meynell

1) **Silvie** Beatrice Selina **Tollemache** (*2 Mar 2016 London)

C) Victoria **Augusta** Lily **von Preussen** (*15 Dec 1986 London) (twin)
= 19 Sep 2015; **Caspar** William **Helmore** (*26 Jan 1987 London) son of Charles Helmore & Rachel Aykroyd
no issue

D) **Frederick** Nicholas Stormont **von Preussen** (*15 Dec 1986 London)

II) **Prince** William **Andrew of Prussia** (*14 Nov 1948 London)
= (morg.) 2 Jan 1979 London; **Alexandra Blahova** (*28 Dec 1947 Brno) daughter of Frantisek Blahov & Vlasta Dokrpilova; =1st Tom Aisbeth

A) **Tatiana** Brigid Honor **von Preussen** (*16 Oct 1980 London)
= 28 Jun 2014 Thorpe Hall, Suffolk; **Philip** Alan **Womack** (*1981 Chichester) son of Richard Womack &

Marie Obradovic

1) **Arthur** Frederick Richard **Womack von Preussen** (*21 Nov 2015)

B) **Frederick** Alexander **von Preussen** (*15 Nov 1984 London)

III) **Princess Victoria** Marina Cecilie **of Prussia** (*22 Feb 1952 London)
= 3 May 1976 Albury; **Philippe** Alphonse **Achache** (*25 Mar 1948 Toulouse) son of Jean Achache & Jacqueline Andrieu

A) **George** Jean **Achache** (*8 Jun 1980 London)

B) **Francis** Maximilian Frederick **Achache** (*30 Apr 1982 London)

IV) **Prince Rupert** Alexander Friedrich **of Prussia** (*28 Apr 1955 London) (twin)
= (morg.) 8 Jan 1982 London; **Ziba Rastigar Javaheri** (*12 Dec 1954 Teheran) daughter of Mortez Rastigar Javaheri & Rabeeh Baghati Kermani

A) **Brigid** Elisabeth Soraya **von Preussen** (*24 Dec 1983 London)

B) **Astrid** Katherine Rabeeh **von Preussen** (*16 Apr 1985 London)

V) **Princess Antonia** Elizabeth Brigid Luise **of Prussia** (*28 Apr 1955 London) (twin)
= 3 Feb 1977 London; Arthur **Charles** Valerian **Wellesley, 9th Duke of Wellington**, etc. (*19 Aug 1945 Windsor) son of Arthur Wellesley, 8th Duke of Wellington & Diana McConnel; suc. father 31 Dec 2014

A) **Arthur** Gerald, **Marquess of Douro** (*31 Jan 1978 London)
= 4 Jun 2005 Barbados; **Jemma** Madeleine **Kidd** (*20 Sep 1974 Guilford) daughter of John Kidd & Wendy Hodge

1) **Lady Mae Madeleine Wellesley** (*4 Jan 2010 London) (twin)

2) **Arthur** Darcy, **Earl of Mornington** (*4 Jan 2010 London) (twin)

3) **Lord Alfred Wellesley** (*10 Dec 2014)

B) **Lady Honor** Victoria **Wellesley** (*25 Oct 1979 London)
= 3 Jul 2004 Stratfield Saye; **Hon. Orlando** William **Montagu** (*16 Jan 1971) son of John Montagu, 11th Earl of Sandwich & Caroline Hayman; =1st Laura Roundell
1) **Walter** Frederick **Montagu** (*3 Dec 2005)
2) **Nancy** Jemima **Montagu** (*Jan 2007)
C) **Lady Mary** Louise **Wellesley** (*16 Dec 1986 London)
D) **Lady Charlotte** Anne **Wellesley** (*8 Oct 1990 London)
= 2016; **Alejandro Santo Domingo** (*13 Feb 1977 New York City) son of Julio Santo Domingo & Beatriz Pumarejo de Vengoechea.
1) due late 2017
E) **Lord Frederick** Charles **Wellesley** (*30 Sep 1992 London)
e. **Princess Alexandrine** Irene **of Prussia** (7 Apr 1915 Berlin – 2 Oct 1980 Starnberg)
f. **Princess Cecilie** Viktoria Anastasia Zita Thyra Adelheid **of Prussia** (5 Sep 1917 Potsdam – 21 Apr 1975 Konigstein)
= 21 Jun 1949 Burg Hohenzollern; **Clyde** Kenneth **Harris** (18 Apr 1918 Maud, Oklahoma – 2 Mar 1958 Amarillo, Texas) son of Bert Harris & Aurora Vandervere
I) **Kira** Alexandrine Brigid Cecilie Ingrid **Harris** (*20 Oct 1954 Amarillo)
= 22 May 1952 Santa Fe, New Mexico (dv.1993); John **Mitchell Johnson** (*12 May 1951 Dallas, Texas) son of Edward Johnson & Blanche Dabney
A) **Philip** Louis **Johnson** (*18 Oct 1985 Ft. Worth, Texas)

Grand Duchess Anastasia had additional issue by **Vladimir** Alexandrovich **Paltov** (1874 – 1944 Menton) son of Alexander Paltov & Catherina Vorobieva:

4. **Alexis Louis de Wenden** (23 Dec 1902 Nice – 7 Jul 1976 Paris)
= 25 Jan 1929 Paris; **Paulette** Marie Constance Henriette Félicie **Seux** (3 Jan 1908 Lyon – 19 Nov 1975 Villejuif) daughter of George Seux & Lucile Poulon
a. **Xenia** Anastasie Germaine **Louis de Wenden** (*26 Feb 1930 Paris)
= 31 May 1952 Paris; **Alain Brulé** (*24 Aug 1925 Paris) son of Alexandre Brulé & Marthe Gault

I) **Christophe Brulé** (*15 Apr 1955 Paris)
= 25 Aug 2000 Roussillon; **Victoria Encio** (*21 Dec 1961 Philippines) daughter of Joachim Encio & Marguerita Empig
A) **Philippine Brulé** (*9 Jul 1998 Paris)
II) **Nicolas Brulé** (*3 Nov 1957 Paris)
= 31 May 1978 Paris; **Pascale Chambolle Tounon** (*Sep 1959 Anvers) daughter of Claude Chambolle Tournon & Beatrice Hickson
A) **Alexia Brulé** (*24 Nov 1979 Costa Rica)
B) **Priscilla Brulé** (*3 Jan 1982 Costa Rica)
= 15 May 2010 Santa Domingo de Heredia; **Eisen Rios** (…):
1) **Isabella Brulé Rios** (*20 Sep 2000 Costa Rica)
2) a child (*2011)
C) **Nathalia Brulé** (7 May 1983 Costa Rica – 4 Jun1985 Costa Rica)
III) **Cyril Brulé** (*2 Aug 1959 Paris)
= 31 May 1978 Paris; **Isabelle Moltzer** (*1 Jul 1966 Boulogne) Kim-Georges Moltzer & Odile de Bailleul
A) **Olympia Brulé** (*10 Sep 2002 Paris)
IV) **Gaspard** Alexandre **Brulé** (*17 Apr 1962 Paris)
= 19 Aug 1989; **Sophie André** (*17 Dec 1963 Ambilly) daughter of Eric André & Monique Chiaro
A) **Arthur Brulé** (*30 Aug 1990 Paris)
B) **Alix Brulé** (*3 Dec 1992 Paris)
C) **Josephine Brulé** (*26 Oct 1998 Paris)
b. **Anastasia** Alexandrine Paule **Louis de Wenden** (10 Jan 1935 Paris – 15 Jul 1995 Paris)
had issue by…:
I) **Dominique Louis de Wenden** (*3 Mar 1954 Sannois)
= 5 Jul 1997 Isenay; **Isabelle de la Forest d'Armaille** (*11 Oct 1965 Paris) daughter of Yves de la Forest, Vicomte d'Armaille & Règine Braun
A) **Anastasia Louis de Wenden** (*7 May 1998 Paris)
B) **Dmitri Louis de Wenden** (*24 Apr 2003 Paris)
C. **Grand Duke Michael** Mikhailovich **of Russia** (16 Nov 1861 Peterhof – 26 Apr 1929 London)

= (morg.) 26 Feb 1891 San Remo; **Countess Sofia** Nikolaievna **von Merenberg** (cr. **Countess de Torby**) (1 Jun 1868 Geneva – 14 Sep 1927 London) daughter of Prince Nikolaus of Nassau & Natalia Pushkina, Countess von Merenberg; Countess de Torby 1891 by the Grand Duke of Luxembourg

1. **Countess Anastasia** Mikhailovna **de Torby** (9 Sep 1892 Wiesbaden – 7 Dec 1977 London)
   = 17 Jul 1917 London; **Sir Harold** Augustus **Wernher, 3rd Baronet** (16 Jan 1893 London – 30 Jun 1973 Luton Hoo) son of Sir Julius Wernher, 1st Baronet & Alice Mankiewicz; suc. brother 1948; upon his death the Baronetcy became extinct
   a. **Georg** Michael Alexander **Wernher** (22 Aug 1918 Edinburgh – 4 Dec 1942 Beja, North Africa) killed in action
   b. **Georgina Wernher** (17 Oct 1919 Edinburgh – 28 Apr 2011 London)
      =1 10 Oct 1944 London; **Harold** Pedro **Phillips** (6 Nov 1909 London – 27 Oct 1980 Alford) son of Joseph Phillips & Mary-Mercedes Bryce
      =2 Dec 1992 London; **Sir George** Arnold Ford **Kennard, 3rd Baronet** (27 Apr 1915 – 13 Dec 1999 London) son of Sir Coleridge Kennard, 1st Baronet & Dorothy Barclay; suc. brother, Sir Lawrence, 1967; =1st Cecilia Maunsell, =2nd Molly Wylie, and =3rd Nicola Carew
      issue of 1st (none by 2nd):
      I) **Alexandra** Anastasia **Phillips** (*27 Feb 1946 Tucson, Arizona)
         = 27 Oct 1966 London; **James Hamilton, 5th Duke of Abercorn** etc. (*4 Jul 1934 London) son of James Edward Hamilton, 4th Duke of Abercorn & Lady Mary Crichton; suc. father 4 Jun 1979
         A) **James** Harold Charles, **Marquess of Hamilton** (*19 Aug 1969 London)
            = 7 May 2004 London; **Tanya Nation** (*30 Apr 1971 Paris)
            1) **James** Alfred Nicholas, **Viscount Strabane** (*30 Oct 2005)
            2) **Lord Claud** Douglas Harold **Hamilton** (*12 Dec 2007)

B) **Lady Sophia** Alexandra **Hamilton** (*8 Jun 1973 London)
=1 7 Sep 2002 London (dv.2006); **Anthony** William Vivian **Lloyd** (*12 Sep 1966 Guildford, Surrey)
=2 2013; **Hashem Arouzi** (...) son of Alireza Arouzi & Firouzeh Rastegar
issue of 2nd (none by 1st):
1) **Caspian Arouzi** (*2015) (twin)
2) **Soraya Arouzi** (*2015) (twin)

C) **Lord Nicholas** Edward Carl **Hamilton** (*5 Jul 1979 Omagh)
= 30 Aug 2009 New York; **Tatiana Kronberg** (*1977 St. Petersburg) daughter of Evgeni Kronberg & Irina Grichtchenko
1) **Valentina** Neva **Hamilton** (*19 Dec 2010 New York)

II) **Nicholas** Harold **Phillips** (23 Aug 1947 London – 1 Mar 1991 Luton Hoo)
= 18 Oct 1975 Salzburg; **Countess** Marie **Lucie Czernin von und zu Chudenitz** (*16 May 1941 Graz) daughter of Count Paul Czernin von und zu Chudenitz & Baroness Elisabeth von Gudenus
A) **Charlotte** Sonia Marie **Phillips** (*12 Dec 1976 Paris)
B) **Edward** Paul **Phillips** (*2 Dec 1981 London)
= 17 Sep 2011; **Marina** Frances Elizabeth **Wilson** (*Jul 1984) daughter of John Wilson & Penelope Mumford
issue ?

III) **Fiona** Mercedes **Phillips** (*30 Mar 1951 London)
= 7 Jul 1971 London; **James** Comyn Amherst **Burnett of Leys** (*24 Jul 1951 Aberdeen) son of Hon. Henry Cecil & Elizabeth Burnett of Leys
A) **Alexander** James Amherst **Burnett of Leys** (*30 Jul 1973 Aberdeen)
= 9 Jul 2005 Aberdeenshire; **Lavinia** Margaret **Cox** (…)
1) **Amaryllis** Susan Rohays **Burnett** (*24 Nov 2006)
2) **Thomas** Henry Amherst **Burnett** (*11 Feb 2008)
3) **Hester** Zia Elizabeth **Burnett** (*11 Apr 2009)
B) **Eliza** Amelia **Burnett** (*13 Jun 1977 Aberdeen)
has issue by **Azzy Asghar**:

1) **Serena** Farzana Georgina **Asghar** (*7 Sep 2013 London)
2) **Theodore** Zachary Pasha **Asghar** (*13 Jul 2016 London)

C) **Victor** Cecil Tobias **Burnett** (*1 Oct of 1982 Aberdeen)

IV) **Marita** Georgina **Phillips** (*28 May 1954 London)
=1 3 Nov 1982 London; **Randall Crawley** (14 Jul 1950 London – 10 Sep 1988 Venaria) killed in a plane crash; son of Aidan Crawley & Virginia Cowles
=2 2006; **Andrew** Stephen Bower **Knight** (*1 Nov 1939) he =1st Victoria Brittain; =2nd Sabilah Rumani Malik
issue of 1st (none by 2nd):
A) **Aidan** Harold Winston **Crawley** (*22 Oct 1983 London)
B) **Cosima** Georgina **Crawley** (*31 May 1985 London)
C) **Galen** Randall George **Crawley** (*13 Nov 1988)

V) **Natalia** Ayesha **Phillips** (*8 May 1959 London)
= 7 Oct 1978 London; **Gerald** Cavendish **Grosvenor, 6th Duke of Westminster** etc. (22 Dec 1951 Omagh – 9 Aug 2016 London) son of Robert Grosvenor, 5th Duke of Westminster & Hon. Viola Lyttleton; suc. father 19 Feb 1979

A) **Lady Tamara** Katherine **Grosvenor** (*20 Dec 1979 London)
= 6 Nov 2004 Chester; **Edward** Bernard Charles **van Cutsem** (*6 Jun 1973 London) son of Hugh van Cutsem & Emilie Quarles van Ufford
1) **Jake van Cutsem** (*21 May 2009 London)
2) **Louis** Hugh Lupus **van Cutsem** (*17 Apr 2012 London)
3) **Isla van Cutsem** (*Dec 2015)

B) **Lady Edwina** Louise **Grosvenor** (*4 Nov 1981 London)
= 27 Nov 2010 Liverpool; **Daniel** Robert **Snow** (*3 Dec 1978 London) son of Peter Snow & Ann Elizabeth Macmillan
a) **Zia Snow** (*13 Oct 2011 London)
b) **Wolf** Robert **Snow** (*9 Sep 2014 London)
c) **Orla Snow** (*Dec 2015)

C) **Hugh** Richard Louis **Grosvenor, 7th Duke of Westminster**, etc. (*29 Jan 1991 London) suc. father 2016

D) **Lady Viola** Georgina **Grosvenor** (*12 Oct 1992 London)

c. **Myra** Alice **Wernher** (*8 Mar 1925 Edinburgh)
= 5 Nov 1946 London; **Sir David** Henry **Butter, KCVO** (18 Mar 1920 London – 29 May 2010) son of Charles Butter & Margarete Clark

I) **Sandra** Elizabeth Zia **Butter** (*26 Jul 1948 London)
= 16 Mar 1983 London; **William** David **Morrison** (*19 Aug 1940 Philadelphia) son of Max Morrison & Mary Chase

A) **Charles** Nicholas **Morrison** (*12 Dec 1985 London)

B) **Sophie** Natasha **Morrison** (*23 Oct 1987 London)

II) **Marilyn** Davina **Butter** (*23 Mar 1950 London)
= 3 Oct 1973 London; **James** Hubert **Ramsay, 17th Earl of Dalhousie** etc. (*17 Jan 1948 London) son of Simon Ramsay, 16th Earl of Dalhousie & Margaret Stirling-Maxwell; suc. father 15 Jul 1999

A) **Lady Lorna** Theresa **Ramsay** (*6 Feb 1975 London)
= 1 Jul 2006 Brechin, Angus; **Fergus Lefebvre** (*4 Nov 1971 Coonamble, NSW, Australia) son of Paul Lefebvre

1) **Archie** James **Lefebvre** (*26 Apr 2007 Sydney)

2) **Henry** Paul **Lefebvre** (*18 Sep 2008 Sydney)

3) **Ned** Fergus **Lefebvre** (*2 May 2011 Sydney)

B) **Lady Alice** Magdalene **Ramsay** (*10 Aug 1977 London)

C) **Simon** David, **Lord Ramsay** (*18 Apr 1981 London)
= 24 Sep 2016; **Kaitlin** Marie **Kubinsky** (*2 May 1985 Ohio) daughter of John Kubinsky & Sheila Torpey

1) **Hon. William** Fox **Ramsay** (*25 Aug 2017)

III) **Rohays** Georgina **Butter** (*9 May 1952 London)
= 7 May 1988 Dunkeld; **Prince Alexander** Peter **Galitzine** (*6 Sep 1945 Marlow, Buckinghamshire) son of Prince George Galitzine & Baroness Anne Marie von Slaten

A) **Princess Sasha** Alice Natalia **Galitzine** (*10 Feb 1989 London)

B) **Princess Nadezheda** Georgina **Galitzine** (*9 Jul 1990 London)

IV) **Georgina** Marguerite **Butter** (*9 Jul 1956 London)
= 4 Dec 1982 Dunkeld; **Count Peter Pejacsevich de Veröcze** (*12 Aug 1954 London) son of Count Markus Pejacsevich de Veröcze & Éva Mariássy de Bátizfalva
A) **Count Alexander** Geza Markus **Pejacsevich de Veröcze** (*15 Jul 1988 London)
B) **Countess Anastasia** Lilias Sophie **Pejacsevich de Veröcze** (*30 May 1992 London)
V) **Charles** Harold Alexander **Butter** (*10 Apr 1960 London)
= 1 Sep 2006 Dunkeld; **Agnieszka Szeluk** (…)
A) **Julia** Davina **Butter** (*20 Dec 2006)
B) **Henry** Archie Alexander **Butter** (*27 Jul 2009)
2. **Countess Nadejda** Mikhailovna **de Torby** (28 Mar 1896 Cannes – 22 Jan 1963 Cannes)
= 15 Nov 1916 London; **George** Louis Victor Henry Serge **Mountbatten** (formerly **Prince of Battenberg**), **2nd Marquess of Milford Haven** etc. (6 Nov 1892 Darmstadt – 22 Jan 1963 Cannes) né Prince of Battenberg, family changed name to Mountbatten 1917; son of Louis Mountbatten, 1st Marquess of Milford Haven & Princess Victoria of Hesse and By Rhine; suc. father 11 Sep 1921
a. **Lady Tatiana** Elizabeth **Mountbatten** (16 Dec 1917 Edinburgh – 15 May 1988 Northampton)
b. **David** Michael **Mountbatten, 3rd Marquess of Milford Haven** etc. (12 May 1919 Edinburgh – 14 Apr 1970 London) suc. father 1963
=1 4 Feb 1950 Washington, DC (dv.1960); **Romaine** Dahlgren **Pierce** (17 Jul 1923 Biltmore, Maryland – 15 Feb 1975 New York) daughter of Ulrich Pierce & Margaret Clark; she =1st William Simpson; =3rd James Orthwein
=2 17 Nov 1960 London; **Janet** Mercedes **Bryce** (*29 Sep 1937 Hamilton, Bermuda) daughter of Francis Bryce & Gladys Mosley
issue of 2nd (none by 1st):
I) **George** Ivar Louis **Mountbatten, 4th Marquess of Milford Haven** etc. (*6 Jun 1961 London) suc. father 1970
=1 8 Mar 1989 London (dv.1996); **Sarah** Georgina **Walker** (*17Nov 1961 London) daughter of Georg Walker & Jean

Hatton
=2 20 Aug 1997 Coatue Point, Massachusetts; **Clare** Husted **Steel** (*2 Sep 1960 New York) daughter of Anthony Steel & Anne Husted; =1st Nicholas Wentworth-Stanley
issue of 1st (none by 2nd):

A) **Lady Tatiana** Helen Georgia **Mountbatten** (*16 Apr 1990 London)

B) **Henry** David Louis, **Earl of Medina** (*19 Oct 1991 London)

II) **Lord Ivar** Alexander Michael **Mountbatten** (*9 Mar 1963 London)
= 23 Apr 1994 Clare, Suffolk; **Penelope** Anne Vere **Thompson** (*17 Mar 1996 Cambridge) daughter of Colin Thompson & Rosemary Edwards

A) **Ella** Louise Georgina **Mountbatten** (*20 Mar 1996 Cambridge)

B) **Alexandra** Nada Victoria **Mountbatten** (*8 May 1998 Bridwell Park)

C) **Louise** Xenia Rose **Mountbatten** (*30 Jul 2002 Bridwell Park)

3. **Count Michael** Mikhailovich **de Torby** (8 Oct 1898 Wiesbaden – 25 Apr 1959 London)

D. **Grand Duke George** Mikhailovich **of Russia** (11/23 Aug 1863 Bielyi-Kliutsch – 30 Jan 1919 St. Petersburg) murdered by Bolsheviks
= 12 May 1900 Corfu; ♦**Princess Maria** Georgievna **of Greece** (3 Mar 1876 Athens – 14 Dec 1940 Athens) daughter of George I, King of the Hellenes & Grand Duchess Olga of Russia; =2nd Pericles Joannides

1. **Princess Nina** Georgievna **of Russia** (7/20 Jun 1901 Mikhailovskoie – 26 Feb 1974 Wellfleet, Massachusetts)
= 3 Sep 1922 London; **Prince Paul** Alexandrovich **Chavchavadze** (16/28 Jun 1899 St. Petersburg – 8 Jul 1971 Wellfleet) son of Prince Alexander Chavchavadze & Maria Rodzinko

a. **Prince David** Pavlovich **Chavchavadze** (20 May 1924 London – 5 Oct 2014 Washington, DC)
=1 13 Sep 1952 Washington, DC (dv.1959); **Helen Husted**

(*1 Feb 1933 New York) daughter of Ellery Husted & Helen McLanahan
=2 28 Dec 1959 Cincinnati, Ohio (dv.1970); Jane **Judith Clippinger** (26 Mar 1929 Cincinnati – 21 Oct 1997 Great Falls, Virginia) daughter of John Clippinger & Jane Becker
=3 23 Jun 1979 Washington; **Eugenia** Vladimirovna **de Smitt** (12 Jul 1939 New York – 30 May 2016 Washington) daughter of Vladimir de Smitt & Irina Magner; =1st … Olkhovsky
issue of 1st:
I) **Princess Maria** Davidovna **Chavchavadze** (*28 Aug 1953 Washington)
= 27 Oct 1990 New York (dv.); **Alexander Rasic** (*31 may 1955 Nouysad, Yugoslavia) son of Milos Rasic & Branka Gudelj
=2 8 Sep 2001 Wellfleet (dv.); **Michael Ensor** (...) son of Albert Ensor & Helen Armstrong
A) **Yelena Rasic** (*16 Dec 1990 New York)
II) **Princess Alexandra** Davidovna **Chavchavadze** (*24 Dec 1954 Berlin)
= 26 Nov 1989 Wellfleet; **Puthukuty Krishman Ramani** (*20 Jan 1956 Carala, India) son of Puluknat Keeszkeveetil Krishman Poduval & Puthukuty Pathmavathy Namian
A) **Alexander Chavachavadze Ramani-Poduval** (*18 May 1991 Cape May, New Jersey)
B) **Caroline Chavchavadze Ramani-Poduval** (*6 Jun 1994 New York)
issue of 2nd (none by 3rd):
III) **Princess Catherine** Davidovna **Chavchavadze** (*29 Dec 1960 Washington)
= 22 Sep 1990 Washington; **John** Alan **Redpath** (*1 Mar 1963 St. Paul, Minnesota) son of Peter Redpath & Barbara Donahue
A) **Sophia Redpath** (*4 Jul 1996 Paris)
B) **Nina Redpath** (*13 Oct 1998 New York)
IV) **Prince Michael** Davidovich **Chavchavadze** (*1 Aug 1966 Washington)
= 21 May 2011 Hartwick, New York; **Colleen** Margaret **Quinn** (*5 Oct 1982 Middleton, New York) daughter of

Michael Quinn & Peggy ...
A) **Prince David** Mikhailovich **Chavchavadze** (*Feb 2016 Watkins Glen, NY)

2. **Princess Xenia** Georgeievna **of Russia** (9/22 Aug 1903 Mikhailovskioe – 17 Sep 1965 Glen Cove, New York)
=1 9 Oct 1921 Paris (dv.1930); **William** Bateman **Leeds Jr.** (19 Sep 1901 New York – 31 Dec 1971 New York) son of William Leeds Sr. & Nancy Stewart (later Princess Christopher of Greece)
=2 10 Aug 1946 Hicksville, New York; **Herman Jud** (14 Feb 1911 Hicksville – 22 Aug 1987 Harrisonburg, Virginia)
issue of 1st (none by 2nd):
I) **Nancy** Helen Marie **Leeds** (4 Feb 1925 New York – 7 Jun 2006 Woodstock, Vermont)
= 22 Dec 1945 Glen Cove; **Edward** Judson **Wynkoop** (23 May 1917 Syracuse – 10 Apr 2009 Woodstock) son of Edward Wynkoop & Florence Niver
A) **Alexandra Wynkoop** (*30 Mar 1959 Stamford, Connecticut)

E. **Grand Duke Alexander** Mikhailovich **of Russia** (1/13 Apr 1866 Tiblisi – 26 Feb 1933 Roquebrune, France)
= 25 Jul/6 Aug 1894 Peterhof; ♦**Grand Duchess Xenia** Alexandrovna **of**
Russia (25 Mar/6 Apr 1875 St. Petersburg – 20 Apr 1960 London) daughter of Alexander III, Emperor of Russia & Princess Dagmar of Denmark

1. **Princess Irina** Alexandrovna **of Russia** (3/15 Jul 1895 Peterhof – 26 Feb 1970 Paris)
= 9/22 Feb 1914 St. Petersburg; **Prince Felix** Felixovich **Yousoupov** (12/24 Mar 1887 St. Petersburg – 27 Sep 1967 Paris) son of Prince Felix Yousoupov & Princess Zenaida Yousoupova
a. **Princess Irina** Felixovna **Yousoupova** (8/21 May 1915 St. Petersburg – 30 Aug 1983 Cormeilles-en-Parisis)
= 19 Jun 1938 Rome; **Count Nicholas** Dmitrievich **Cheremetev** (15/28 Oct 1904 Moscow – 5 Feb 1979 Paris) son of Count Dmitri Cheremetev & Countess Irina Vorontzova-Dashkova
I) **Countess Xenia** Nikolaievna **Cheremeteff** (*1 Mar 1942 Rome)

= 20 Jun 1965 Athens; **Elia Sfiris** (*20 Aug 1932 Athens) son of Ioannis Sfiris & Maria Paizi

A) **Tatiana Sfiris** (*24 Aug 1968 Athens)
=1 May 1996 Athens; **Alexis Giannakoupoulos** (*1963)
=2 ...; **Anthony Vamvakidis** (...)
issue of 2nd (none by 1st):

1) **Marilia Vamvakidis** (*17 Jul 2004)

2) **Yasmine-Xenia Vamvakidis** (*7 May 2006)

2. **Prince Andrew** Alexandrovich **of Russia** (12/24 Jan 1897 St. Petersburg – 8 May 1981 Provender, Kent)
=1 (morg.) 12 Jun 1918 Yalta; **Donna Elisabetta Ruffo** dei principi di Sant'Antimo (renamed **Elizabeth** Fabrizievna) (27 Dec 1886/8 Jan 1887 Snamenskoie – 29 Oct 1940 London) daughter of Don Fabricio Ruffo, Duke of Sasso-Ruffo & Princess Natalia Mestcherskya; =1st Alexander de Friderici
=2 (morg.) 21 Sep 1942 Norton, Kent; **Nadine** Sylvia Ada **McDougall** (5 Jun 1908 Lynsted, Kent – 6 Jun 2000 Provender) daughter of Herbert McDougall & Sylvia Borgstrom
issue of 1st:

a. **Princess Xenia** Andreievna **Romanoff** (10 Mar 1919 Paris – 22 Oct 2000 St.-Cernin)
=1 17 Jun 1945 London (dv.1954); **Calhoun Ancrum** (28 Apr 1915 in the Philippines – 21 Feb 1990 Charlestown, Massachusetts) son of Calhoun Ancrum & Dixie Quarles
=2 7 Apr 1958 Teheran; **Geoffrey** Cuthbert **Tooth** (1 Sep 1908 London – 28 Feb 1998 St-Cernin) son of Howard Tooth & Helen Chiver; =1st Olga Galitzine (sister of Princess Vassili of Russia)
no issue

b. **Prince Michael** Andreievich **Romanoff** (15 Jul 1920 Versailles - 21 Sep 2008 Sydney, Australia)
=1 24 Feb 1953 Sydney (dv.1953); Esther Blanche (**Jill**) **Murphy** (*21 Oct 1921 Horsham, Victoria)
=2 23 Jul 1954 Sydney; **Shirley** Elizabeth **Crammond** (4 Mar 1916 Brisbane – 20 Jun 1983 Sydney) daughter of Gordon Crammond & Dorothee-Elisabeth Chapman
=3 14 Jul 1993 Sydney; **Guilia Crespi** (*7 Mar 1930 Milan)

daughter of Giuseppe-Maria Crespi & Beatrice Martinegro
no issue

c. **Prince Andrew** Andreievich **Romanoff** (*21 Jan 1923 London)
=1 9 Sep 1951 San Francisco (dv.1959); **Helen** Constantinovna **Dourneva** (7 Mar 1927 Tokyo – 1 May 1991) daughter of Constantine Dournev & Felixa Zapalsky
=2 21 Mar 1961 San Francisco; **Kathleen Norris** (1 Mar 1935 San Francisco – 8 Dec 1967 San Francisco) daughter of Fran Norris & Alice McCreery; =1st Gilbert Roberts
=3 17 Dec 1987 Reno, Nevada; **Inez** Mary **Bachelin** (*11 Oct 1933 Santa Monica, California) daughter of Franz Bachelin & Anita Hirtfield; =1st Thomas Storer
issue of 1st:
I) **Prince Alexis** Andreievich **Romanoff** (*27 Apr 1953 San Francisco)
= 19 Sep 1987 Oakland Cal.; Zoetta (**Zoe**) **Leisy** (*25 Nov 1956 Memphis, Tennessee) daughter of Robert Leisy & Ellen Telfer
no issue
issue of 2nd:
II) **Prince Peter** Andreievich **Romanoff** (*21 Nov 1961 San Francisco)
= 2 May 2009 Marin County, California; **Barbara** Anne **Jurgens** (*1968)
no issue
III) **Prince Andrew** Andreievich **Romanoff** (*20 Feb 1963 San Francisco)
= 12 Jun 1989 Point Reyes Station, California; **Elizabeth Flores** (*25 Apr 1964 San Francisco) daughter of Armand Flores & Cecil Sherrod
A) **Princess Natascha** Catherine **Romanoff** (*2 Feb 1993 Greenbrae, California)

issue of 2nd:

d. **Princess Olga** Andreievna **Romanoff** (*8 Apr 1950 London)
= 1 Oct 1975 London (dv.1989); **Thomas Mathew** (*8 Jul 1945 London) son of Francis Mathew & Emma Bowen-Davis
I) **Nicholas Mathew** (*6 Dec 1976 London)

= 6 Dec 2002 Houston (civil) & 14 Dec 2002 Killanen Kirk, Scotland (rel.); **Judith** Aird **Stanley** (...) daughter of Michael Stanley

A) **Thomas Mathew** (*18 Nov 2004)

B) **Lucy Mathews** (*10 Jul 2006)

C) **Isabella** Florence **Mathew** (*4 Jan 2011)

II) **Francis** Alexander **Mathew** (*26 Sep 1978 London)

III) **Alexandra Mathew** (*20 Apr 1981 London)

IV) **Thomas Mathew** (27 Nov 1987 London – 20 Apr 1989 London)

3. **Prince Feodor** Alexandrovich **of Russia** (11/23 Dec 1898 St. Petersburg – 30 Nov 1968 Ascain)
= (morg.) 31 May 1923 Paris (dv.1936); ♦**Princess Irene** Pavlovna **Paley** (21 Dec 1903 Paris – 15 Nov 1990 Biarritz) daughter of Grand Duke Paul of Russia & Olga Karnovich, Princess Paley; =2nd Hubert de Monbrison

a. **Prince Michel** Feodorovich **Romanoff** (4 May 1923 Paris – 21 Sep 2008 Paris)
=1 15 Oct 1958 Paris (dv.1992); **Helga Staufenberger** (*22 Aug 1926 Vienna) daughter of Ludwig Staufenberger & Frederika Schmoll
=2 14 Jan 1994 Jossé; **Mercedes Ustrell Cabani** (*26 Jul 1960 Hospitalet, Spain) daughter of Ramon Ustrell & Carmen Cabani
issue of 1st:

I) **Prince Michel** Mikhailovich **Romanoff** (31 Jul 1959 Paris – 24 Jan 2001 Mumbai, India)
has issue by **Mercedes Ustrell Cabani** (later his step-mother, see above):

A) **Tatiana** Mikhailovna **Romanoff de Russie** (*21 Oct 1986 Bayonne) adopted by grandfather/step-father 20 Mar 1995

4. **Prince Nikita** Alexandrovich **of Russia** (4/17 Jan 1900 St. Petersburg – 12 Sep 1974 Cannes)
= (morg.) 14 Feb 1922 Paris; **Countess Maria** Illarianovna **Vorontzova-Dashkova** (31 Jan/13 Feb 1903 Tsarskoie-Selo – 15 Jun 1997 Cannes) daughter of Count Ilarion Vorontzov-Dashkov & Irina Narishkina

a. **Prince Nikita** Nikitich **Romanoff** (13 May 1923 London – 3 May 2007 New York)
= 14 Jul 1961 London; **Janet** Anne **Schonwald** (*24 Apr 1933 Oklahoma City) daughter of Michael Schonwald & Ethel Dimond
I) **Prince Theodor** Nikitich **Romanoff** (30 Nov 1974 New York – 25 Aug 2007 Pompano Beach, Florida)
b. **Prince Alexander** Nikitich **Romanoff** (4 Nov 1929 Paris – 22 Sep 2002 London)
= 23 Feb 1971 New York (civil) & 18 Jul 1971 Cannes (rel.); **Donna Maria** Immaculata Rosalia Emmanuela Stanie Margherita **Valguarnere** dei principi de Nescemi (*29 Nov 1931 Palermo) daughter of Don Carrado Valguarnere, Prince of Nescemi & Margaret Hirsh
no issue
5. **Prince Dmitri** Alexandrovich **of Russia** (2/15 Aug 1901 Gatchina – 7 Jul 1980 London)
=1 (morg.) 24 Nov 1931 Paris (dv.1947); **Countess Marina** Sergeievna **Golenisheva-Kutuzova** (7/20 Nov 1912 St. Petersburg – 1969 Sharon, Connecticut) daughter of Count Serge Golenishev-Kutuzov & Maria Besobrasova
=2 (morg.) 29 Oct 1954 London; Margaret **Sheila** MacKellar **Chisholm** (9 Sep 1898 Sydney, Australia – 13 Oct 1969 London) daughter of Harry Chisholm & Margaret MacKellar; =1st Franc, Lord Loughborough; =2nd Sir John Milbanke, 12th Baronet
issue of 1st (none by 2nd):
a. **Princess Nadejda** Dmitrievna **Romanoff** (4 Jul 1933 Boulogne – 17 Sep 2002 Vancouver, British Columbia.)
=1 20 Dec 1952 London (dv.1976); Anthony **Brian Allen** (6 May 1931 Connah's Quay, Wales – 2 Apr 2015 Victoria, B.C.) son of Samuel Allen & Jane Fletcher
=2 May 1977 San Francisco; **William** Thomas Hall **Clark** (17 Mar 1924 Montreal – 16 Feb 1995 Victoria, British Columbia)
issue of 1st (none by 2nd):
I) **Penelope Allen** (*27 Feb 1953 London)
= 6 Sep 1981 London; **Prince Emmanuel** Emmanuelovich **Galitzine** (*11 Mar 1951 Montevideo) son of Prince Emmanuel Galitzine & Gwendoline Rhodes

A) **Princess Victoria** Emmanuelovna **Galitzine** (*23 Apr 1985 Eastbourne, Sussex)
= 24 Apr 2011 Salinas, California; **Robert** Harold **Hanson** (*11 Sep 1978 Eastbourne, Sussex) son of Robert Hanson & Nancy Perlman
1) **Alexander** Bowie **Hanson-Galitzine** (*25 Jun 2016 Dominican, Cal.)
B) **Prince Michael** Emmanuelovich **Galitzine** (*2 Feb 1993)
II) **Marina Allen** (*10 Jul 1955 London)
=1 20 Jul 1974 Victoria, British Columbia (dv.1978); **Franklin** Daniel **Hudson** (*1 Feb 1952 Winnipeg, Manitoba)
=2 11 Nov 1978 Cambridge, Massachusetts (dv.); **Michael** Peter **Otis** (*10 Nov 1948 Boston)
issue of 1st (but born after 2nd divorce):
A) **Ryan Hudson** (*31 Jul 1981 Vancouver, British Columbia)
= ...; **Hella Woeckener** (…) daughter of Hartmut Woeckener & Lori Threlfall
1) **Carter** Reid **Hudson** (*2008 Vancouver)
2) **Chloe Hudson** (*2010 Vancouver)
III) Alexandra (**Alex** Mark) **Allen** (*10 Dec 1958 Redruth, Cornwall) legally changed name and gender ca.2009
6. **Prince Rostislav** Alexandrovich **of Russia** (11/24 Nov 1902 Ai-Todor – 31 Jul 1978 Cannes)
=1 (morg.) 1 Sep 1928 Chicago (dv.1944); **Princess Alexandra** Pavlovna **Galitzine** (7/20 May 1905 Marijno, Novgorod – 5 Dec 2006 Lake Forest, Illinois) daughter of Prince Paul Galitzine & Princess Alexandra Mestcherskya; =2nd Lester Armour
=2 (morg.) 24 Nov 1944 Chicago (dv.1951); **Alice Eilken** (30 May 1923 Chicago – 21 Oct 1996 Skokie, Illinois) daughter of Alvin Eilken & Rose Schultz; =2nd William Steuber
=3 (morg.) 19 Nov 1954 London; **Hedwig** Maria Gertrud Eva **von Chappuis** (6 Dec 1905 Habelschwerdt – 9 Jan 1997 Grasse) daughter of Carl von Chappuis & Baroness Gertrud von Richthofen; =1st Berkeley Gage (later Sir Berkeley)
issue of 1st:

a. **Prince Rostislav** Rostislavovich **Romanoff** (3 Dec 1938 Chicago – 7 Jan 1999 London)
=1 9 Sep 1960 Winnetka, Illinois (dv.1978); **Stephena** Verdel **Cook** (*15 Dec 1938 Maracibo, Venezuela) daughter of Edgar Cook & Sidney Hunt
=2 12 Aug 1980 Lake Forest; **Christia Ipsen** (*3 Apr 1949 Rockford, Illinois) daughter of Harold Ipsen & Lorraine Wrobel; =1st John Odell; =3rd David Russell, 5th Baron Ampthill
issue of 1st:
I) **Princess Stephena** Rostislavovna **Romanoff** (*21 Jan 1963 Chicago)
= 23 Dec 1988 Lake Bluff, Illinois; **William Porter Boggess III** (*31 Mar 1960 Lake Forest) son of William Boggess II & Judith Norton
no issue
issue of 2nd:
II) **Princess Alexandra** Rostislovavna **Romanoff** (*9 Jun 1983 Lake Forest)
III) **Prince Rostislav** Rostislavovich **Romanoff** (*21 May 1985 Lake Forest)
has issue with **Foteini** Maria Cristina **Georganta** (*1979 Athens):
A) **Mikhail** Rostislavovich **Romanoff** (*2013)
IV) **Prince Nikita** Rostislavovich **Romanoff** (*24 Mar 1987 Lake Forest)

issue of 2nd (*was not granted any titles*):

a. **Nicholas Romanoff** (8 Sep 1945 Chicago – 9 Nov 2000 Las Vegas) killed in a car crash
=1 24 Aug 1966 Wheaton, Illinois (dv.); **Pamela Kuzinkowska** (*7 Jul 1944 Chicago) daughter of Matthew Kuzinkowski & Estelle Slowik
=2 12 Mar 1994 Las Vegas; **Lynn Panniero** (...)
issue of 1st (none by 2nd):
I) **Nicholas** Christopher **Romanoff** (*30 Jul 1968 Oak Park, Illinois)
=1 13 May 1995 Rolling Meadows, Illinois (dv.); **Lisa Marie Glowa** (*28 Mar 1971 Chicago) daughter of Thomas

Glowa & Linda Lesiewicz
=2 16 Jun 2001 Las Vegas (dv); **Sheryl Buffet** (…)
issue of 1st:
A) **Cory** Christopher **Romanoff** (5 Dec 1994 Arlington Heights, Illinois – 5 Jan 1998 Memphis, Tennessee) murdered
issue of 2nd:
B) **Karlyn Romanoff** (*5 Apr 2000 San Diego, California)
C) **Chelle Romanoff** (*7 Mar 2003 San Diego)
II) **Daniel** Joseph **Romanoff** (*19 Mar 1972 Chicago)
= 9 Apr 2006 Maui, Hawaii; **Soo Kim** (…)
A) **Madison Romanoff** (*9 Jul 2007 Chicago)
B) **Jackson** Daniel **Romanoff** (*9 Jan 2009 Chicago)
III) **Heather** Noel **Romanoff** (*6 Nov 1976 Park Ridge, Illinois)
= 14 Jul 2006 Bartlett, Illinois; **Joseph Munao** (*2 Jun 1976 Chicago) son of Joseph Munao & Joanne…
A) **Jack** Joseph **Munao** (*29 May 2008 Hoffman Estates, Illinois)
B) **Alexandra** Rose **Munao** (*13 Apr 2010 Hoffman Estates)
g. **Prince Vassili** Alexandrovich **of Russia** (24 Jun/7 Jul 1907 Gatchina – 24 Jun 1989 Woodside, California)
= 31 Jul 1931 New York; **Princess Natalia** Alexandrovna **Galitzine** (13/26 Oct 1907 Moscow – 28 Mar 1989 Woodside) daughter of Prince Alexander Galitzine & Lubov Glebova
I) **Princess Marina** Vassilievna **Romanova** (*22 May 1940 San Francisco)
=1 8 Jan 1967 Woodside (dv.); **William** Lawrence **Beadleston** (*31 Jul 1938 Long Branch, New Jersey) son of Alfred Beadleston & Sylvia White; =2nd Charlotte Beers
=2 ...; **Daniel** Leslie **Stanberry** (*10 Aug 1946) =1st Alta ...
issue of 1st (none by second):
A) **Tatiana Beadleston** (*18 May 1968 San Francisco)
= 21 Jun 1998 Southwest Harbor, Maine; **Charles** Wheeler **Erdmann** (*3 Jun 1967 Boston) son of Rubin Erdmann & Cinda Wheeler

1) **Alexander** Romanov **Erdmann** (*18 Jan 1997 Los Angeles)
2) **Sebastian** Wheeler **Erdmann** (*2000)
3) a daughter (*Aug 2010 Los Angeles)

B) **Alexandra Beadleston** (*19 May 1970 New York)
= 25 Jul 1996 Somerset, Colorado; **Peter** DeWitt Mason **Blake** (*11 Mar 1970 Charlottesville, Virginia) son of Everingham Blake & Elizabeth Schvetsova
1) **Serena Blake** (*30 Jul 1997 Aspen, Colorado)
2) **Fynn** Everingham **Blake** (*7 May 1999 Grand Junction, Colorado)

C) **Nicholas** Romanov **Beadleston** (*22 Nov 1971 New York)

D) **Natalia Beadleston** (*30 Sep 1976 New York)
= 22 Mar 2003 Charleston, South Carolina; **John Steinle** (…) son of John Steinle & Diane Hoeffer
1) **Marina Steinle** (*2004)
2) **Nicolai** Nash **Steinle** (*22 Feb 2007 West Palm Beach, Florida)
3) **Alexander** William **Steinle** (*14 Jul 2010 West Palm Beach)

F. **Grand Duke Serge** Mikhailovich **of Russia** (25 Sep/7 Oct 1869 Norjam, Georgia – 17 Jul 1918 Alapaievsk) murdered by Bolsheviks

G. **Grand Duke Alexei** Mikhailovich **of Russia** (28 Dec 1875 Tiblisi – 2 Mar 1895 San Remo)

Other Books by Daniel A. Willis

NON-FICTION:

WILLIAM IV, MRS. JORDAN, AND THE FAMILY THEY MADE

THE ARCHDUKE'S SECRET FAMILY

LEGENDS, HALF-TRUTHS, AND CHERISHED MYTHS OF THE DRANE FAMILY

THE DESCENDANTS OF CHARLES II
VOLUME 1: MONMOUTH
VOLUME 2: DACRE
VOLUME 3: SOUTHAMPTON & DERWENTWATER
VOLUME 4: GRAFTON
VOLUME 5: SEYMOUR

HABSBURGS IN THE 21ST CENTURY

FICTION:

IMMORTAL BETRAYAL

IMMORTAL DUPLICITY

IMMORTAL REVELATION

PROPHECY OF THE AWAKENING

CPSIA information can be obtained
at www.ICGtesting.com
Printed in the USA
LVHW07s1437080418
572693LV00020B/201/P